T0373601

Routledge Revivals

Liberal Neutrality

Originally published in 1989 *Liberal Neutrality* approaches the recommendation of neutrality by confronting the abstract prescription (that we should be neutral) with the implications for particular people and institutions. This not only identifies what neutrality involves logically, but also exposes the practical difficulties that may be encountered in pursuing it. In some cases, such close examination shows that neutrality is not desirable, and in others that it is attainable only within certain limits. Although neutrality has become a fashionable term in political theory, this is the only volume to subject the idea to systematic scrutiny. It will be useful not only to specialists in diverse disciplines – political scientists, philosophers, sociologists, lawyers and educationalists.

Liberal Neutrality

Edited by Robert E. Goodin and
Andrew Reeve

Routledge
Taylor & Francis Group

First published in 1989
by Routledge

This edition first published in 2018 by Routledge
2 Park Square, Milton Park, Abingdon, Oxon, OX14 4RN
and by Routledge
711 Third Avenue, New York, NY 10017

Routledge is an imprint of the Taylor & Francis Group, an informa business

Publisher's Note
The publisher has gone to great lengths to ensure the quality of this reprint but
points out that some imperfections in the original copies may be apparent.

Disclaimer
The publisher has made every effort to trace copyright holders and welcomes
correspondence from those they have been unable to contact.

A Library of Congress record exists under LCCN: 89006232

ISBN 13: 978-1-138-32403-9 (hbk)
ISBN 13: 978-0-429-44705-1 (ebk)

Liberal neutrality

edited by

Robert E. Goodin

and

Andrew Reeve

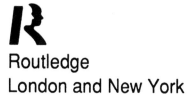

Routledge
London and New York

First published 1989 by
Routledge
11 New Fetter Lane, London EC4P 4EE
29 West 35th Street, New York, NY 10001

Typeset by LaserScript Limited, Mitcham, Surrey
Printed in Great Britain by TJ Press (Padstow) Ltd, Padstow, Cornwall

British Library Cataloguing in Publication Data

Liberal neutrality
   1. Political ideologies, liberalism, neutrality
   I. Goodin, Robert E. II. Reeve, Andrew
   320.5'1

   ISBN 0 415 00145 5

Library of Congress Cataloging in Publication Data

Liberal neutrality.
The essays result from deliberations of the Liberal Political Theory Specialist
Group of the Political Studies Association of the United Kingdom – Acknow.
   Includes index.
   1. Equality before the law. 2. Liberalism. 3. Apathy. 4. Autonomy.
5. Pluralism (Social sciences) I. Goodin, Robert E. II. Reeve, Andrew.
III. Political Studies Association of the United Kingdom. Liberal Political
Theory Specialist Group.
JC578.L53   1989   323.42   89–6232
ISBN 0 415 00145 5

Contents

Acknowledgements

The essays result from deliberations of the Liberal Political Theory Specialist Group of the Political Studies Association of the United Kingdom. The members of this group have no collective view or common ideological persuasion. They are brought together only by their concern to explore liberal thought in the context of modern political theory. This volume is the first fruit of that concern.

Several of the essays were originally presented to meetings of that group, either at the 1985 PSA Annual Conference in Nottingham or at a special meeting of the group convened in London in 1986. We should here record our gratitude to the PSA for financial support, and to the LSE's Suntory-Toyota International Centre for Economics and Related Disciplines for hosting our London meeting.

Robert E. Goodin
Andrew Reeve

August 1988

Liberalism and neutrality

Robert E. Goodin and Andrew Reeve

The discussion of 'neutrality' as a – much less the – defining characteristic of liberalism is a fairly recent development. One of our contributors dates it, with a precision that is not altogether spurious, to 1974. Earlier liberals may well have been less concerned to identify the 'true core' of liberalism, and they may well have been less expansive on the merits of the notion of neutrality in that regard, than contemporary authors are. Still, liberals have long been keenly aware of something very closely akin to the virtue of neutrality on the part of the police, the judiciary and the military: unless they dispense justice without fear or favour, liberal theory in practice simply does not work.[1] Thus while it is only in the last decade or so that the term has come into particular focus as a general issue, apparently similar notions have long figured largely in recognizably liberal political discourse.

This volume sets out to explore what exactly is involved in the idea of neutrality as it is deployed in liberal political thought. One question addressed, given this background, is whether anything new is being said by those who employ the concept of neutrality, or whether this is simply another example of new wine in old bottles. 'Neutrality' may be no more than recent terminology for ideas with a longer pedigree; hence we will naturally need to trace its relations with similar concepts. The essays presented here locate neutrality by reference to ideas like impartiality, even-handedness, absence of bias, equality of treatment, and indifference.

Whether a concern with neutrality is a defining characteristic of liberalism is a question to be addressed shortly. It is, however, undeniable that both critics and defenders of liberalism as a political ideology have focused on neutrality and cognate notions. Those who see neutrality as a virtue have associated it with intellectual honesty in relation to unsettled issues, with tolerance of those with different ideas, with the accommodation of a variety of values or lifestyles, with securing the conditions of intellectual or material progress, and with providing for the equal rights of citizens. Those who have seen the commitment to neutrality as a weakness have claimed that it masks vacillation, the absence of intellectual or political courage, an unwillingness to make hard decisions and difficult choices, an abdication of responsibility, and an indifference to the actual fate of the individuals whom it makes a formal claim to cherish.[2] This is, no doubt, one reason for John Stuart Mill's fierce denial that neutrality, at least in the sense of 'no coercive interference', was in any way connected with indifference to the faults of individuals, and thus with their well-being.[3]

I.A

At least some of the disagreement about the value of neutrality results from a pair of connected problems. The first is that 'neutrality' can be associated with a number of other concepts which have an evaluative element. As we have seen, two such notions are 'equal treatment' and 'indifference'. Obviously, it would not be surprising if those who relate neutrality to the achievement of equal treatment find it more valuable than those who interpret it as indifference. This problem is exacerbated by the ubiquity of the idea of neutrality. It has been invoked in a variety of contexts, from prescriptions about the proper use of state power, to requirements placed on state officials, to recommendations to scientists, teachers and journalists, to support for the value of market institutions. Both the meaning of neutrality, and the practical consequences of adopting it, may be expected to alter with the context in which it is invoked. As a result, one source of disagreement about the value of neutrality may well be failure to specify this context.

It is therefore helpful, in assessing arguments about neutrality, to ask who or what is to be neutral, and what they are supposed to be neutral about, and what objective their neutrality is supposed to secure. Such a protocol draws attention to a number of important 'variables' in the specification of neutrality. It also helps to diagnose the sources of disagreement and the difficulties of conceptual clarity in this area.

Using such a three-part formulation of the notion of neutrality will not only lead to a more precise specification of the context and of why neutrality is thought to matter in that particular area. It will also bring out some other problems.

First, if we look at who or what is supposed to be neutral we shall find the prescription varying over individual agents (for example, a teacher or civil servant), institutions in a conventional sense (for example, the civil service), and networks of practices which involve individuals, institutions, and complexes of social relations (for example, science). Clearly, the senses in which these individuals, agencies and practices can be neutral, and the point of proposing that they are or should be, will need to reflect the different sorts of analysis needed to deal with individual agents, institutions and practices.

Second, although it is obvious that liberal neutrality is directed in some way at the well-being of citizens, the immediate object of neutrality may not be concrete individuals. For example, neutrality towards ideas in education, or neutrality towards interpretations of events in journalism, is not so immediately directed towards individuals as are the requirements of state neutrality. To be sure, the point of the neutrality in question must be some contribution to the quality of citizens' lives. But equally, the content of the requirements of neutrality must reflect what it is to which neutrality is directed. Again, even if individuals are the direct object of concern, what aspect of their individuality is at issue? Their interests, their welfare, their self-esteem, their rights are all plausible candidates.

Third, the formulation asks what good neutrality is supposed to secure. Here it is worth isolating two issues. In the first place, this formulation presupposes that neutrality is an instrumental value, that it does not have the same status as the goals it is designed to secure. Its value is therefore parasitic on those goals. If the neutrality of a judge is instrumental in securing justice, then it is valuable because just outcomes are valuable. This helps dispel some of the wariness about liberal neutrality that clearly follows from a suspicion that an instrumental (rather than fundamental) value is being put at the centre of the stage.

I. B

This leads to the second issue. Neutrality in different contexts plausibly aims at different goals: truth, progress, and justice are amongst them. The value of neutrality can then be contested for two quite different reasons.

On the one hand, there can be reasonable disagreement about the substantive value served – particularly how valuable it is in the light of other liberal commitments. This point is connected to one of the central features of liberalism, a concern to allow individuals to pursue their own views of the good, to which we shall return shortly. On the other hand the value of neutrality can be contested on the much more empirically grounded claim that, even where it exists as the theory requires, it does not in fact secure the good which it is allegedly (instrumentally) aimed at. This may be because of countervailing considerations in the social system, or because of institutional considerations not properly absorbed into the abstract theory.

II

Let us now turn to the place of neutrality in liberalism. It is notoriously difficult to discuss the content of a political ideology like liberalism. All approaches suffer from some methodological defect.[4] Nevertheless, since neutrality is at least a candidate for consideration as one of its defining values, especially since both proponents and critics of liberalism give it such emphasis, it is worth asking about its status in relation to liberalism generally.

We have already acknowledged that the present ubiquity of the terminology does not (necessarily) entail any novelty in the ideas presented. It is one objective of this volume to address this issue. We have also argued that neutrality is an instrumental value, rather than a fundamental one; and on the face of it this would seem to defeat its claim to be central to liberalism. It is odd, it might be argued, to regard a 'second level' commitment as in any way a defining feature of a political ideology.

But perhaps this argument goes too quickly. First, both the concern to allow individuals to pursue their own view of the good life, mentioned earlier, and a commitment to an open-ended plurality of values suggest that liberalism aims to achieve what individuals value: and while this notoriously leads to difficult judgements and assorted social dilemmas, when values are incommensurate or when one version of the good life clashes with another, it also suggests that the distinctiveness of liberalism is unlikely to be captured by a shortlist of value commitments. Plainly, we shall want to recognize that liberals, both historically and at the present day, value liberty, justice, the welfare of citizens, and so on. But so do many non-liberals. These commitments are not themselves distinctively liberal.[5]

The argument just presented is far from novel. A recognition that the liberal is not necessarily distinctive in the values he or she holds leads easily enough to a 'second level' concern: is there something distinctive about the means the liberal favours to secure those goals, or their ranking? Hence essays on liberalism are led to focus on the way in which liberals have thought the goals might be secured. The obvious methodological difficulty of this is that writers who thought of themselves as liberals, or who were perceived by their critics to be so, have not agreed on the best approach. Partly, of course, this reflected their particular historical context. It is not surprising, for example, that threats to freedom were first perceived in oppressive government and religious intolerance, and only more recently in economic organization, private power and public opinion. All this makes a consensus on 'the best approach' rather chimerical. Nevertheless, such essays examine a commitment to private property and the market, to individual rights, or to liberty (often by contrast with welfare or equality) in an attempt to locate the distinctiveness of liberalism.[6]

It is not being claimed that neutrality will provide the answer in this search for a second-level commitment which truly reflects the special features of the liberal position. There are good reasons to suppose that that particular holy grail will remain elusive. What is claimed, though, is that whether we start at the first or second level of discussion, we shall quickly run into neutrality in various contexts. In addition, we can see that other candidates for the role of definitive value commitments will bring up issues of neutrality. Let us take these points in turn.

If we start from value pluralism and the commitment to allow individuals to pursue their own views of the good life, we encounter problems of agnosticism about how values should be made commensurate, how legislation should be constructed to facilitate the realization of these commitments, and how the state should conduct itself to recognize the equal worth of conceptions of a valuable life. These issues involve the neutrality of the state, addressed by Peter Jones in Chapter 2, and the neutrality of legislation, examined by Jeremy Waldron in Chapter 4.

If we begin from the institutional commitments associated with liberalism, we shall equally encounter problems of neutrality. For example, the market has been favoured by some liberals as a device which secures the dispersal of power and which is in some sense neutral between individuals. The meaning and limits of this claim are explored by A. T. O'Donnell in Chapter 3. Similarly the liberal theory of the state relies upon the notion that state power is indifferent to the substantive commitments of particular individuals (although, of course, there may be a filter on the legitimacy of those commitments deriving from the need to reconcile different conceptions of the good life). In such a theory, the neutrality of the civil service is obviously crucial. The assertion that political power is available to all who establish a legitimate claim is not compatible with collective administrative bias. Adrian Ellis explores the tensions between the claims of neutrality and those of loyalty in the civil service, in Chapter 5.

Again, there is an aspect of liberal thought which stresses progress or amelioration as an end of our associative endeavour. This progress could be moral, material, or cognitive. Hence liberals have been concerned with the emergence of truth through dialogue and controversy. They have thought of knowledge as something to be valued either for itself or for its contribution to the improvement of the human condition. The neutrality of science, discussed by Hugh Ward in Chapter 8, has, therefore, been hotly contested by liberals and their radical critics. Equally, liberals have relied upon education to produce both the sort of citizen upon which the political ideology relies, and the opportunity to promote or support individual conceptions of the good life. Coupled to its commitment to value pluralism, to diversity of ways of life, this reliance leads to particular injunctions to the teacher. The coherence of these proposals is Peter Gardner's topic in Chapter 6. Since the dissemination of information is part of the educative process for a concerned citizenry, and since progress is thought to rely on the proposal and defence of opinion, the presentation of news and information is equally vital. Ken Newton discusses the neutrality of the media in Chapter 7.

Finally, if we examine other candidates for the role of the focus of distinctiveness, we shall find that they lead us back to neutrality. For example, some assessments of liberalism have given a central place to the value of autonomy. A concern with autonomy, with self-determination, immediately requires the insulation of the individual from certain sorts of interference and external pressures. The value of autonomy is intimately linked to that of a self-chosen conception of the good life, and suggests the same prescriptions about the use of political (and even social) power and influence.

All this points to the need to investigate neutrality both in specific contexts and in the social and political system as a whole. That is the aim of this collection of essays. The problem of aggregation, of moving between specific contexts and the system as a whole, is the subject of the concluding essay. But there are a number of questions which need to be answered in each context, which provide the themes common to the particular essays. First, what has neutrality been taken to mean in this context? What else might it involve? Second, given that conception of neutrality, is the ideal coherent? And, if it is, can it be put into practice? Finally, given that meaning and those practical implications, is it something which we should value?

A number of reasons for disagreement about the value of liberal neutrality were identified earlier. Still more arise in connection with these issues. First, neutrality, whether at the level of the disposition of a particular agent, such as a civil servant, or at the level of an institution, such as the civil service, or at the level of a practice, such as that of science, is likely to be a matter of degree. Certainly individuals and institutions can be more or less neutral. This suggests that evaluating neutrality will be troublesome. On the one hand, it seems obvious that more neutrality is better than less. But on the other, two doubts might arise. The first doubt concerns liberalism's focus on the individual. If a particular individual has received non-neutral treatment, it seems a poor response to say that the system which so treated him is more neutral than others, and, as it were, someone inevitably draws the short straw. From the individual's point of view, neutrality is an all-or-nothing matter; but from the point of view of institutional design, we may want to have as much as possible without supposing we shall achieve perfection. In many ways, this dilemma reproduces the dispute about neutrality as a surrogate for indifference (x can still be badly treated with a high level of neutrality) compared with neutrality as a political virtue (given everything, institutions are the best, on balance, that can be devised).

A second doubt concerns problems of evidence. The possibility of greater neutrality relies on mental experiments and counterfactual propositions. This is clear from Ward's discussion of science and technology, but it has an application in the other particular contexts as well. First, we have to decide whether identifiable failures of neutrality are ineradicable, and, if so, how we should respond to them. O'Donnell draws attention to the need for a theory of the second best in the context of market neutrality, and this point may be generalized. If we are confronted with such failures, we stand in need of countervailing measures, which themselves are non-neutral. But, second, we have a problem of aggregation. If, for example, some political opinions are likely to be more widely canvassed than others, given the structure of ownership and control of the media, what can we put in the balance against this? Should we try to do something about that, within its own context, or attempt to redress the balance through, for example, education? Is a strategy of countervailing influence a genuine realization of the second best, or merely an exacerbation of the problem of non-neutrality? We shall return to these issues in our closing chapter.

Notes

1 This concern is most explicit in the discussion of the 'rule of law' but exercised jurisprudence before that term became the focus for discussion. See, for example, Lon Fuller, *The Anatomy of Law*, New York: Praeger, 1968, Part 1 especially pp. 19–22. A recent statement of liberalism which is sceptical of 'neutrality' is Joseph Raz, *The Morality of Freedom*, Oxford: Oxford University Press, 1986, especially pp. 110–33.
2 Such criticisms need not be directed at the intellectual integrity of proponents of neutrality. They may be treated as assertions about the practical consequences of institutions designed to embody neutrality. See section I.B, pp. 3–4.
3 John Stuart Mill, *On Liberty*, London: Dent, 1910, p. 132.
4 The difficulties are mentioned in, for example, D. J. Manning, *Liberalism*, London: Dent, 1976, pp. 11–13, and R. N. Berki, *Socialism*, London: Dent, 1975, pp. 9–22.
5 Compare the account in R. N. Berki, *Socialism*, pp. 25–9.
6 For example, John Gray, *Liberalism*, Milton Keynes: Open University Press, 1986, Part Two.

2

The ideal of the neutral state

Peter Jones

The phrase 'neutral state' is one that occurs most commonly in the context of international disputes. A neutral state is one that refrains from taking sides in an international conflict. However, within liberal political theory, the phrase 'neutral state' has come to describe not the external posture of a state but an idea of what its internal arrangements should be. A neutral state is one that deals impartially with its citizens and which remains neutral on the issue of what sort of lives they should lead. Those who endorse the idea of the neutral state hold that it is not the function of the state to impose the pursuit of any particular set of ends upon its citizens. Rather the state should leave its citizens to set their own goals, to shape their own lives, and should confine itself to establishing arrangements which allow each citizen to pursue his own goals as he sees fit – consistent with every other citizen's being able to do the same.

Thus, neutralists conceive the state as having an essentially secondary role in the lives of its citizens. A referee in a game of football does not himself play football, he simply administers the rules within which others play the game. Similarly, the state is not itself to pursue the good life – whatever that may be – it is simply to establish and maintain the ground-rules within which others can engage in that pursuit. Hence, too, the preoccupation of neutralists with justice. States are not to be judged in terms of their promotion of some overall conception of the good for that is not their proper concern. Rather states are to be judged by the quality of the arrangements they establish enabling individuals to pursue their own conceptions of the good. The most important quality that these arrangements should display is that of justice.

Neutralism has gained the allegiance of some of the most prominent political philosophers of the last twenty years. The best known of these are John Rawls, Robert Nozick, Ronald Dworkin, and Bruce Ackerman. In examining the neutral state I shall concentrate on that idea as it occurs in the writings of Rawls, Dworkin, and Ackerman.[1] The conception of the neutral state advanced by these three writers is both importantly similar and importantly different.

In Rawls's *Theory of Justice* neutrality, of the relevant sort, is written into the foundations from which his principles of justice are derived. Individuals are obliged to choose the principles that will govern their lives in a hypothetical original position in which they are ignorant of what their own sex, race, natural endowments, social position, and so on, will turn out to be. They are also ignorant of their conceptions of the good. Rawls's belief is that choice, under these conditions of uncertainty, will necessarily yield principles which are neutral between individuals and their conceptions of the good because individuals are ignorant of what they would need to know if they were to be partial.

Ackerman rejects Rawls's contractarian approach and seeks instead to develop a theory of the liberal state as one that would be arrived at by individuals engaged in a constrained dialogue about what social institutions there should be. The most significant constraint that he imposes upon justification is that it must be neutral. In arguing for a particular distribution of power, an individual is not allowed to hold either (a) 'that his conception of the good is better than that asserted by any of his fellow citizens', or (b) 'that, regardless of his conception of the good, he is intrinsically superior to one or more of his fellow citizens'.[2]

Dworkin's approach is different again. He regards neutrality as something required by the fundamental principle that a state must treat its citizens with equal concern and respect. A neutral condition is to be achieved by ensuring that, as far as possible, the resources available to one life should be no greater than those available to another life, and by allowing political processes to be influenced only by individuals' preferences concerning their own lives and not by preferences they may have about the status to be accorded to other individuals or about the lives that they would like others to lead.

In spite of these differences in approach, Rawls, Dworkin, and Ackerman do adopt a broadly similar conception of the neutral state and one which, for example, marks them off as a group from the likes of Nozick. Henceforth when I speak of 'neutralists' without qualification, it is this trio of neutralists that I shall have in mind. As far as possible, I want to examine the neutral state as an idea shared by these three and to avoid becoming embroiled in the merits or demerits of their particular versions of that idea. However, before doing that I must briefly notice one other issue.

Several of the advocates of neutralism regard it as the defining feature of liberalism: a liberal state *is* a state which imposes no conception of the good upon its citizens but which allows individuals to pursue their own good in their own way.[3] That last phrase is J. S. Mill's and it is possible, though controversial, to read Mill's *On Liberty* as espousing a neutralist position. John Locke's *Two Treatises* and his *Letter on Toleration* might also be interpreted in that way. The state is authorized to interpret and apply the laws of nature and to punish violators of those laws; but, within the bounds of the laws of nature, it must leave individuals free to live their lives as they see fit. Locke's favourite image for government is that of an 'umpire'. However, I shall not take up questions of the historical identity of liberalism. Those are separate from critical questions about the neutral state. That is, it is possible that neutralism is a defensible position but that it is not the common ingredient of the liberal tradition, or that neutralism is not a defensible position but that it is, nonetheless, the ideal central to liberalism. I shall concern myself only with the idea of the neutral state itself.

That idea gives rise to three sorts of questions:

1 What is a neutral state? What is it for a state to be neutral?
2 Is that a coherent notion? Can there be a neutral state?
3 If it is a coherent notion, is it one that we should embrace?

These are large questions and I shall deal only with the first two. However, the answer to the second question may pre-empt an answer to the third: if the idea of the neutral state turns out to be incoherent, there is no point in considering whether it is one that we should adopt. What then is the neutral state to be neutral among? I have already indicated that the answer is individuals and their conceptions of the good.

Neutrality among individuals

Neutralists offer differing formulations of this requirement, some of which are more satisfactory than others,[4] but the idea that they share in common is that individuals are to be regarded as of equal worth. No person, or class of persons, enters the world with a claim upon the state to be treated more or less favourably than others. That is not a

11

particularly remarkable view, nor one exclusive to neutralists. But there are a number of points worth making about it.

First, there is considerable significance in individuals being chosen as the objects of neutrality. That is, it makes a difference that individuals are identified as the parties amongst whom the state is to act as a neutral arbiter and not, for example, groups or cultures. Suppose a culture accorded women an inferior status. A government which was trying both to promote equal opportunities for individuals and to respect cultural diversity would then encounter a conflict of policies. However, if the principle underlying its policies were that no person should be less favourably treated than any other whatever their sex or cultural background – in other words neutrality among *individuals* – it is clear which policy should have priority.[5]

Second, there is some scope for argument over who is to count as an 'individual' for purposes of neutrality. Ackerman, for example, extends neutral political concern not to human individuals as such but only to those who are dialogically competent, i.e. those who can assert claims and engage in argument. Idiots, the dead, foetuses, the unborn, young infants are therefore excluded from neutral political concern for reasons, and with consequences, that many would find quite unacceptable.

Third, and implicit in all this, is that what parties the state is to be neutral between is not something dictated by the idea of neutrality itself. Thus the doctrine of neutrality stands in need of some principle which indicates why it is *individuals* that the state should be neutral amongst.

Neutrality between conceptions of the good

The more distinctive, and more controversial, claim of neutralism is that the state should remain neutral amongst competing conceptions of the good. What are these 'conceptions of the good' that the state is to treat neutrally? That is a potentially complicated matter and I shall confine myself to some fairly informal comments on it.

The phrase 'conception of the good' may suggest a commitment to a form of life which is the product of careful reflection and which is, in some sense, a moral commitment. A conception of the good can be like that but, in a comprehensively neutralist theory, it need not be. It should also be taken to include all of those things that we ordinarily dub a person's preferences such as a liking for cycling, Beethoven, pizzas, etc. As Dworkin says, 'the scholar who values a life of contemplation' has a conception of the good, but 'so does the television-watching, beer-drinking citizen who is fond of saying "This is the life", though of course he has thought less about the issue and is less able to describe or defend his conception'.[6] In fact it is easier to be sure of what the notion of a conception of the good should be taken to include at this more mundane level than when one enters the higher reaches of beliefs, ideals and commitments.

For one thing, a neutralist theory has to make a sharp distinction between the right and the good; that is, between the rules of right (or principles of justice) within which conceptions of the good are to be pursued, and conceptions of the good themselves. It is not always clear whether these are supposed to have mutually exclusive contents – so that, for example, a person's beliefs about the just society should not be included in his conception of the good – or whether the distinction is not necessarily one of content but one turning on the special status and role ascribed to certain principles of right. I shall return to that issue later.

The boundaries of a 'conception of the good' are subject to question in another way. Within theories of justice, an individual's conception of the good is typically regarded as something in which that individual has an interest such that, when individuals come forward with different and competing conceptions, we confront a conflict of demands calling for a just resolution. That is not to say that an individual's conception of the good must be narrowly self-interested but only that, if A and B have opposing and competing conceptions of the good, then, in some sense, the realization of A's conception must be good for A and bad for B and the realization of B's conception must be good for B and bad for A. If their interests were not in competition in this way, no issue of distributive justice would arise. But it would not seem appropriate to regard every conflict of view amongst individuals in that way. Suppose that A and B are citizens of the same state and that both desire international peace. A believes that peace will be best promoted by his state's giving up nuclear weapons while B believes the contrary. Do these differences in belief constitute differences in conceptions of the good? It would seem very odd to hold that unilateral nuclear disarmament was good for A but bad for B while the retention of nuclear weapons was good for B but bad for A. In this sort of case A and B are not rival claimants in pursuit of competing conceptions of the good, they have simply given different answers to a common question. Their dispute arises not from competing interests but merely from their having arrived at different judgements about the one best strategy in which they are both interested. The general issue to which this points is that of how and where one sets the boundary between, on the one hand, matters on which conflicts of view should be treated as endeavours to answer common questions and on which public judgements may be reached and, on the other hand, matters on which conflicts of view constitute conflicts amongst goods which are private to their holders and on which the state is to remain neutral. Is that boundary set by the nature of the case? E.g. is there something about the very nature of religious faith which makes it good for each individual to be able to live in accordance with his own beliefs rather than in accordance with beliefs formed by others (perhaps on the basis of better information)? Or is that boundary set merely by prevailing political circumstances? Are individuals' religious beliefs to be included in their conceptions of the good simply because that is how they have come to be regarded in the modern world and that is, for all practical purposes, the form in which they confront the modern liberal democratic state?[7] I do not intend to answer these questions here but only to indicate that they need to be asked.[8]

One further point of clarification. The neutral state need be neutral not between all possible conceptions of the good but only between conceptions of the good as these are held, or are likely to be held, by its citizens. For what I shall take to be the primary conception of the neutral state, that distinction is of no great significance. But, for other possible interpretations of the neutral state, it might be. Thus, consider the view that a neutral state must promote all conceptions of the good equally. On that view it matters greatly that we require this only for conceptions of the good actually held by citizens rather than (impossibly) for every imaginable conception of the good. Or suppose that the neutral state were conceived not as one which handled conflicts by neutral rules but one which resolved conflicts by neutral processes such as voting. It would then matter greatly that a particular conception of the good was held by 55 per cent rather than by 5 per cent of the population.

Neutrality and the equal promotion of conceptions of the good

How must a state act if it is to be neutral between its citizens and their conceptions of the good? Clearly it must not favour some citizens and some conceptions of the good more than others. In some sense, it must treat them equally. Thus Alan Montefiore holds that 'to be neutral in any conflict is to do one's best to help or to hinder the various parties concerned in an equal degree'.[9] We might therefore infer that, if a state is to remain neutral between individuals' conceptions of the good, it must promote these in equal degree or, perhaps, provide individuals with opportunities to promote these in equal degree. A state would therefore fail to be neutral to the extent that some citizens found their conceptions of the good less promoted, or less easily promoted, than those held by others. If that is what a state has to achieve in order to be neutral, there are a number of reasons for dismissing the ideal of the neutral state from the outset as misconceived or impracticable or both.

What should we understand by the 'equal promotion' of conceptions of the good? Suppose that we take it to mean that individuals are to attain, or are to have equal opportunities of attaining, equal levels of satisfaction understood in a Benthamite or mental-state sense.

(i) How are we to know that individuals have attained equal levels of satisfaction? In asking this I do not mean to join forces with those who doubt the possibility of any interpersonal comparison of utility. But there are clearly formidable difficulties in measuring and comparing the all-inclusive, life-time satisfactions of individuals. Individuals being assessed in this way would have an incentive to understate their satisfaction levels. But, even if we assumed that all individuals were scrupulously honest, it is difficult to see what mechanism they could use to reveal their relative levels of overall satisfaction to one another.

(ii) The equal satisfaction approach seems to assume that people's satisfaction levels increase in smooth curves. But sometimes the goods that people want are 'lumpy' so that without them they are at a low level of satisfaction but, on receipt of them, they immediately jump to a high level of satisfaction. In such cases there may be no scope for an intermediate level of satisfaction of the kind required by an equalizing principle.

(iii) What if some individuals choose goals which are intrinsically less satisfying than others? Are these goals to be more fully realized because they are less satisfying? These questions are indicative of a larger objection which is that to judge individuals' lives in terms of 'satisfaction' itself presupposes a particular conception of the good – the conception that the ultimate good is utility understood in a Benthamite sense. But individuals may reject that view and attribute greater value to other goals, such as the proverbial truth and beauty, which they therefore pursue for reasons other than their own hedonic condition and whose pursuit may not, in fact, maximize their personal satisfaction. The evaluation of individuals' lives by the criterion of satisfaction therefore itself violates neutrality for it judges individuals in terms of a conception of the good that they themselves need not share.

How else then might we understand the enterprise of promoting individuals' conceptions of the good equally? If individuals' conceptions have to be assessed by their own standards, we might adopt a principle of equal fulfilment. That is, we could establish what the complete fulfilment of each individual's conception of the good would consist in, set out a scale of stages towards complete fulfilment, and then try to ensure that each individual was at the same point on that scale. However, this too would prove highly problematic.

(i) The good which is the object of each individual's concern need not be a single, unitary good. It can be, and for most individuals is likely to be, a large variety of states of affairs to which value is attributed. Thus, we encounter the familiar issue of commensurability. It may be that an individual's conception of the good is internally diverse in a way that does not permit a single measure of fulfilment for that individual.

(ii) For the equal fulfilment principle to be practicable, individuals' conceptions of the good must be sufficiently fixed and settled for us to be able to establish a scale of fulfilment. But individuals' conceptions are likely to change and shift over the course of their lives so that we cannot treat them as if they were engaged upon a lifetime's journey to a fixed destination. The notion of a 'plan of life' which is frequently used in discussions of this subject must not be taken too literally if it is to relate to lives as people actually live them.

(iii) It may be that identical stages of fulfilment themselves have different significances for different individuals. Some people may set a high premium upon fulfilment itself and so adopt goals that are easily attainable. Others might set themselves more difficult and distant goals because the very process of striving to attain them is something which they value. Thus individuals will value identical stages of fulfilment differently. In that case, placing people at identical points on a scale of fulfilment will, like equalizing satisfaction, cease to be neutral between their conceptions of the good. However, that may be less of an objection than a complication indicating that we have to build the different value of different degrees of attainment into the idea of fulfilment itself, so that individuals can be equally fulfilled even though they are at different distances from their adopted goals.

(iv) Finally, it may be, as Dworkin suggests,[10] that the whole enterprise of using individuals' conceptions of the good to determine their claims upon a society puts things an impossible way round. People normally adopt a form of life in the light of the resources (wealth, liberty, etc.) available to them. To ask them to form conceptions of the good with no indication of the resources that are to be at their disposal may be a meaningless exercise. But if we have to establish a principle which allocates resources to individuals *in advance of* their adopting conceptions of the good, that distributive principle cannot be the equal fulfilment principle. For that principle presupposes that individuals' conceptions of the good are already in place.

There are, then, large objections to requiring a neutral state, or indeed any state, to promote each individual's conception of the good in equal measure. In fact both Dworkin and Ackerman articulate several of the objections that I have instanced and explicitly reject the principles of equal satisfaction and equal fulfilment.[11] So too does Rawls.[12] However, Rawls's position requires some comment. He assumes that individuals, who were unaware of their conceptions of the good, would choose to distribute primary goods in a manner which ignored differences in the content of conceptions of the good. But would they? If, as he supposes, rational individuals in the original position would be overwhelmingly concerned to minimize the worst possible outcome for themselves, they might well be attracted towards the equal fulfilment principle. Although they would be ignorant of their own conceptions of the good, they could know that the fulfilment of some conceptions would require more resources than the fulfilment of others. They could therefore know that, if primary goods were distributed equally (subject to the difference principle) and if they turned out to possess a more than averagely 'expensive' conception of the good, they could be worse off than if they had adopted a principle which took account of the different demands of different conceptions. Maximin would therefore seem to dictate the principle of equal fulfilment. Rawls himself does not embrace that conclusion. He rejects the equal fulfilment principle not merely because of the philosophical and practical difficulties that it presents, but also because he believes it to be the wrong principle. I shall therefore understand him to adopt the same stance on this issue as Dworkin and Ackerman even though a different stance may be inferred from his original position.

If we set aside the equal promotion of conceptions of the good, what sort of neutral position remains available to the state? One possibility is that the state could deal neutrally with individuals' claims upon it but, whatever sort of neutrality that was, it could not be said to extend to the consequences for different conceptions of the good. Consider the following remarks of Rawls.

> We should not speak of fairness to conceptions of the good, but of fairness to moral persons with a capacity for adopting these conceptions.... Fairness to persons may be achieved by a well-ordered society even though all (admissible) conceptions of the good do not flourish equally and some hardly at all. This is because it is fairness to persons that is primary and not fairness to conceptions of the good as such.[13]

Rawls here speaks of fairness rather than neutrality but we might suppose that we could translate his remarks into the language of neutrality. We would then understand him to be saying that the state is to be neutral amongst persons but that that does not entail its being neutral amongst conceptions of the good. Yet for the neutralist to concede that would be for him to concede the central tenet of his doctrine. As I commented earlier, the distinctive element in liberal neutrality is not so much neutrality with respect to persons as neutrality with respect to their conceptions of the good. In order to see how that claim can be advanced without resort to the equal promotion of conceptions of the good, we need to return to the concept of neutrality.

Two forms of neutrality

Consider first how we use the term in the context of international conflict. Suppose that nations A and B are at war and that nation C opts to remain neutral in relation to that war. What does C's being neutral mean here? It means that C refrains from seeking to advance the cause of either party to the conflict. The simplest way that C can do that is by staying out of the conflict, by neither helping nor hindering either side. Now it is arguable that neutrality in this situation does not require that C should steer clear of the conflict altogether. Recall Montefiore's definition of neutrality: 'to be neutral in any conflict is to do one's best to help or hinder the various parties concerned in an equal degree'. On this definition C could intervene in the war and remain neutral provided only that it did so in a way that helped or hindered nations A and B in equal measure.[14] That possibility immediately raises awkward questions about what helping or hindering in 'equal degree' would mean in this context. Would it mean, for example, that C should deal in identical terms with A and B; e.g. by making food or arms available to both on the same commercial terms? Or would it mean that C should intervene in such a way as not to alter the chances of A and B being successful? (These may require very different sorts of intervention: if C makes identical commercial offers of food or arms to A and B, that may alter their chances of success if one side needs food or arms more than the other, or if one side has more money with which to purchase food or arms.) However, for my present purposes, I need not resolve that issue. All I need draw attention to is what neutrality, in international contexts, is ordinarily thought *not* to require. It does not require that C should intervene in the conflict and, more particularly, it does not require C to intervene to even up the odds between A and B. That is, C, in order to remain neutral, is not called upon to establish conditions such that A and B have equal chances of success. I shall call neutrality of this form 'negative neutrality'.

Now consider the case of the neutral referee. A neutral referee is not one who steers clear of conflict or competition for to be a referee is to occupy a particular role in relation to a competition – the role of interpreting and applying the rules of the game. A neutral referee is one who administers the rules in an even-handed manner; he applies the rules no more severely to one side than to the other. To that extent, he helps or hinders both sides 'in an equal degree'. Obviously there are limits to that equality. The rules that the referee administers are not designed to eliminate every form of inequality. The rules of soccer, for example, are not designed to eliminate the effect of all differences of skill, strength, fitness and luck. But the rules do eliminate certain forms of rough play such as tripping or punching, and a referee, in applying the rules even-handedly, would be endeavouring to eliminate any advantage a team might gain by resorting to those illegal tactics. In the case of a referee therefore, neutrality does not entail having no influence or impact upon a conflict or competition; it is a matter of ensuring that the rules of the game are observed in equal measure by both sides.

I must concede that the case of the referee is not entirely satisfactory for the contrast I have in mind, for referees do not determine all of the constraints within which a game is played. They simply administer rules set by others. Perhaps a better example of what I have in mind is our conception of an ideal judicial process. Neutrality, of a certain sort, is a central feature of that process. That is, individuals' chances of being convicted or acquitted in a criminal trial, or of having a civil suit decided in their favour, should not be affected by whether, for example, they are black or white, male or female, rich or poor. A well designed judicial process would be one constituted so that any influence those differences might have upon its proceedings would be eliminated. Here again being neutral is not a matter of turning one's back or washing one's hands. It is a matter of establishing conditions of equality amongst individuals, conditions which 'neutralize' certain factors that might otherwise enable one individual to fare better than another. I shall call this sort of neutrality 'positive neutrality'.

In using the terms 'negative' and 'positive' neutrality, I do not mean to imply that these are two distinct concepts of neutrality. I mean to suggest only that 'being neutral' can take different forms in different contexts. In some cases it requires, or is satisfied by, refraining from having any impact upon a conflict. In other cases it can involve intervening in a conflict in a regulative role, though, to satisfy neutrality, that role must be neither designed, nor executed, so as to favour one side more than another.[15] There may be some doubt about whether what I have called 'positive neutrality' should be described as a form of neutrality at all. On some interpretations, neutrality entails not intervening in a conflict in any way, so that there is no scope for 'positive' neutrality. Interventions could be impartial but they could not be neutral.[16] But that highly restrictive view does not accord with ordinary usage and, more importantly, it overlooks the root idea, common to negative and positive neutrality, that of not taking sides. Of course, in intervening to regulate a conflict one cannot remain neutral on the issue of the terms upon which that conflict should be conducted. But that is not the same as ceasing to be neutral between the *parties* to the conflict. It may also be that the terms upon which a conflict should be conducted is itself a controversial matter. That is certainly true within the idea of the neutral state as I hope to show shortly. But again that does not show that a conflict cannot be regulated neutrally, that is, in a way which favours neither one side nor the other. It shows only that what constitutes 'favouring neither one side nor the other' will itself sometimes be a matter of controversy.[17]

The distinction between the two forms that neutral conduct can take – negative and positive – is of central importance to the idea of the neutral state. However, whereas the form of neutrality appropriate to international conflicts or judicial processes is usually uncontroversial, there is no similar consensus concerning the way a neutral state should relate to its citizens. Views of what form of neutrality is required of a neutral state will depend upon views of the proper scope of that state's responsibilities.

Thus neutralists who regard every aspect of individuals' well-being as the proper concern of the state will hold that the neutral state should ensure that the well-being of each of its citizens is promoted equally. In other words, it should act on the equal satisfaction or equal fulfilment principles that I have already considered. Only thus can it be said to favour none of its citizens more than others. Since the state can wash its hands of nothing that relates to its citizens' well-being, there is no scope for it to be negatively neutral on anything.

At the other extreme we might imagine someone who held that the state's neutrality should be complete but entirely negative. But to hold that would be to hold that there should be no state; for a state which could not intervene to regulate any aspect of its citizens' lives would be a state that could do nothing at all.

Between these two extremes there is a continuum of intermediate possibilities.[18] Thus a minimal state theorist who was also a neutralist would hold that the state should make equally available to its citizens a system of security of person and property. Beyond that his claim that the state should remain neutral amongst its citizens would amount only to the negative claim that it should not intervene to influence the conduct of their lives or their dealings with one another.

Rawls, Dworkin, and Ackerman set the threshold of proper state activity considerably higher than that, but they too set it at a point that makes the distinction between positive and negative neutrally crucial. Roughly speaking they hold that the state should ensure that resources such as liberty and wealth are apportioned in a way that is no more favourable to one individual than to another. Each person is regarded as having an equal claim upon resources and, as far as possible, the state should ensure that that claim is honoured. More particularly, the state should ensure that individuals are not disadvantaged in their access to resources by 'morally arbitrary' characteristics such as their race, gender, talents and abilities (in so far as those talents and abilities are the products of a genetic lottery rather than the results of their own endeavours). This general characterization of their position is subject to a variety of qualifications such as Rawls's difference principle, but their theories do entail the general sort of commitment to equality that I have described. In performing this role, the state can be said to be acting neutrally amongst its citizens in that it is merely securing, or endeavouring to secure, an equality of life-chance amongst them. No citizen should be able to complain that he is treated less favourably *qua* citizen than any other.

However, when we move to the content of individuals' conceptions of the good, the particular lives they choose to lead, the state's neutrality assumes a different form. Individuals' conceptions of the good are their own affair. The state is not called upon to adjust its arrangements to suit the particular conceptions of particular individuals, nor to adjust its distribution of resources to match the different demands of different conceptions. In other words, the just state of Rawls, Dworkin, and Ackerman remains neutral with respect to its citizens' conceptions of the good not by promoting them all equally but by making them none of its business. In that respect its neutrality assumes a negative form. The different merits and different demands of different conceptions of the good are outside its jurisdiction and it assumes a neutral posture on these matters simply by treating them as extraneous to its own proper concerns.

It may be, indeed it will be, that within the more or less equal arrangements secured by this form of neutral state, some conceptions of the good will be more easily pursued than others. Cheap conceptions will be more easily attained than those which make heavy demands upon material resources. Individualist conceptions, which demand no more than one's allotted share of liberty, will be more readily pursuable than those which require the widespread agreement and co-operation of others. But to infer from that fact alone that the allegedly neutral state is a fraud is to mistake the character of the neutrality that is being asserted. Nagel complains of Rawls's theory that 'the model contains a strong individualistic bias' and that his original position 'seems to presuppose not just a neutral theory of the good, but a liberal, individualistic conception according to which the best that can be wished for someone is the unimpeded pursuit of his own path'.[19] But the brand of neutralism represented by Rawls does not make individualist conceptions more easily pursuable because it regards those as better conceptions. Rather that is merely a consequence of its apportioning primary goods amongst individuals in an even-handed way (subject to the usual qualifications concerning the difference principle). His state is designed to be neutral amongst conceptions of the good against a background of resource-allocation which is itself neutral amongst individuals as persons capable of pursuing conceptions of the good. And it should not be surprising that rules designed to be neutral between *individuals* in this way should have the consequence of making individualist forms of life easier to pursue, even though those rules do not proscribe non-individualist forms of life. Of course, someone whose conception of the good requires more than his allotted share of liberty or wealth might object to the state's being neutral, or to its being neutral between individuals, or to its being negatively neutral between conceptions of the good. But he cannot simply point to the frustration of his aspirations as evidence of the state's lack of neutrality.

Neutrality and responsibility

I want now to use the distinction between negative and positive neutrality to clarify a number of features of neutralism. First, that distinction shows how there can be disagreement not only over whether a state can, or should be, neutral between individuals and their conceptions of the good, but also, within the idea of the neutral state, over the form that that neutrality should take. In other words, it indicates how neutralists can be at odds with one another as well as with those who reject neutralism. Second, it indicates that a theory of the neutral state rests crucially upon a theory of the state's responsibilities. Earlier I pointed out that the claim that the state should be neutral amongst individuals must rest upon some principle, not provided by the idea of neutrality itself, which indicates why it is *individuals* that the state should be neutral between and not, say, groups or cultures. Similarly, we can now see that the question of what *form* the state's neutrality should take on various matters must be answered by reference to something other than the idea of neutrality itself. That answer must be provided by a theory of the state's responsibilities which itself will normally be part of a larger moral theory. Only by reference to some such theory can the boundary be set between negative and positive neutrality. Broadly speaking the trio of neutralists I am concerned with assign the state responsibility for ensuring that individuals' life-chances – that is, their ability to pursue a conception of the good – are not prejudiced by features of the world or of themselves that are not of their own making. However, a sharp distinction is drawn between that and the particular conceptions of the good that particular individuals pursue. Individuals are conceived as themselves determining their own conceptions of the good. That is why, although an individual's choice of a conception of good must be respected as his chosen conception, no special account need be taken of the particular conception he chooses.[20] Having chosen goals against the background of resources set by the state, he must look to himself and to other like-minded individuals to attain those goals. He cannot expect the burden of their attainment to be shared by others who possess different conceptions of the good.

Indeed, on this view not only *need* not the state (or individuals *qua* citizens) take account of the specific content of individuals' conceptions of the good, it also *should* not. Suppose A possessed a more expensive conception of the good than B. ('Expensive' here could mean more demanding of liberty as well as of material resources.) Suppose too that A and B moved from a condition in which each possessed equal resources to one in which resources were held in proportion to the demands of their conceptions of the good (that is, in accordance with the equal fulfilment principle). A would now receive more resources, and B fewer, than formerly. The more expensive A's conception was, or became, the more B's bundle of resources would dwindle. Under that regime, B would clearly suffer because of the conception of the good that A had chosen and he would have reasonable ground for complaint. The equal fulfilment principle would allow the cost of A's choice to be imposed unilaterally upon B. That would contravene the principle that individuals should bear the responsibility for their own choices – not only in that they are culpable for what they choose, but also in that they must themselves bear the burdens consequent upon those choices. That is why a state which sought to equalize levels of fulfilment would be pursuing a form of neutrality that was not only different from that espoused by Rawls, Dworkin, and Ackerman, but also one that was, in their view, wrong.

Obviously, there is much in all this that is open to argument. The particular neutralist position that I have sketched relies heavily upon a distinction between those aspects of an individual's life that he can be said to have chosen and those which he cannot. That is a very difficult distinction to draw. In so far as it can be drawn, it may not coincide with the distinction between the content of an individual's conception of the good and the baseline of resources from which he pursues that conception. Dworkin, for example, although he argues broadly in the terms that I have described, is forced to accept that an individual's tastes and preferences are not wholly voluntary in origin.[21] Even if we set those difficulties aside, the centrality of the distinction between the chosen and the unchosen to an individual's entitlements remains open to argument.[22] I do not wish to plunge into this vast undergrowth of issues.

All I want to make plain is how critical they are to any specific conception of the neutral state.

Can a state be neutral?

Finally, there is the relation between the positive and negative segments of the neutral state. Can a state set the terms, either wholly or in part, within which individuals are to pursue conceptions of the good and yet remain neutral, in some credible sense, with respect to all particular conceptions of the good? The idea of a neutral state confronts a special difficulty here which takes us back to what it means to 'be neutral'. To illustrate that difficulty, let me return to the international example in which nations A and B are at war with nation C remaining neutral. Suppose that A is far stronger than B so that, without C's intervention, A is certain to crush B. Why can C's non-intervention be deemed neutral in spite of A's and B's manifestly unequal chances of success? The answer is that the example supposes that C bears no responsibility for the war nor for the relative standings of A and B. We suppose, for example, that C has not set the terms of the conflict between A and B and that it has been assigned no special responsibility for regulating international conflicts. Because it bears no responsibility either for or in relation to the conflict, its failure to intervene cannot be deemed its either helping A or hindering B. (One could reject that reasoning but, to do so, would be to hold that neutrality could never exist as an option for nations situated like C.) But suppose now that nation C had, somehow, set the terms of the conflict between A and B and set them in such a way as to make A's chances of success far greater than B's. In that case C's claim to be neutral would seem plainly fraudulent even if C itself took no active part in the hostilities between A and B.

Yet is it not just some such questionable claim that is being asserted on behalf of the neutral state? The allegedly neutral state sets the terms within which individuals are to pursue their conceptions of the good and those terms, as we have already noticed, will make some conceptions easier to pursue than others – the cheap easier than the expensive, the individualist easier than the communitarian. The neutral state is not therefore in an equivalent position to nation C in my international example. It cannot and does not disclaim responsibility for the terms upon which people pursue their conceptions. How then can it claim to remain neutral, albeit negatively neutral, on the issue of which conceptions of the good individuals are to pursue?

On some understandings of what neutrality requires, that claim would indeed be fraudulent. If the actual effect of a state's rules is to help or to hinder the pursuit of some conceptions of the good more than others, it could not claim to be neutral amongst them. The critical issue here is how intentions or reasons or purposes (which ever is appropriate to the context) bear upon 'being neutral'. Neutrality is often said to be an intentional concept in the limited sense that the intention to be neutral is a necessary condition of being neutral. That is, one should not be said to be neutral in relation to a conflict of which one is simply unaware. Being neutral entails being aware of a conflict and opting not to become a party to it. The question is whether intentions or reasons or purposes are relevant to neutrality in more than this limited way. Suppose nation C refrains from taking sides in the conflict between A and B but does something the actual effect of which is to assist A. Should we therefore say that C has ceased to be neutral? On one view we should. In the language of Montefiore's definition, C has helped A more than B and has therefore acted non-neutrally between A and B. Thus suppose that C had sold arms to A not because it wanted A to win the war but merely to make a commercial profit. As Joseph Raz observes,[23] that C's act was impelled by that reason would not ordinarily be regarded as sufficient to render the act neutral. But not every case is as straightforward as that. Suppose that A were financially indebted to C. If C were to demand repayment of the debt, A's war effort would be adversely affected. Is C therefore to be branded non-neutral in demanding repayment even though it is quite plain that C is not aiming to hinder A in its conflict with B but merely wants its money back? Or suppose that A becomes embroiled in two separate conflicts: one with B, the other with D. C adopts a neutral stance on the conflict between A and B, but sides with D in its conflict with A. Yet if C assists D in its conflict with A that will inevitably, if incidentally, adversely affect A in its conflict with B. Does C's non-neutrality with respect to the conflict between A and D mean then that it cannot be deemed neutral in the conflict between A and B in spite of the fact that C is sincerely and unequivocally committed to not taking sides in the conflict between A and B?

I am not sure what the correct answers to these questions are or whether they have 'correct' answers. It may be that we have to make yet another distinction within the general idea of neutrality; this time between (a) a strong concept of neutrality according to which C, to remain neutral between A and B, must do nothing the actual effect of which is to help or hinder either side unequally, and (b) a weaker concept of neutrality according to which C's being neutral between A and B requires that C must not take sides in their conflict but which allows that C's 'not taking sides' is consistent with its sometimes acting in ways whose incidental consequence is, but whose actual purpose is not,[24] to help one side more than the other.[25] According to the strong concept of neutrality, the just state of Rawls, Dworkin, and Ackerman is not neutral amongst conceptions of the good because its rules do not help or hinder all conceptions equally. The only sort of state that could properly claim to be neutral on that matter would be one structured in accordance with the equal fulfilment principle and, as I have already argued, such a state does not seem feasible and might be found objectionable even if it were feasible.

However, the weaker concept of neutrality does not obviously remove the possibility of a neutral state. If we were to adopt that concept, a state could be held neutral amongst conceptions of the good if the rules it laid down were set without reference to any particular conception of the good. That is, its basic structure would have to be founded upon a justification which was independent of any particular conception of the good. Only then could it be said not to take sides on the merits and demerits of rival conceptions. Only then could differences in the attainability of different conceptions of the good be deemed, not an attempt by the state to steer individuals towards particular goals, but a purely incidental consequence of arrangements which embodied no view on the use to which individuals should put the resources at their disposal. It is a state founded upon this weaker concept of neutrality that is the usual aspiration of neutralists. I therefore want to conclude by examining the feasibility of a state which is neutral in this more limited sense, while accepting that someone who understood 'neutrality' in its stronger sense could object that this sort of state is not properly described as neutral at all.[26]

I shall consider three sorts of reservation that may be expressed about the possibility of a state that is uncommitted to any conception of the good.

1 Neutral and anti-neutral commitments

How does the neutral state stand in relation to political views which challenge its own foundations? Can it claim to deal neutrally with views which challenge the principle that all individuals are to be treated as equals and which demand that different statuses be accorded to different individuals, e.g. on grounds of race or sex? Can it claim to deal neutrally with those who assert that they have indeed perceived the good and that because it is the good, societies should be devoted to its attainment to the exclusion of other, mistaken, conceptions of the good?

The answer is, of course, that the neutral state does not pretend to deal neutrally with those views. But that does not undermine its claim to be neutral; that merely indicates where it takes its stand. It is a state founded upon the rightness of treating individuals and their conceptions of the good neutrally; it is not intended to be, nor is it logically required to be, neutral on *that* matter.

It is possible to contemplate a different sort of neutral doctrine – one which took its stand 'further back'. Such a doctrine might hold that competing conceptions of the right society should be decided amongst by a neutral process – perhaps a lottery or a popular vote in which the majority was to be decisive. But that is not the doctrine we are considering. Neutralism as propounded by Rawls, Dworkin, and Ackerman is not a doctrine about the process by which a constitution should be selected, but a doctrine about what that constitution should be. Thus views which challenge the neutralist's conception of the right society are not to be dealt with even-handedly by the neutral state. They are to be ignored because they address an issue that has already been settled in establishing a neutral state.

However, that is not quite the last word on this question. The right and the good as used in this context may be sharply separated by the standing given to each but they are not therefore sharply separate in content. Conceptions of the good will often be social in character and may therefore be closely bound up with conceptions of the right society. The effect of the neutral state's setting aside alternative principles of right will therefore be to exclude conceptions of the good which are tied to those principles. That exclusiveness can be more or less severe. In its more severe form, principles of right which contradicted those to which the neutral state was itself committed would be ruled out of consideration in any form, as would conceptions of the good which embodied or which were dependent upon those principles. That, for example, is what Rawls intends when he asserts the priority of the right over the good.[27] But what a neutral state implies could also be understood less severely. Clearly, it could not accord full status to alternative principles of right *as* principles of right. But it might allow that those principles could figure as ingredients in individual's conceptions of the good. As such they could count for no more than, and no other than, conceptions of the good and they could be acted on only in so far as that was possible within the terms set by the neutral state. Thus, on this less severe interpretation, individuals could become involved in forms of life which treated some individuals as of less consequence than others, or in which some individuals surrendered basic freedoms to others, *provided* that all concerned entered into those forms of life from the position of equal standing established by the neutral state. What I have in mind here is something like Nozick's idea of 'utopia' in which social arrangements which would otherwise violate individuals' rights can be rendered legitimate if they are voluntarily entered into by all who live under them.[28]

2 Neutrality and wealth

I want now to turn to the neutral state's handling of resources, understanding that term to cover two broad sorts of resource: wealth and liberty. Can a state determine how those resources should be available to its citizens without resorting to a particular conception of the good?

Given the background assumptions of the neutralists' position, the fact that one conception of the good may prove more expensive, and therefore less attainable, than another need not impugn the neutrality of a more or less equal distribution of material resources. However, there are other issues which warrant special attention.

One is the large practical problem involved in operationalizing the neutralist's position. Even though the wealth notionally available to each life simply as a life should be equal, the amount actually available to individuals throughout their lives need not be. That is because the wealth at each individual's disposal will not be entirely independent of the form of life he adopts. For example, an individual who places a high premium on leisure relative to income, or who opts for more satisfying but worse-paid employment, will accumulate less wealth than one who opts for a life which combines little leisure, high risks and higher financial returns. The neutralist finds nothing wrong in that. But he does then have to discriminate between (a) those inequalities in wealth which result from natural and social factors beyond individuals' control and (b) those inequalities which result only from individuals' choices. The first should be corrected, the second should not. Even if we could be sure which inequalities resulted from what, it would be extremely difficult to establish a mechanism that would correct for the first but not for the second. Rawls's difference principle, for example, even though it is combined with a principle of equal opportunity, would seem ill-suited to that task.[29]

A second issue it that wealth, beyond a basic minimum, need not be a resource necessary for certain forms of life and, beyond that minimum, may be regarded as a positive evil. That would be true, for example, for an individual who chose to live a life of ascetic self-denial for religious or other reasons. There are two sorts of reply that the neutralist can make to objections based on that possibility. One is that the neutral state would make resources available to all but would not compel individuals to receive them. Consequently, those who wish to live the life of Diogenes could simply turn their backs on the wealth that the state was willing to secure for them.[30] The other reply is that, the mere fact that the state concerns itself with the distribution of a resource that is not valuable for all forms of life, does not entail that it attributes value only to forms of life which employ that resource. Provided the supply of that resource is not at the expense of other forms of resource, and provided its supply does not prejudice forms of life which do not value that resource, the state can remain neutral between wealthy and wealthless forms of life.

However, those qualifications point to a third issue – that of how far individuals can be insulated from the consequences of one another's wealth. If the reality of life is that they cannot, such that the prevailing level of wealth will actually favour some forms of life more than others, the issue ceases to be one about how wealth should be distributed and becomes one about the extent of wealth that should be available in a society at large. That is, a society then confronts a choice between different levels of wealth, a choice grounded in conflicting evaluations of the different forms of life to which those different levels of wealth are conducive. It is difficult to see how that choice could be made without choosing between conceptions of the good.[31] I will not pursue that issue further partly because it involves large and complex empirical questions but also because it arises again, in a more obvious form, in relation to liberty.

3 Neutrality and liberty

If we ignore my last point, we may say that wealth is an indefinitely divisible asset and that the neutral state need be concerned only to ensure that that asset is available in equal quantities to each life. Is it not the same with liberty? By 'liberty' here I understand the scope, the personal space, each individual has with respect to others to pursue his conception of the good. We may infer that, in the neutral state, each individual is to have as much liberty as possible subject to everyone's enjoying the same liberty. Thus Rawls's first principle: 'each person is to have an equal right to the most extensive total system of basic liberties compatible with a similar system of liberty for all'.[32] However, it would be a mistake to suppose that this can be a purely quantitative matter comparable to doling out sums of money. Setting rules governing the distribution of liberty in a society also involves inescapably qualitative judgements. Different sorts of freedom conflict with one another so that different complexes of freedom can be put forward all of which satisfy the principle of equal distribution. Consider, for example, the choice between the freedom of individuals to associate with whom they choose and the freedom of individuals not to associate with whom they choose – a choice which has been very important in relation to racial discrimination. It seems unlikely that we shall be able to decide between these two different complexes of freedom in a purely quantitative way. If some complexes are judged preferable to others that is because they are reckoned more valuable, but their value must then depend upon the kind of life one wants to lead or believes should be led.

Moreover, liberty comes into competition with other goods which rank importantly and differently in individuals' lives. One person may want no limits upon freedom of expression while another may prefer limits to be tightly drawn in the interests of public order and stability, personal security, protection of reputation, and protection from the offensive, disturbing and embarrassing. On a generous definition of freedom, some of these apparently competing goods might be included within the scope of freedom itself. In that case they would simply add to the range of competing complexes of freedom. But suppose that we treat them as goods other than freedom. It is still not clear how that could make a difference. How, consistent with neutrality, can a life which combines extensive freedom and high risks be regarded more favourably than one which places a high premium upon personal security?

These points are commonplace enough and I need not labour them. They have been frequently urged against Rawls in relation both to the priority he gives to liberty and to his equivocations over the content of that liberty.[33] They are linked to the common observation on Mill's harm principle: that it may seem to offer a simple empirical criterion for the limits of liberty but it does not. For what we are to consider harmful will itself be founded upon judgements of value.[34]

Together they raise serious difficulties for the neutralist's project. The problem is not that, under an equal distribution of liberty, some lives might be more liveable than others. Nor is it that individual liberty, as such, might be more valuable to some forms of life than to others. Rather the problem is whether a state can establish a structure of freedoms without making qualitative choices between different freedoms and between freedoms and other goods. If it cannot, the distinction between universal resources and particular goods breaks down and the state confronts a choice which intrudes into the area of the good.

It may be for this reason that Rawls, in his more recent writings, has recast some of the foundations of his theory of justice.[35] Individuals in his original position are now characterized as possessing two sorts of moral power: the capacity for a sense of justice and the capacity to form and rationally to pursue a conception of the good. They are also conceived as possessing 'highest-order interests' in the realization and exercise of those moral powers, and primary goods are now to be understood as goods which are instrumental to the exercise and realization of those powers. Such a view can, no doubt, still accommodate a wide variety of conceptions of the good but, given the conception of individuals' 'highest-order interests' to which Rawls is now explicitly committed, it is hard to see how his position can still be viewed as a thoroughly neutralist one.

The same difficulty is illustrated not so much by the theory of rights that Dworkin develops as by the theory that he does not.[36] The main way in which Dworkin suggests that political processes should be rendered neutral is by eliminating the influence of 'external preferences' – preferences that individuals have about how others should be treated or about the kinds of lives others should lead. The main device he proposes for screening out external preferences is a bill of rights. The rights included in such a bill would override or 'trump' decisions that were likely to embody external preferences. However, notice that, on this argument, the only right a person has, *in principle*, is the right not to have his life shaped to meet the external preferences of others. Thus, ideally, such a bill would give me no right to free expression as such; it would give me only the right not to have my freedom of expression curtailed to satisfy the external preferences of others. If my freedom were to conflict with the 'personal' preferences of others, it should have

no special status. Thus no special place should be given to my freedom
of expression as against others' personal preferences for personal
security, public order, a quiet life and (I would include though Dworkin
would not) their desire not to be offended or upset. This may seem odd
in a theorist who gives such prominence to rights. The explanation, I
believe, lies in Dworkin's neutralism. For to discriminate amongst
goods so that one's claim to some (e.g. freedom of expression) was a
matter of right, while one's claim to others (e.g. not being offended) was
not, would be to violate the principle that the state should remain neutral
between individuals' personal preferences.

One further possibility centring on rights deserves mention. It might
be possible to identify those freedoms to which individuals have rights
by approaching this question in a more proprietorial spirit. Up to now I
have treated freedom as though it were a resource separate from
individuals which needed to be distributed amongst them in some
satisfactory way. But it may be that the freedom to do certain things with
their lives could be held simply to 'belong' to individuals. If so, the task
would be not one of distributing freedoms but one of identifying or
recognizing the boundaries of that liberty over which each individual
had a right of ownership. The freedoms to be available in a society
would then be established not by a judgement of what set of liberties was
most conducive to the good, but by what might be called, mimicking
Nozick, an 'entitlement' theory of freedom. Freedom would be placed
within the boundaries of the selves amongst whom the state was to be
neutral. This view is implicit in Ackerman's treatment of freedom. He
appears to regard the traditional problem of the apportionment of
freedoms as a problem of practice rather than of principle. That problem
would be solved if we had a 'perfect technology of justice' which
provided complete protection for each individual's liberty.[37] The
treatment of this matter as a purely technical one implies an entitlement
or proprietorial conception of individual freedom because it simply
takes as given the identity of the freedom around which each
individual's protective shield is to be cast. If rights over freedoms could
be specified in this way, they could be asserted independently of any
conception of the good. But the problem with the proprietorial approach
is that it is liable to be merely dogmatic.

There does then seem to be a real difficulty in maintaining the sharp
distinction between the right and the good that the neutralist position
requires. The challenge facing neutralists is to show either that, in spite
of appearances to the contrary, the basic structure of a liberal society can

be set without making qualitative judgements that draw upon a theory of the good, or that, if such judgements are inescapable, they can nevertheless be sufficiently 'thin' for the liberal state to remain largely, if not comprehensively, neutral between rival conceptions of the good. There are, of course, many contemporary exponents of liberalism who believe that that challenge cannot be met and who remain unperturbed since they believe that liberalism both is and should be founded upon a theory of the good.[38] There are also many others (myself included) who still hope that something approximating to the neutralist position can be sustained for, if liberals have ultimately to accept that they, no less than their opponents, seek merely to impose a favoured form of life upon others, liberalism will have lost much of its distinctiveness and appeal.

Notes

I am grateful to Richard Bellamy, Tim Gray, Joseph Raz, Ella Ritchie, Hillel Steiner, and to the members of the Liberal Political Theory Group for many helpful comments on earlier versions of this chapter.

1   John Rawls, *A Theory of Justice*, Oxford: Clarendon Press, 1972. Rawls has subsequently revised his argument in ways which make his position less straightforwardly neutralist. For the main body of this chapter I shall take Rawls's position to be as stated in his *Theory of Justice*. I take account of Rawls's revised position towards the end of the chapter. Bruce A. Ackerman, *Social Justice in the Liberal State*, New Haven and London: Yale University Press, 1980. Of Dworkin's writings, those most directly concerned with neutralism are *Taking Rights Seriously*, London: Duckworth, 1978; 'What is equality?' 'Part I: Equality of welfare', 'Part 2: Equality of resources', *Philosophy and Public Affairs*, 10 (1981), pp. 185–246, 283–345; *A Matter of Principle*, Cambridge, Mass. and London: Harvard University Press, 1985, Parts 3 and 6. For other statements of liberalism sympathetic to the neutralist position, see Thomas Nagel, 'Moral conflict and political legitimacy', *Philosophy and Public Affairs*, 17 (1987), pp. 215–40; David A. J. Richards, 'Human rights and moral ideals: an essay on the moral theory of liberalism', *Social Theory and Practice*, 5 (1980), pp. 461–88.
2   Ackerman, *Social Justice*, p. 11.
3   This view is taken by all three neutralists but see especially Dworkin, *A Matter of Principle*, ch. 8 'Liberalism', and Rawls, 'Justice as fairness: political not metaphysical', *Philosophy and Public Affairs*, 14 (1985), pp. 245–9.
4   For example, Ackerman's embargo upon an individual's asserting that he is intrinsically superior to others leaves unclear how we should

respond to an individual who asserts that he is intrinsically inferior to others. See Bernard Williams, 'Space talk: the conversation continued', *Ethics*, 93 (1982–3), pp. 367–71.

5 While neutrality between individuals is inconsistent with some individuals being compelled to accept an inferior lot in life, that neutrality could tolerate individuals themselves, from a position of equality, opting for an inferior position out of respect for their culture – provided that that was genuinely their own choice.

6 Dworkin, *A Matter of Principle*, p. 191. Rawls is more ambivalent about the inclusion of 'mere' desires: 'conceptions of the good are not in general self-interested, although some of them are, nor are they mere preferences and personal tastes', 'Fairness to goodness', *Philosophical Review*, 84 (1975), p. 537.

7 Rawls's position as outlined in 'Justice as fairness: political not metaphysical' would seem to rely, at least partly, on this second criterion.

8 I explore some aspects of these questions in 'Intense preferences, strong beliefs and democratic decision-making', *Political Studies*, 36 (1988), pp. 7–29, and in 'Liberalism, belief and doubt', *Archiv fur Rechts und Sozialphilosophie Beiheft* 36 (1989) , pp. 51–69. For an argument that the liberal's claim to neutrality is vitiated by the very way in which he conceptualizes conceptions of the good, see Patrick Neal, 'A liberal theory of the good?', *Canadian Journal of Philosophy*, 17 (1987) pp. 567–82. See also Michael J. Sandel, *Liberalism and the Limits of Justice*, Cambridge: Cambridge University Press, 1982, especially pp. 59–65, 154–68.

9 Alan Montefiore (ed.), *Neutrality and Impartiality*, Cambridge: Cambridge University Press, 1975, p. 5.

10 Dworkin, 'Equality of welfare', p. 205.

11 Dworkin, 'Equality of welfare', pp. 186–244; Ackerman, *Social Justice*, pp. 45–53.

12 Rawls, 'Fairness to goodness', pp. 551–4.

13 Rawls, 'Fairness to goodness', p. 544.

14 For an illuminating discussion of this idea, see Joseph Raz, *The Morality of Freedom*, Oxford: Clarendon Press, 1986, pp. 120–3.

15 The difference between positive and negative neutrality is not simply that between intervention and non-intervention. When nation C sells food to the combatants A and B in a way which helps each in equal degree, it intervenes in the conflict but still remains negatively neutral in that it has no impact upon the terms of the conflict. The difference is therefore between assuming and not assuming a regulative role in relation to a conflict.

16 See, for example, Leszek Kolakowski, 'Neutrality and academic values', in Montefiore, *Neutrality and Impartiality*, pp. 72–3. The meaning of 'impartiality' and its relation to neutrality is too complicated a matter to be dealt with here. Clearly the two may not be identical in what they require. For example, C may impartially assess the merits of A's and B's conflicting claims and come to the conclusion that A's are more justified

than B's; i.e. C may adopt an impartial but non-neutral stance as between A and B. On the other hand, in many contexts neutral conduct and impartial conduct would come to much the same thing. For a discussion which brings out the intricacies of this subject, see Montefiore's analysis, pp. 3–30, 199–245.

17 Cf. Montefiore *Neutrality and Impartiality*: 'Impartiality is concerned with equal dealing in a situation of conflict – not only with treating all sides alike, but with treating them alike in terms of rules whose general application tends not to deflect or distort the development of such conflicts from their "natural course" ', p. 214. 'What constitutes the "natural" or "normal" order or orders ... is an essentially disputable question', p. 217.

18 In using the term 'continuum', I do not mean to suggest that differences amongst neutralists over the proper role of the state can be reduced to a single quantitative scale.

19 Thomas Nagel, 'Rawls on Justice', in Norman Daniels (ed.), *Reading Rawls*, Oxford: Basil Blackwell, 1975, pp. 9–10.

20 Rawls, 'Fairness to goodness', p. 554: 'as citizens the members of a well-ordered society take responsibility for dealing justly with one another on the basis of a public measure of (generalized) needs, while as individuals they and members of associations take responsibility for their preferences and devotions'.

21 'Equality of welfare', pp. 232–3.

22 It is questioned, for example, by Nozick, *Anarchy, State and Utopia*, especially pp. 213–31.

23 *The Morality of Freedom*, p. 116.

24 I use 'purpose' rather than 'intention' here to avoid the issue of whether someone should be said to intend the known but unwanted consequences of their actions.

25 This simple distinction will serve my purpose. But usage of neutrality may be still more complex. It might be held that certain sorts of action (e.g. sales of arms) could not be compatible with neutrality whatever the reasons for their performance, while other sorts of actions which have consequences for a conflict (e.g. requiring repayment of a debt) could 'reasonably' co-exist with neutrality. That distinction might rest upon evidence of what people's real reasons for these actions *generally* tend to be. Or it might simply rest upon features of the actions themselves, e.g. the immediacy of their impact upon the conflict. Cf. Raz's distinction between comprehensive and narrow neutrality, *The Morality of Freedom*, p. 122.

26 Thus Raz distinguishes between the doctrine of the neutral state properly so-called and this doctrine which he describes as 'the exclusion of ideals'. *The Morality of Freedom*, pp. 114–24, 134–7.

27 'The principles of right, and so of justice, put limits on which satisfactions have value; they impose restrictions on what are reasonable conceptions of one's good .... In justice as fairness one does not take man's propensities and inclinations as given, whatever they are, and

then seek the best way to fulfil them. Rather, their desires and aspirations are restricted from the outset by the principles of justice which specify boundaries that men's systems of ends must respect. We can express this by saying that in justice as fairness the concept of the right is prior to that of the good.' *Theory of Justice*, p. 31. See also pp. 395–6, 425, 447–52.

28 Nozick, *Anarchy, State and Utopia*, ch. 10.

29 For a discussion of this issue and an attempt to solve it by using the idea of a hypothetical insurance market, see Dworkin, 'Equality of resources'. Whether Dworkin succeeds in dealing with this issue in a manner consistent with liberal neutrality is questioned by Larry Alexander and Maimon Schwarzchild, 'Liberalism, neutrality and equality of welfare vs equality of resources'. *Philosophy and Public Affairs*, 17 (1987), pp. 85–110.

30 Cf. Rawls, *Theory of Justice*, pp. 142–3; Ackerman, *Social Justice*, pp. 59–61.

31 For a fuller statement of this sort of objection, see Adina Schwartz, 'Moral neutrality and primary goods', *Ethics*, 83 (1972–3), pp. 294–307, especially p. 304. See also Brian Barry, *The Liberal Theory of Justice*, Oxford: Clarendon Press, 1973, pp. 119–20.

32 *Theory of Justice*, p. 250.

33 See, for example, H. L. A. Hart, 'Rawls on liberty and its priority', in Daniels (ed.), *Reading Rawls*, pp. 230–52; Onora O'Neill, 'The most extensive liberty', *Proceedings of the Aristotelian Society*, 80 (1979–80), pp. 45–59; Barry, *The Liberal Theory of Justice*, pp. 120–7.

34 Raz, *The Morality of Freedom*, pp. 412–29; John Horton, 'Toleration, morality and harm', in John Horton and Susan Mendus (eds), *Aspects of Toleration*, London: Methuen, 1985, pp. 113–35.

35 'Kantian constructivism in moral theory', *Journal of Philosophy*, 77 (1980), pp. 515–72; 'Social unity and primary goods', in Amartya Sen and Bernard Williams (eds), *Utilitarianism and Beyond*, Cambridge: Cambridge University Press, 1982; 'Justice as fairness: political not metaphysical'. Rawls applies his amended approach to freedom in 'The basic liberties and their priority', *The Tanner Lectures on Human Values*, III, Cambridge: Cambridge University Press, 1982, pp. 3–87. While Rawls describes his theory as 'ideal-based' ('Justice as fairness: political not metaphysical', p. 236n), he seems no less hostile to perfectionism ('Kantian constructivism', p. 551; 'The basic liberties', pp. 6, 8).

36 I draw here upon Dworkin's ideas as set out in *Taking Rights Seriously*, chs 9 and 12, and *A Matter of Principle*, ch. 17. My interpretation of Dworkin's position is not wholly consistent with some of his remarks on rights in ch. 7 of *Taking Rights Seriously*. That, I believe, is because ch. 7 was originally an essay written some years before the chapters on which I draw and is not wholly consistent with them.

37 Ackerman, *Social Justice*, pp. 174–95.

38 For example, Raz, *The Morality of Freedom*; Vinit Haksar, *Liberty, Equality and Perfectionism*, Oxford: Oxford University Press, 1979; William Galston, 'Defending liberalism', *American Political Science Review*, 76 (1982), pp. 621–9; Steven Shiffrin, 'Liberalism, radicalism and legal scholarship', *UCLA Law Review*, 30 (1983), pp. 1103–217.

3

The neutrality of the market

A. T. O'Donnell

Economists spend a great deal of effort analysing markets. They classify them as competitive, monopolistic, oligopolistic, or whatever. They rarely talk about neutral markets. Discussions of distortions or biases tend to take perfect competition, not perfect neutrality, as their reference point. This chapter attempts to define the meaning and limits of neutrality when applied to a market process, considers whether neutrality is a desirable objective and then looks at some examples of important markets and products to explore how neutrality, or its absence, affects the outcome of the market process.

What is a neutral market?

Market neutrality is defined here as the absence of *discrimination* among customers or among suppliers. In a neutral market the same prices, and other conditions, are offered to all potential purchasers or suppliers of a particular good or service, subject only to differences in transactions or transport costs. In order to make this definition a little more precise it is useful to establish a more formal definition. Let $_iP_{ab}$ denote the price in market i at which a can buy a particular product from b. *Consumer neutrality* is obeyed if $_iP_{ab}$ is the same for all a, i.e. the price is the same for all consumers. Similarly *producer neutrality* requires that $_iP_{ab}$ is the same for all b. The i th market is defined as completely neutral if both these conditions are fulfilled. Within such a market, there will be a single fixed price for the product.

Even in a completely neutral market there is a distinction between producers and consumers. In certain cases, particularly in financial markets, a greater degree of neutrality is possible, which is perhaps best described as a *symmetry* requirement. In a symmetrical market, if the buyer and seller were to swap places, yet were unchanged in all other respects, the nature (and price) of the transaction would be identical. The following example may help to show the strength of the symmetry requirement. Imagine that a poor academic has inherited a BMW from a deceased parent and wants to sell it as the upkeep of the car is prohibitively expensive. A stockbroker contacts the academic and, after negotiating over the price, purchases the car. The next day the stockbroker, having been given a BMW by his company, goes back to the academic to try and reverse the transaction. The matrix below sets out plausible maximum and minimum prices for these transactions. In this example the swapping of roles will almost certainly result in different prices i.e. the transaction is not symmetrical. Symmetry would be guaranteed if all the prices in the matrix were the same, which would only happen if there were no consumers' or producers' surplus to be distributed between the contracting parties.

	Academic	Stockbroker
(i) Academic selling	Reservation (min.) price = 8K	Maximum purchasing price = 11K
(ii) Academic buying	Maximum purchase price = 8K	Reservation price = 7K

In contrast, consider a bank purchasing foreign exchange from another bank. Ignoring transactions costs for the moment, the nature and price of the transaction should be the same whether bank A is selling to bank B or *vice versa*. In this latter example the two parties to the transaction have similar knowledge about the product, and the same bargaining power. This situation can be described as one of *partial symmetry* which occurs if $P_{ab} = P_{ba}$ for all a, b. It is of course possible to have many different prices in such a market. For example large banks may trade foreign exchange at a certain price and smaller banks may trade with each other at a different price. A more likely split would be based on the size of transaction. It is generally the case that small amounts of foreign exchange (or shares) are traded at different prices to large amounts. In the case of equity trading this effectively means that institutional (wholesale) purchasers get better prices than individual (retail) traders. It is a moot point whether to define such differences as market imperfections (or non-neutralities) or whether it would be more illuminating to say that there are two markets for equities: a wholesale and a retail one. This makes it clearer that the existence of different prices demonstrates, in part, the administrative and other costs of distributing the product in small amounts. Nevertheless the existence of a proliferation of markets for a single product suggests the present of inefficiencies.

The ideal, from an efficiency standpoint, is a single market. Consider, for example, the market for a particular type of car, say a Honda Accord. This car is sold in many countries and within each country the market is fairly neutral.[1] However, the price in each country is rather different as a result of various factors, including voluntary quotas, so the market as a whole is non-neutral. There would clearly be efficiency gains in this kind of situation from establishing a single market. (Indeed this is one of the major reasons for the moves to break down the internal barriers in the European Community by 1992.) It therefore makes sense to concentrate on a product, e.g. Honda Accords, when defining a market and, as far as possible, to resist the temptation to apply neutrality definitions separately to sub-markets, even if each market is itself neutral.

In the notation described above this means that *full neutrality* of the market for a product requires that $_i P_{ab} = {}_j P_{cd}$ for all i, j, a, b, c, d. In other words the 'law of one price' must hold among individuals and among markets. There is a danger that this requirement is taken too literally. There will of course be transport costs and other factors which may lead to divergences between prices in different areas. Neutrality is not violated simply because it costs more money to send coal from A to B than to C. If, however, the transport cost is the same from A to B as from A to C neutrality would require that the same price prevail in B and C. A further, more stringent, requirement would be to compare the markup for transport costs of products of similar size, weight, fragility etc. in each direction. If markups on goods going from A to B are different from those going in the opposite direction there is *prima facie* evidence of non-neutrality.

More formally, this slightly weaker version of neutrality requires that $_i P_{ab} = {}_j P_{ab} + x_{ij}$ (for all i, j, a, b). The price at which a can buy from b in market i is the same as in market j apart from a markup x *which is independent of a or b*. In other words prices must be *anonymous*, i.e. they should not vary with the identity either of the supplier or the consumer.

There will, however, be cases where the identity of the transactor will legitimately affect the nature of the transaction. Smokers have to pay more for life insurance than non-smokers, but this does not mean that the insurance companies are violating neutrality. The *identity* of the consumer needs to be defined carefully so as to include all relevant factors. Anonymity is achieved if an unknown person would receive the same treatment (e.g. be offered the same insurance policy at an identical cost) as another individual who was identical as regards all the factors that the company has previously stated to be relevant.

In practice markets are often not neutral and this can often be discovered by testing whether any departures from anonymity can be easily justified. Particular customers or suppliers are often relatively favoured or disfavoured, for reasons such as trade protection, imperfect information, social or personal priorities or prejudices, or commercial exploitation.

Limitations to market neutrality

The definitions above have been structured in terms only of prices and in most cases this is all the information that is required to understand what has taken place. But what about situations where there are restrictions on the quantities sold, e.g. quotas? In general whenever there is rationing we need to know not only the prices at which transactions take place but also the method by which the products are allocated to understand fully the market process. The allocation system often takes the form of queuing which creates the possibility of an apparently neutral market in fact involving biases, as certain individuals are allowed to jump the queue. This is an important consideration when considering the distributional merits of planned versus market economies.

The discussion above also concentrated on neutrality between *transactors* in a market but it is possible that markets will treat transactors in a neutral fashion when dealing with certain *preferences* but not others. For example neutrality is likely to be much easier to achieve for preferences relating to competitively marketed, rather than *public*, goods. There are wide differences, for example, in the amount that individuals would like to spend on defence. It is not possible to let each person purchase the desired amount because public goods are, by definition, non-excludable and non-rival, i.e. you get defended whether you pay or not and the amount of defence enjoyed by any person does not diminish the amount left for the others.

Miller has described another class of preferences,[2] namely 'group oriented desires', which market systems fail to treat in a neutral fashion. The desire to work in a co-operative is a good example of a preference that is unlikely to be satisfied in a predominantly market economy. This is because, as Miller shows quite convincingly, co-operatives are likely either to invest too little or to evolve into capitalist forms of production. Miller argues that this bias towards certain forms of production demonstrates that the market mechanism is not neutral and that its efficiency in satisfying these kinds of preferences is not great.

The market mechanism, however, tends to favour production of goods *by the most efficient means possible.* If a socialist economy, or one dominated by collective enterprises, produced a good at a lower price than that charged by capitalist firms it would be able to export that product to the capitalist country. The market is neutral with respect to the *efficiency,* not the method, of production. In a market economy it is quite apparent that certain public goods are not produced efficiently by competitive firms, hence the proliferation of mixed economies. The predominantly capitalist form of production in the United States and many European countries has not prevented the existence of large public and/or non-profit sectors. This argument implies that the market mechanism is neutral over *efficient* methods of satisfying *all* preferences. Certain public goods cannot be provided efficiently by competitive markets so neutrality requires that they be provided in some other, more efficient, manner.

How then should neutrality be defined in relation to the provision of public goods? By definition each person consumes the same amount of a public good irrespective of the individual's desired level of consumption. Hence there is little point in worrying about neutrality in meeting the consumers' demands as this is impossible. This suggests that neutrality needs to be defined in relation, first, to the total amount of the public good to be supplied and, second, to the method of financing.

One possibility is that the state is charged with deciding on the level of provision. Each administration would determine what it regards as the appropriate level and the electorate would be allowed to express periodically whether or not it was happy with this level and the size of current (or future) taxes required to finance the public good. The neutrality of this system depends upon the nature of the political decision-making mechanism which is discussed in more detail in chapter 4. It is necessary to add, however, that neutral provision should be accompanied by neutral financing. Since all are provided with the same amount, an obvious definition of neutral financing is for everybody to pay the same amount. The main objection to this solution is that the benefits of public goods are often unevenly distributed amongst individuals. For example, expenditure on defence and internal security services may well provide greater benefit to those with more wealth to lose.

Neutrality in the provision of public goods is therefore rather more difficult to interpret than in the case of goods provided by traditional profit-oriented companies. There is, however, an intermediate category of growing importance. There are goods and, frequently, services provided by 'non-profit' organizations.[3] Non-profits frequently step in to alleviate the problem mentioned above, i.e. that the provision of public goods may leave some consumers wanting more of that particular good. The private sector is unlikely to fill the gap because of the difficulties of excluding non-payers but a non-profit organization may be able to operate successfully. As Weisbrod puts it, 'non-profits are useful in providing collective goods when consumer demand is heterogeneous'.[4]

The existence of organizations that lie between the private and public sectors can be explained by recognizing again that market systems tend to result in *efficient* solutions. The non-profit organizations are able to discover individuals' demands for public goods more efficiently and can therefore target their product at those with unsatisfied demand. This results in an important non-neutrality in the provision of public goods. Those who want the level of provision provided by the state are in the best position. Those wanting to consume more of the public good will be somewhat worse off because the non-profit organization will generally require some kind of payment, possibly in the form of a 'donation' to cover its costs. The main losers are those who regard the provision of the particular good as excessive. They gain nothing from the existence of non-profits and may even have to support their existence either directly through donations (possibly solicited by moral blackmail) or indirectly through the taxes needed to finance the subsidies given to non-profits.

The advantages and disadvantages of neutrality

Neutrality is often, though not always, a prerequisite for both fairness and efficiency. This is so in particular where markets are non-neutral because of prejudice. Such biases may be *personal* if based, say, on race, class or nepotism, or *national*, as in the case of protectionist legislation. Markets which avoid such prejudices are generally fairer, as among different suppliers and customers, and more efficient, in the sense that transactions are chosen only to provide the best available value for money.[5]

Neutral markets are also efficient in that transactors do not have to waste time sampling prices in different markets and haggling over prices. There is also no possibility of experiencing regret when you realize that you have paid 'too much' for something, or satisfaction from having negotiated a 'good' price.

Anonymity can also be a blessing when buying products that are embarrassing, possibly because of social taboos adopted by a particular society. Vending machines allow greater anonymity when buying condoms, thereby probably increasing total sales and the purchaser's welfare. The use of computerized medical diagnosis is beginning to show advantages over personal interviews because there is perceived to be less danger of embarrassment when confiding to a machine.

The *option* of anonymity will usually result in Pareto improvements, i.e. someone is made better off and no-one is made worse off. The *imposition* of neutrality is unlikely to result in Paretian gains. The removal of trade protection, for example, may well put the less efficient producers out of business.

There are situations in which a non-neutral market might be preferable to a neutral one, although as we shall see these situations generally involve some people losing out while others gain. Affirmative action programmes obviously involve a move away from neutrality as defined here. There will also be occasions when the distribution of initial endowments is so skewed that it might be worthwhile having non-neutral transactions in the hope of improving the distribution of wealth. If country A has a non-neutral market then it is possible that country B will need to follow suit to offset the effects of A's non-neutrality on B's market. This is of course a special example of the second-best theorem which has made practical welfare economics so much more complex,[6] although potentially more relevant.

It is also useful to distinguish between neutrality at a single point in time, or 'current' neutrality, and what might be called 'long-run' neutrality. Perfectly competitive markets achieve current neutrality but they tend to preserve the inequalities and biases inherited from earlier periods. These earlier imperfections may have been caused by a skewed distribution of initial endowments or prior non-neutralities in markets. Whatever the cause it is probable that current neutrality will need to be violated to offset these problems thereby aiding the achievement of long-term neutrality. This can be regarded as the *inter-temporal* equivalent of the second-best theorem.

A side effect of neutral markets is that they make it harder for the authorities to check up on criminal behaviour. Swiss banks are known for the strict confidentiality of the bank-customer relationship, yet it is frequently alleged that Swiss bank accounts hold the proceeds of illegal transactions. Indeed financial transactions can be among the most anonymous of all. This has enormous efficiency advantages yet ensures that, for example, money laundering is never too difficult and certain illegal behaviour, such as insider trading, is difficult to detect and even harder to prove.

Anonymity can also be less fun. The element of personal discretion in transactions, which can allow prejudice to thrive, also provides the innocent benefit of personal communication between buyer and seller which is lost in a totally impersonal system.

Neutrality within a market may sometimes be achieved only at the cost of restricting its participants – for example to those with the resources to fulfil contracts arranged instantaneously, or qualified to provide professional services.

The alternative to a neutral market is one in which prices for an identical product vary between consumers. This situation, known as price discrimination, may arise if the market for a product can be split into separate sectors and it is difficult to transfer either demand for, or supply of, the product between sectors. There must also be some restriction on entry to the industry to ensure that the supplier has a degree of monopoly power. A number of products meet these conditions, especially in the area of services. Doctors can charge patients different fees because the patient frequently cannot go elsewhere for treatment and cannot easily transfer the treatment to patients with the same problem. Similarly legal, hotel, and transport services are all commonly provided under conditions that encourage price discrimination.

From the supplier's point of view the ability to discriminate between different persons or groups is an advantage in that a discriminating monopolist will always earn profits that are at least as high as one that cannot discriminate. (This is because the discriminator could always charge everybody the same price in which case he would make exactly the same profit as an ordinary monopolist.) From the consumer's point of view discrimination generally means higher prices as profit-maximizing price discriminators can obtain up to all the consumer's surplus. In practice some monopolists who could charge different prices to different consumers often choose to offer a single, or relatively few, prices. One reason for voluntarily limiting the exercise of the power to discriminate is simply that there can be enormous administrative and time costs associated with agreeing individual prices. A second problem, noted by Pigou, is that 'it opens the way, not only to error, but also to the perversion of agents through bribery'. He added that monopolists were also constrained by what society deemed fair.

> But in practice the monopolist's freedom of action is limited by the need, already referred to, of acting on general rules.... Moreover, since a hostile public opinion might lead to legislative intervention, his choice must not be such as to outrage the popular sense of justice.[7]

In practice, states sometimes adopt price discrimination to provide products at lower prices to those with lower incomes (e.g. medical prescriptions, housing). Discriminatory pricing of goods supplied by public enterprises can also be defended on the grounds that it may be more efficient to raise revenue in this way than by the usual alternative of general taxation. In addition the state may discriminate between consumers in order to prevent certain individuals or states acquiring particular goods. Few would welcome nuclear weapons or dangerous drugs being available to anonymous purchasers. These examples demonstrate that although many economists start with a firm presumption in favour of neutral markets, few, if any, would favour them in all cases. Some examples are considered below to bring out the kinds of considerations that determine the relative desirability of neutrality in different markets. First it is worth considering the factors that create the possibility of establishing neutral markets.

Preconditions for market neutrality

A major precondition for neutrality is that *information* on prices at which transactions have taken place is publicly and easily available. It is much more difficult to discriminate between potential purchasers, charging each what you think they will pay, if they know not only what has been charged for identical products in the past but also the current prices being offered by other sellers. Another necessity is that payments be enforceable. This is an area where less sophisticated markets that operate strictly for cash have an advantage over some financial markets that tend to have a variety of means of payment, most of which involve a risk that payment will not be received. In financial markets the rules tend to be designed to ensure that the seller can deliver the product, and the buyer can pay for it, in a timely fashion. The regulatory organizations, in policing these rules, often require a great deal of information about the financial well-being of the transactors. This can be costly to collect but if transactors have confidence in the regulators they can choose who to transact with on the basis solely of price, and will not favour any particular buyer or seller.

An effective way of trying to achieve neutrality is to set up a system which ensures anonymity for transactors. Screen-based trading systems – where qualified purchasers and sellers transact through a computer – are an increasingly popular way of maintaining anonymity. Certain types of auctions produce similar results. But for these kinds of anonymous systems to function effectively access to the market has to be limited to 'qualified' traders (i.e. those who can meet their obligations). It is also necessary to monitor the traders continuously to ensure that they meet the relevant standards at all times.

Another important precondition is that the government does not impose taxes or regulations that bias choices. Government procurement rules that favour domestic suppliers will clearly upset neutrality. Transactions taxes present a more complex case. Such taxes reduce the number of trades and prevent welfare gains where the gap between the purchaser's maximum offer price and the supplier's minimum selling price is smaller than the transaction tax. Such taxes may appear to be non-neutral in that they are often paid by only one party to the transaction, i.e. the buyer or the seller. However this does not generally mean that the party that pays the tax will bear the full burden of it. Some of the cost will be passed on to the other party, the amount depending on the shape of the supply and demand curves for the product in question.

Practical examples

Informal and formal markets

There are, of course, many different kinds of markets. At one extreme there are street markets at which no fixed prices are posted, transactions take place using cash or by barter, and there are few guarantees about the characteristics of the product. Prices can be very competitive in such circumstances because sellers face low overheads. Informal markets of this kind are unlikely to be neutral in that prices depend on the bargaining skills and information available to participants. In more formal markets, such as stock exchanges, transactions take place at prices which are broadly the same at any point in time for all potential transactors. There are rules to ensure that both sides of the transaction meet their obligations and regulatory organizations designed to stop cheating. The markets are competitive, but reflect the fairly large overhead costs associated with the regulatory regime. Neutrality is virtually assured for those who can afford to participate in the market.

It is clear from this simple discussion of two rather different markets that neutrality need not always be associated with minimum prices. The examples that follow attempt to show how the degree of neutrality in each market affects the type and nature of transactions that take place.

Open-outcry markets

Futures exchanges around the world are organized in the form of open-outcry auction markets. The Chicago Mercantile Exchange (CME), for example, handles trading in futures of the Standard & Poor's 500 index, *inter alia*, in a pit where buyers and sellers shout their bid and offer prices. Self-regulatory organizations ensure that the members do not default by a system of margin requirements. In addition the Exchange acts as the counterparty to both sides of the trade (i.e. if Merrill Lynch wants to sell 100 futures contracts then a buyer is found in the pit but in fact Merrill's have sold their contracts to the Exchange which in turn sells them to the buyer). This is an interesting way of making buyers and sellers behave as if the market were anonymous. Sellers care nothing for the identity of the ultimate buyer, and vice versa, since their direct counterparty to the trade is the Exchange, in which they have complete faith. Hence exchange by open outcry – which at first sight seems the reverse of anonymity as the buyers and sellers meet face to face in the pit – is actually quite anonymous.

The open-outcry market, as operated by the CME, meets most of the conditions for market neutrality. It is a highly efficient market in that transactions costs are low and it is probably one of the cheapest places in the world to buy the particular products it sells. Nevertheless open-outcry markets are quite rare, although they remain popular for certain financial transactions such as futures and options. Their physical limitations, coupled with the scope for human error, suggest that even for financial transactions they may soon be phased out in favour of computerized trading. This has already happened with the disappearance of the London Stock Exchange floor, ousted in favour of a totally computerized system. But the performance of the futures and options markets during the stock market crash in October 1987 was in many ways superior to the spot markets, so it would be premature to expect their demise for the next few years at least.

Screen-based markets

The markets for buying and selling shares on the International Stock Exchange in London and through the National Association of Securities Dealers Automated Quotations (NASDAQ) system are becoming largely 'screen-based'. This means that qualified dealers are required to post the prices at which they will buy and sell specific shares. Anonymous, but qualified, purchasers can then transact with the dealers at these prices. There are restrictions regarding the permitted size of trades which rule out administratively costly small transactions and prevent massive purchases which would be beyond the scope of some dealers, but these limits are very wide and rarely binding.

These are perhaps the most neutral markets in existence at the moment and seem destined to take over a larger share of total sales in their markets. They have an analogue in 'home shopping'. This is a merchandizing system popular in the US where products are displayed on TV and consumers can purchase them by making a phone call using methods of payment such as credit cards. The kinds of products sold in this way are sometimes available elsewhere, but the market exists because it offers lower transactions costs in the form of convenience. The buyers are anonymous but of course this kind of shopping does not involve the possibility of obtaining the prices at which the dealer is prepared to buy *and* sell before revealing which kind of transaction you intend to make. This aspect of neutrality is one of the impressive features of screen-based markets like NASDAQ.

Auction markets

In an auction prices are not, of course, fixed beforehand, although the owner may well impose a reservation price below which he will not part with the product. The absence of fixed prices is often a good indicator of non-neutrality but the virtue of auctions is that the bidding process reintroduces some of the benefits of neutrality. In a 'normal' (English) auction bids are sequential and the highest bid above the reservation price secures the product. In a sealed-bid auction bidders put their offers in at the same time without knowing the amount of any of the other bids. It seems sensible to define a 'neutral' strategy on the part of the seller as one which treats all identical bids equally. If the seller's strategy is to maximize expected receipts this implies in most cases simply accepting the highest bid, irrespective of who makes that bid.

Economists have devoted considerable effort recently to analysing the outcome of different styles of auction.[8] One of the strongest theoretical results is the 'Revenue-Equivalence Theorem' which asserts that sealed-bid auctions generate the same expected revenue as open auctions under certain fairly strong assumptions.[9] This is a reassuring result for potential sellers as it means that they can use either form of auction and still get on average the same price. However, Maskin and Riley show that the 'optimal' auction – defined as the one that maximizes revenue – differs from the open and sealed-bid varieties by prohibiting bidders from making certain bids.[10] In particular they find that bids from certain types of bidders need to be disallowed to achieve maximum revenue (i.e. the objective of maximizing expected revenue is not possible if the auctioneer has to be neutral).

A number of empirical studies have attempted to test the revenue-equivalence theorem. One problem is that it is difficult to find examples of auctions of the same product that were conducted in both open and sealed-bid forms. Fortunately, due to a change in federal law, the US Forest Service conducted both sealed-bid and open auctions for contracts to harvest timber in 1977. Hansen concluded, on the basis of this data set, that 'the joint hypothesis implied by revenue equivalence cannot be rejected at the 95 per cent level'.[11] (The reference to a joint hypothesis refers to the need to model first the process of deciding whether to use a sealed bid or open auction and second the value of the highest bid conditional on the choice of auction method.)

Against this brief theoretical background it is informative to look at how governments have actually organized auctions and whether they have adopted 'neutral' strategies. The regular auctions of US government securities are interesting examples of the sealed-bid approach. The products are well understood by the bidders and there are regular auctions so that learning is possible. The government adopts the rule of accepting bids, starting from the highest price and going down to lower prices until the amount for sale is exhausted. For example, imagine that the Treasury is selling $100 million of 20-year bonds and has bids worth $50 million at a price of 100, $50 million at a price of 90, and $10 million each at prices of 85 and 80. The bids at 100 and 90 would be accepted and the bidders would have to pay these different prices. The bidders offering below 90 would get nothing. The result is that the product is sold at a variety of prices, reflecting the strength of the demand for these particular bonds by the different bidders. This strategy can be defined as neutral in that all bids at a given price are treated equally. It also probably maximizes revenue, but it is interesting to note that in this case neutrality does not imply that all purchasers pay the same price for an identical product. After the auction, once the bonds are traded in the secondary market, the law of one price reasserts itself and the market becomes neutral in the sense defined at the start of this chapter.

The auction has been refined to help non-professional bidders. They are allowed to enter 'non-competitive' bids which are allocated in full at the average price of the successful competitive bids (95 in the previous example). This feature ensures that private investors are not elbowed out by the professionals. But it violates neutrality and probably lowers expected revenue. The professional dealers operate mainly through a network of specialists known as primary dealers, who have certain advantages in auctions.[12] Such dealerships are allocated by the Federal Reserve taking account of numerous factors. Increasingly the emphasis has been on whether primary dealerships are equally available to foreign firms in the country of the applicant. This can be interpreted as an attempt to force 'international neutrality' by applying reciprocity standards (i.e. you can bid in our auctions if we can bid in yours). The imposition of reciprocity requirements has probably reduced the number of primary dealers and, to a marginal extent, it may have reduced the number and value of bids at auctions.

The method of selling houses in Scotland provides a good example of a special type of sealed-bid auction. Purchasers make sealed bids which are all opened on a given day but the seller's choice of the winning bid is often influenced by non-price factors like whether the purchaser can pay immediately or must await the sale of another property. This is a perfectly valid reason for discriminating between potential purchasers but the system leaves open the possibility that sellers will take into account considerations that we would rather they ignored e.g. race or colour. But at least the seller is made aware of the direct financial loss (measured by the difference between the highest and the chosen bids) incurred as a result of his or her prejudices.

Non-competitive markets

Even in those countries most committed to capitalism, some products are produced in a non-competitive environment. This may be the result of a 'natural monopoly' or of a government decision to have only one supplier. In such circumstances the prospects of achieving any of the benefits of neutrality are bleak. The most common examples concern products which are either extremely expensive, for example, the space shuttle, or which may have limited sales potential because of government restrictions, such as certain defence products, like the Stealth bomber.

Defence ministries have generally coped with this problem by awarding contracts on a cost-plus basis. The drawback of such contracts is that the profits earned by the manufacturers increase with the costs of production. The incentives are clearly in the wrong direction. One contract that resolves this incentives problem has been described by Nalebuff and Stiglitz.[13] They consider the case where there are two potential producers of, say, a prototype weapon. Neither the government nor the companies can accurately predict how much the weapon will cost to build. Their suggestion is to give a contract to firm A that promises to pay a fixed amount plus whatever it costs firm B to produce the product and similarly give firm B a fixed amount plus firm A's production cost. If firm A is efficient, and manages to produce the weapon at a lower cost than B, it will keep any savings. Similarly firm B knows that its profit will be reduced pound for pound by the amount by which its production cost exceeds that of firm A.

This system is more neutral than single firm contracts in that it discriminates less between firms. It has the added advantage of telling the government how much the product really costs to produce which can be used to help price future contracts for further supplies of the weapon. There is, of course, a cost in that the government has had to pay for some unnecessarily duplicated expenditures, but this may be a small price to pay for obtaining a more accurate guide to the true production costs.[14]

The nature of the modification introduced by this contract into the neutrality condition can be understood by looking at the equations that determine the prices received by companies j and k from the purchaser i.

$$P_{ij} = C_k + x$$
$$P_{ik} = C_j + x$$

where C denotes the cost incurred by the producer and x is the fixed amount given to each contractor. Since the price received by j is independent of any item under his control, profits are maximized by minimizing his own costs. The law of one price is violated, so there is not perfect neutrality, but the incentive structure has been greatly improved.

Labour markets: discrimination and affirmative action

The labour market is perhaps the least anonymous of all markets. In cases where the distinction between the transactors and the product ceases to exist, anonymity ceases to be possible. Prostitution is an obvious example. Buyers, while possibly keen to be anonymous themselves, are not indifferent between different suppliers. In theory a system could be devised where firms indicate the skills that are required for a specific job, and a job centre or a recruitment agency could match these against individuals searching for a job. But it is rare for a personnel manager to be willing to hire someone without conducting a face-to-face interview. There are good reasons for interviewing but it is always possible that interviews are used to provide information that should be irrelevant and which the firm would not dare request on a printed form.

The anti-discrimination legislation that has been passed in the UK can be regarded as an attempt to move towards greater anonymity in the hiring and firing process. In the US affirmative action measures are a good example of a second-best solution. For various reasons certain minorities are disadvantaged in the labour market in ways that cannot be directly and immediately rectified. Given these distortions it is possible to improve matters by biasing choices in ways that offset the existing distortions. Viewed in this light affirmative action programmes involve a trade-off whereby efficiency losses are accepted in order to promote the objective of greater equity. However, the policies are perhaps better interpreted as necessary, temporary measures designed to speed up the achievement of long run neutrality.

It is not clear how imposing non-neutrality of this kind will affect output or efficiency. Consider Mr K, an employer who has a prejudice against blacks. Given a choice between two individuals who would perform a job equally well (i.e. have the same marginal products) Mr K would choose the non-black applicant. If an affirmative action programme now makes him hire the black person there will be no change in the company's output or efficiency since by assumption the marginal products of both applicants are the same. There may be some cases in which affirmative action laws in the form of quotas may result in the hiring of some workers with lower marginal products but it is also likely that some more efficient workers will be hired. Remember, Mr K would prefer a non-black to a more productive black worker so his prejudice will in some cases result in lower output.[15] It is also likely that employers *learn* about the actual productivity of workers and may revise their views. Mr K may come to realise that his prejudices are not borne out in practice and may as a result revise his prior beliefs. This suggests that, while neutrality may well be the appropriate long term goal for labour markets, its achievement may be hastened by apparent departures from neutrality to enable one of its preconditions to be achieved, namely the absence of irrelevant considerations in the decision process.

Labour markets: contract neutrality

During the 1970s and 1980s economists have increasingly concentrated on situations where the traditional market assumptions of certainty and full information do not always prevail.[16] Much of the literature has focused on the labour market and the problems facing an employer trying to choose the person who will be most productive without any direct information on that person's abilities. One strand of the literature has concentrated on the choice of labour contract that will achieve the best result. Consider a firm that wants to hire the salesperson who will sell the most. Assume that applicants know exactly how well they will do but in the firm's eyes they all start off as equal. The simple solution is to offer a contract based only on commission (increasing the commission rate until one person accepts) or it could conduct an auction hiring whoever agrees to accept the lowest commission rate.

How does this procedure fit in with our notions of neutrality? An obvious definition of neutrality in labour contracts is to require that applicants that are judged *ex ante* to be identical are offered the same contract. In the hiring example the firm suspects that the applicants are *not* all the same and it wants to use the information (or signal) provided by their responses to different types of contracts to learn more about them. The final contract is offered to all, so neutrality is preserved, while the firm is able to discriminate between the good and bad sellers. More complex contracts can help to distinguish other features of the applicants such as their attitudes to risk.[17]

Complex contracts are rare and with good reason. The more that the contract is refined to select exactly the 'right' candidate, the greater are the chances that the contract will choose the wrong person because of even small changes in the underlying conditions. Consider the previous example, amended so that commission accounts for only half of the salary, and add the assumption that the best salespeople happen to be the most risk-averse. It is now unlikely that the most able person will get the job. A contract offering a high basic element with a small element of profit-related pay would best fit this situation. But if we assume, as seems plausible, that the effort put in by the salesperson is proportional to the size of the profit-related portion of the pay, it makes sense to increase this portion. As Leonard and Zeckhauser note, 'Adding even a small payoff from effort to a contract context that originally involved only selection and risk aversion could dramatically alter the contract stipulations required to achieve optimality'. They conclude that it is not surprising that most contracts are fairly simple. Complex contracts are 'like creatures too carefully adapted to a particular ecological niche ... vulnerable to small changes in conditions'.[18]

These kinds of contracts are neutral in that identical applicants are offered the same contract but they are not neutral between certain characteristics of people, such as their ability to sell. Once discrimination is allowed on the basis of a particular characteristic the merit of neutrality is potentially considerably diminished. An employer could argue, for example, that he treats all white applicants equally, or the Nazis could point out that all Jews were treated equally. This highlights the need for some means of determining that the characteristic used as the basis for discrimination is legitimate (or acceptable to society). This is unlikely to be at all easy in practice particularly given that employers could argue that their contract design reflected uncomfortable compromises made necessary by the need for robustness. Further research is clearly needed and a great deal is being carried out in the US where the interface between law and economics is proving to be a highly fertile area.

International dimensions of market neutrality

As we have seen, non-auction markets that are perfectly neutral will obey the law of one price. In general products sell for different amounts in different countries because neutrality is violated in various ways. Factors such as transport costs affect prices but are generally relatively unimportant compared to the distortions caused by tariffs and quotas.

Governments tend to be unwilling to allow foreign products to compete on a perfectly neutral basis with domestic ones for numerous reasons. First, many believe that domestic production creates jobs, while purchasing imports results in a loss of jobs. If all countries adopt rules of this kind everybody is likely to be worse off. Yet it may pay no one country to drop its barriers to foreign goods in the absence of action from its competitors (for in so doing it is throwing away a bargaining point to help drive down protective barriers elsewhere). This is the *raison d'être* for the General Agreement on Tariffs and Trade (GATT) which attempts to negotiate multilateral agreements to reduce barriers to trade. Second, there may be strategic reasons for favouring a domestic producer to ensure that some production capability remains in the economy in case the products are needed urgently and will not be supplied by other countries for some reason.

Those making the argument about losing jobs to foreigners tend to ignore the possible job losses as a result of retaliation. The job gains are usually more visible and localized than the job losses which tend to be spread around various exporting companies. The protection of the domestic industry is also likely to result in inefficiencies and higher costs for domestic producers. The strategic argument is often deployed regarding weapon systems or other defence products. Its validity is questionable as there may well be other ways of meeting the strategic requirement such as building stockpiles or making arrangements with alternative suppliers.

The moves toward dismantling internal trade barriers in Europe by 1992 represent a significant step towards greater neutrality. The efficiency gains, as estimated by the European Commission, should be substantial. The same is true of the US–Canada Free Trade Agreement. The one potentially worrying aspect of these developments is that neutrality *between* the large trading blocks may suffer. But if the gains from the removal of barriers within these regional areas are as large as expected, there will surely be a strong presumption in favour of reducing barriers between the blocks to achieve further improvements in efficiency.

Conclusions

On efficiency grounds there is a strong presumption in favour of neutral markets. The more surprising conclusion that seems to emerge from considering various kinds of markets is that there is often a strong case for neutrality based on equity considerations. If we accept that neutrality is desirable how can it be fostered? One plausible answer is that no action is required. Consumers will seek out neutral markets, producers will adopt neutral hiring rules and sellers will use neutral auction strategies because to do otherwise would reduce their welfare. In certain cases, however, the achievement of neutrality may require some prodding by governments. (This may mean, paradoxically, implementing legislation that requires apparent violations of neutrality to achieve it in the end.) In markets that are already fairly neutral, further gains can probably be achieved by modifying the rules and regulations to make transactions as anonymous as possible.

In addition, any measures which make transactions more visible will probably make markets more neutral. It is particularly important that the prices at which transactions take place are available publicly at low cost. (One curious feature of the English housing market is the difficulty of discovering actual prices paid for specific houses.)

Finally there may well be cases when government decide that they prefer the outcome of a non-neutral market. This could reflect social or distributional objectives or it might be an attempt to offset non-neutralities in related markets. Even in these circumstances it will be important to be able to define and measure the deviations from 'neutral' prices to see whether the policies are achieving the desired objectives, and at what cost.

Notes

The views expressed in this chapter are my own and do not necessarily represent the views of any government department. I am extremely grateful to the editors and to Michael Spackman for comments and suggestions.

1 In the UK there are divergences between the prices paid by individuals and those paid by companies for fleets of cars. These reflect quantity discounts and other factors, such as differences in price elasticities of demand.

2 D. Miller, 'Market neutrality and the failure of co-operatives', *British Journal of Political Science*, 11, pp. 309–29.

3 The term 'non-profits' has become widely accepted, particularly in the US but it is really too narrow to cover the kinds of organizations that fill the gap between public and private provision. They are more accurately described as 'intermediate organizations' which Ware defines as 'organizations which in law are private institutions but which take a legal status that prevents the distributions of any profits they make'. A. Ware, *Between Profit and State*, Oxford: Polity Press, 1989, p. 1.

4 B. Weisbrod, *The Nonprofit Economy*, Cambridge, Mass: Harvard University Press, 1988, p. 25.

5 H. Varian, 'Equity, envy and efficiency', *Journal of Economic Theory*, 9, pp. 63–91.

6 R. G. Lipsey and K. Lancaster, 'The general theory of second best', *Review of Economic Studies*, 24, pp. 11–32. The theory states that if there is a constraint preventing attainment of one of the Paretian conditions, then an optimum position can generally only be achieved by departing from all the other conditions.

7 A. C. Pigou, *Economics of Welfare*, 4th edn, London: Macmillan, 1932, pp. 280–1.

8 W. Vickrey, 'Counterspeculation, auctions and competitive sealed tenders', *Journal of Finance*, 16, pp. 8–37; J. G. Riley and W. G. Samuelson, 'Optimal auctions', *American Economic Review*, 71(3), pp. 381–92; E. S. Maskin and J. G. Riley, 'Auction theory with private values', *American Economic Review*, papers and proceedings 75(2), pp. 150–5.

9 The assumptions are that each bidder's reservation price for a unit of an indivisible good is an independent draw from the same distribution and that bidders are risk neutral.

10 E. S. Maskin and J. G. Riley, 'Auction theory with private values', *American Economic Review*, paper and proceedings 75(2), pp. 375–80.

11 R. G. Hansen, 'Empirical testing of auction theory', *American Economic Review*, papers and proceedings 75(2), pp. 156–9.

12 There are also rules governing payment which ensure that successful bidders meet their financial obligations. The professional bidders, such as primary dealers, have special arrangements while non-competitive bids have to be accompanied by cheques.

13 B. J. Nalebuff and J. E. Stiglitz, 'Information, competition and markets', *American Economic Review*, papers and proceedings 73(2), pp. 278–83.

14 Pigou, *Economics of Welfare*, chapter XVII.

15 On the potential inefficiency of racial discrimination see G. Becker, *The Economics of Discrimination*, 2nd edn, Chicago: University of Chicago Press, 1971.

16 See, for example, K. Arrow, *Essays in the Theory of Risk Bearing*, Chicago: Markham, 1971 and M. Spence, *Market Signalling*, Cambridge, Mass.: Harvard University Press, 1974.

17 Pigou, *Economics of Welfare*, chapter XVII.

18 H. B. Leonard and R. J. Zeckhauser, 'Financial risk and the burden of contracts', *American Economic Review*, papers and proceedings vol. 75(2), pp. 156–9.

4

Legislation and moral neutrality

Jeremy Waldron

I

In this paper, I want to discuss some aspects of the modern liberal theory of legislation and state action. In particular, I want to consider what I shall call '*the doctrine of liberal neutrality*', expounded by philosophers like Ronald Dworkin, Bruce Ackerman, and Robert Nozick.[1] But though I shall be concentrating on the suggestions that have been made in these recent writings (together with some rather less explicit arguments in John Rawls's *A Theory of Justice*[2]), the themes that I shall be discussing have a rich heritage. The idea of neutrality is only the most recent attempt to articulate a position that liberals have occupied for centuries: the ancestry of the idea may be traced back through John Stuart Mill's essay *On Liberty* and Immanuel Kant's *Metaphysical Elements of Justice* at least as far as John Locke's *Letter Concerning Toleration* and maybe even further.[3] It is the latest expression of a view that liberals have always held about the attitude the state should take to the personal faith and beliefs of its citizens.

We talk about *the* liberal view and *the* doctrine of liberal neutrality, but one of the points I hope to make in this paper is that there are in fact *several* such views, each based on premises and yielding practical requirements that differ subtly from those involved in each of the others. It is not my intention to single out and defend any one of these views in particular as the one that we ought to adopt. I am taking on the more modest task of sorting out the work that needs to be done before *any* view of this kind can be defended.

II

We have to start somewhere. Perhaps the clearest expression of the modern doctrine is to be found in Ronald Dworkin's paper 'Liberalism'. As Dworkin put it, the doctrine requires that legislators (and other state officials)

> must be neutral on what might be called the question of the good life, or of what gives value to life. Since the citizens of a society differ in their conceptions [of what makes life worth living], the government does not treat them as equals if it prefers one conception to another, either because the officials believe that one is intrinsically superior, or because one is held by the more numerous or powerful group.[4]

The idea that Dworkin is getting at here is quite familiar to anyone who has read their Locke or their John Stuart Mill. It is the idea of tolerance, of secularism, of the state standing back from religion and personal ethics. But it is worth remarking that Dworkin's *formulation* of the liberal position is quite new; I mean its formulation in terms of the image of *neutrality*. I am not aware of the use of this image by any liberal writer to express such a position prior to 1974. In a book published just before the Second World War, T. S. Eliot occasionally referred to the secular conception of the state which he opposed, and which he believed existed in Britain in 1939, as 'the idea of a neutral society'.[5] But I have managed to find no evidence that any liberal view that Eliot was opposing was ever actually formulated in these terms. The image of neutrality, then, is relatively new to the liberal tradition. I believe it is a promising and helpful image (helpful not only in expressing the liberal position but also in highlighting some of its difficulties). But it is an image which is easy to misunderstand – the more so because it may be discredited automatically by being associated with other contexts in which the image of 'neutrality' has been deployed, particularly in relation to the discredited chimera of 'value-neutrality' in the social sciences which was widely canvassed in the 1950s and 1960s and which remains alive in some shadowy corners even today.[6] I hope that in this paper I can dispel some of the more obvious and more probable misunderstandings that may arise from the use of this image to express the liberal attitude towards ethical diversity.

III

The first thing to note about the use of the neutrality image is that neutrality itself is far from a straightforward concept. Certainly the course of the recent debate has shown that it is not one that is particularly amenable to uncontroversial logical analysis.[7] We can say a bit about it by way of analysis, but not much.

The concept of neutrality presupposes a *contest* between two or more sides (two or more people, parties, teams, nations, religions, ideals, values) and it focuses attention on a third or additional party whose actions and status are in question and to whom either the term 'neutral' or the term 'non-neutral' is to be applied. It is not necessarily the judicial or quasi-judicial image of the 'triad' – plaintiff, defendant, judge – though of course that is an area where the image is often invoked. The third party's status and actions which are in question may or may not include an attempt to mediate between the other two. (Sometimes the concern is merely whether the third party can go 'neutrally' about her own business ignoring the conflict between the other two as far as possible.)

The neutrality of the third party is a matter of her relation to the contest between the other two. In attempting to pin this down, two points of reference can be identified. (1) If the third party takes part in the contest in the same way and on the same terms as the sides by whose actions and interactions it is constituted, she can never be described as neutral. (2) If the actions or existence of the third party can have no impact on the contest at all, either on its course or on its outcome, then the question of her neutrality does not arise. Those are our fixed points. In between we have all the cases in which the third party has or might plausibly be thought to have an effect on the contest to the detriment or frustration of the interests of either side. That is the situation of most third parties in relation to most disputes, and that is, so to speak, the *domain* of the concept of neutrality. The concept of neutrality is the concept of a range of actions open to the third party which are not to count (for some purpose – to determine, for example, whether it is appropriate to retaliate, or whether the contest is fair) as involvement or participation in the contest. The immediate function of the concept is to mark a division in the domain somewhere between our two fixed points, between a status and actions that count as non-involvement and a status and actions that count as involvement in the contest.

There is always some point to this division of the middle area into a realm of non-involvement and a realm that counts as being involved. In the context of international law, for example, one can think of various reasons we have (we, the international community) for wanting to draw such a line: the containment of conflict; preservation of the possibility of mediation and 'honest broking'; the need to allow international trade and diplomacy to proceed on some sort of basis even while a conflict between nations is going on; and 'so on. These reasons will be different in different contexts. A particular set of reasons, together with the sorts of demarcations they suggest, will define, as it were, a particular *conception* of neutrality.[8] Thus in international law, the reasons which make it seem desirable to the international community that there be such a thing as a neutral status provide the basis of a particular conception of how and where the line between third parties' involvement and non-involvement in a conflict is to be drawn. Inasmuch as people may give different accounts of those reasons, or map them out as a demarcation in different ways, there will be competing conceptions of neutrality at work in international law.

As well as the reasons that there are for having such a thing as neutral status, there will also be reasons which particular third parties – in international law, reasons which particular nations – have for wanting to be on one or other side of that line. Just as the idea of neutrality is not self-evident, so a policy of neutrality is not self-justifying. Some states are neutral out of distaste for war; others for reasons of survival; others for reasons of domestic politics. It is obviously crazy in international affairs to expect a neutral state to have 'neutral' reasons for its neutrality. Neutrality is not vitiated by the fact that it is undertaken for partial or self-interested reasons. One does not, as it were, have to be neutral all the way down. This point, as we shall see, is very important for an understanding of the logic of the liberal doctrine.

As I have indicated, the idea of neutrality is probably most at home in the context of international law – in the doctrine that any sovereign state may opt to be neutral in relation to any war or conflict between other nations in which it is not *ab initio* involved, and that if it publicly exercises this option, it acquires certain duties, rights and powers which are in theory enforceable in international tribunals. But even in international law, the meaning of 'neutrality' is not fixed and uncontroversial (mostly because of the changes and shifts that take place in the two sets of reasons I mentioned in the preceding paragraphs). Two illustrations of the way the doctrine changes may be of some interest.

On the traditional doctrine, a neutral government has a duty to refrain from helping either of the belligerent powers; but it is not required to prohibit or prevent its private citizens from trading with one of the belligerent countries or offering loans or whatever. Now that doctrine works fine in a world in which most economies are organized on a *laissez-faire* basis and in which there is a clear distinction between government action and private trade. But what conception of neutrality are we to adopt for cases where the putatively neutral state itself controls the economic activity of its society – directly or indirectly through nationalized agencies? No easy answer is available; it is partly a matter of what it is reasonable to expect from a country if it is to secure the advantages of neutrality (should the price be economic self-immolation?), and, on the other hand, of what it is reasonable for the other belligerents to put up with before acting against the putatively neutral party. No amount of purely logical analysis can tell us how the concept is to be deployed to deal with problems like this.[9]

Second, it may be worth saying something about the precarious history of the doctrine of neutrality in international law. If one reads Hugo Grotius or any of the natural law writers of his generation, one will find that the modern doctrine of neutrality is rejected at least in relation to those conflicts that can be classified under the heading of 'just wars'. The traditional idea of the just war is profoundly hostile to the doctrine of neutrality, for it is the idea of a war which one of the belligerents is morally justified in waging and in respect of which it may reasonably expect the support and co-operation of other powers. In that circumstance, the idea that a nation was entitled to stand back impartially, helping and hindering one party no more than the other, was regarded as morally misguided.[10] The modern doctrine of neutrality emerged only as the idea of a just war – or rather the idea of a *demonstrably* just war – became discredited. (The work of the Swiss jurist Emeric de Vattel was seminal in this respect.[11]) If there was no clear way of picking and choosing between the justice of the belligerents' causes, then there was no way states could be thought to be under a *duty* to intervene, and so a liberty to sit on the sideline, and the attachment of rights and duties to the exercise of that liberty, was the logical conclusion. But, by the same token, whenever the doctrine of the just war is resurrected (even implicitly as it was in the latter stages of the Second World War, or as in the claim that a war – like the Korean War – might have the status of an 'international police action') then again the doctrine of neutrality goes into decline. For evidence of this, we need only look at the wholesale and flagrant violation of what would normally be neutral duties by the United States in 1940–1, parading itself both as neutral in the conflict between Britain and Germany and, at the same time, 'the arsenal of democracy', supplying enormous amounts of military equipment and intelligence to the British. We may look also at the considerable international criticism that was directed at the decision of a state like the Irish Republic to remain aloof from the war against the Nazis *pour épater les anglais.*

It would be fascinating to draw a parallel between the disrepute of neutrality in relation to just wars, and the criticisms that are directed at the doctrine with which we are concerned – the liberal doctrine of moral neutrality – in relation to what certain moralists would see as the 'just war' being waged (say) by Christian values against the values of secular humanism. But I will not pursue the analogy any further.

What I did mean to stress was that even on its home turf, so to speak, neutrality is far from a straightforward or uncontested concept. And that is to say nothing of its use in other contexts: the concept of neutralism (as distinct from neutrality) in international diplomacy; the idea of neutrality as a judicial ideal; ideas of neutral colours, neutral tastes, neutral chemicals; the alleged neutrality of meta-ethical analysis; the idea of value-neutrality in the social sciences (with which, as I said, liberal neutrality is often confused); neutrality in education; and so on. All of this means that we are dealing with a host of images of neutrality, not a single image. If they are united by anything at all, it is by their all being conceptions of the abstract concept I outlined earlier (and it has to be pretty abstract to fit some of them in!). Thus, when liberals talk then about the desirability of morally neutral legislation, it is simply not clear so far which of these conceptions they want us to bring to mind.

One issue of definition, in particular, is very important. When a liberal like Dworkin says that a legislator must be neutral as between competing conceptions of the good life, is he talking about neutrality so far as the legislator's *intention* is concerned, or is he talking about the neutrality of the *effects* of the legislator's actions?

A number of writers – Alan Montefiore, for example, and I think, Joseph Raz – have interpreted liberal neutrality as concerning primarily the *consequences* of legislative action: the legislator must take care that her laws are even-handed in their effects on competing conceptions of the good life.[12] On this account a neutral law must not increase the chances of, say, a hedonistic lifestyle flourishing at the expense of adherence to traditional Christian values. It must enhance or retard the prospects of these lifestyles to the same degree. But this conception gives rise to enormous problems. The main theoretical difficulty is that it involves the postulation of some baseline relative to which differential effects of legislation or other state action may be measured. That aside, in practical terms it is a very difficult requirement to live up to, because it is so hard to predict what the effect of a law is going to be on lifestyles and mores. If that is how neutrality were to be understood, we should have grave doubts about whether it was ever reasonable to require legislators to be neutral.

However, instead of that, the liberal may be talking instead about neutrality of intention – that is, neutrality in relation to the motives and reasons that the legislator uses to justify her laws. She may say – and I think this was John Stuart Mill's view (at least in Chapter One of *On Liberty* – the argument in Chapter Two points in the other direction) that power must not be exercised over people for non-neutral reasons.[13] Thus, for example, the fact that a law against Sunday trading would accord with the requirements of a sabbatarian faith is not a good reason for having such a law; but the fact that it is necessary to prevent shop employees from being overworked may be. And the latter reason can be a good reason, and the legislation neutral on that account, even though the law undoubtedly benefits sabbatarianism over other sects. John Locke gives another example in his *Letter on Toleration*: a prohibition on the slaughter of cattle may particularly disadvantage a religious sect that focuses on animal sacrifice; but it will be justified nevertheless if, say, an economic or public health reason can be given for the ban.[14] One and the same law, then, would be permitted or not permitted by the neutrality constraint depending on what the reasons for it were.

This looks as though it should also be a hard doctrine to apply in practice, because of the difficulty of telling what the reasons behind a particular piece of legislation were. But that may be an unnecessary problem to worry about. Perhaps the doctrine of liberal neutrality ought to be understood primarily as a basis of political morality in a narrow sense – that is, as a basis for each law-maker to evaluate her own intentions – rather than as a doctrine for evaluating legislation as such. Or perhaps it can be seen as a constraint on the reasons *we* deploy in our reconstruction of the justification of some rule we support (whatever its original intention was). We should not think of political morality simply as a set of principles for judging outcomes. Its primary function is to guide action and to constrain practical thought.

Which of these conceptions should the modern liberal adopt? Nozick seems to favour the second;[15] so it seems does Dworkin, though he is not entirely consistent on this.[16] Bruce Ackerman oscillates freely between the two, depending on what he wants to use the neutrality constraint to rule out.[17] Certainly, Raz and other critics of liberalism are happier attacking the first (equality of consequences) conception than the second (motivational) one.

My hunch is that this is not a matter we can simply *decide*. And it is not a matter of peering at the rival conceptions of neutrality to see which is most congenial to our 'intuitions' or which best approximates some dictionary definition. Rather, it is a question of the ultimate argument or justification that we want to bring forward in favour of liberal neutrality. Is our argument for neutrality based on moral scepticism? Is it based on a commitment to the positive value of ethical diversity? Is it based on a faith in moral progress like that of John Stuart Mill? Is it based on the importance of autonomy and the evil of coercion? Is it based on political worries about entrusting legislators with the moral authority perfectionism would involve? Or is it, as Dworkin suggests, derived from some deep ideal of equal respect? All these are arguments that can be, and have been, made in favour of the doctrine. The thing to remember is that a policy of liberal neutrality, in the sense of conception *X*, may not be susceptible to the same line of justification as a policy of liberal neutrality, in the sense of conception *Y*.

For example, the argument from moral scepticism may yield or justify one conception of neutrality (arguably the intentionalist one), while the pluralistic line of argument may be more congenial to consequentialist concern, and so on. If moral scepticism yields an argument for neutrality (which, by the way, I doubt),[18] it is (presumably) because there is something irrational about acting on moralistic reasons which in the nature of things cannot be known to be true; but then there is nothing irrational about action which differentially affects some moral creed if that is not the reason motivating one's action. If the value of moral pluralism yields an argument for neutrality, it proceeds presumably *via* the claim that we ought to be careful that our legislative action (whatever its intentions) does not accidentally diminish the diversity of moral lifestyles.

Different lines of argument for the liberal position will generate different conceptions of neutrality, which in turn will generate different and perhaps mutually incompatible requirements at the level of legislative practice. Since we cherish our deep values and our justificatory arguments much more dearly than we cherish any particular posited conception of neutrality, it will be the justification we favour which determines our interpretation of the concept, rather than the other way round.

This, by the way, is sufficient to destroy much of the basis of Bruce Ackerman's book, *Social Justice in the Liberal State*. Ackerman believes that it is possible, and indeed desirable, for us to be as liberally non-committal about the justification of neutrality as we are about the issue of the good life itself. He thinks we should be neutral not only about ethical ideals, but about the justification of neutrality as well.[19] But if there are two or more competing conceptions of neutrality, and one is the upshot of one line of argument, and another the upshot of another, then Ackerman's 'liberal' strategy is simply a recipe for incoherence.

What emerges, then, is the centrality and inescapability of argument and justification so far as the liberal is concerned. The proponent of liberal neutrality cannot afford to be negligent about the task of justifying the position she wants to embrace (as Dworkin is, for example[20]), because justifying it is part and parcel of the task of articulating it. By the same token she cannot afford, like Ackerman, to be indifferent about it or promiscuous across an array of different justifications. Neutrality is not a straightforward concept and we are in no position to say what conception of it we have adopted unless we have some idea already of why neutrality should be thought to matter. (This, I take it, is a general point about conceptual analysis. The study of concepts like *law*, and *freedom*, and *power*, and *democracy* cannot be undertaken in a practical or normative vacuum. Unless, for example, we have some idea of why it might *matter*, why it might be thought a matter of *concern* whether something is a law or not, we cannot sensibly choose among rival conceptions of this concept. Unless we have an idea of the difference it makes whether a given relation counts as a power relation or not, we cannot specify a particular conception of power. Justificatory argument in political theory and jurisprudence must precede conceptual analysis, not the other way round.)[21]

IV

I have argued that in order to illuminate the concept of neutrality, an adequate liberal theory has to indicate why neutrality is required. Apart from this vital task, an adequate theory also has to explain two other things. (1) It has to explain exactly *who* is required to be neutral. If the answer focuses on legislators and those who have political power, then some explanation has to be given of why the duty of neutrality is *particularly* incumbent on them. (2) It has to explain who or what exactly the legislator (or whoever) is required to be neutral between. The latter task means saying something about what a conception of the good life is, and how conceptions of the good life may differ from those other values and principles (like justice, for example) that no legislator could possibly be expected to be neutral about. Let me say a little about each of these tasks.

The first point to note is that although the liberal insists that *legislators* should be neutral on the question of what constitutes the good life, she does not insist that people in general should be neutral on that question, or that neutrality is, in general terms, some sort of moral or intellectual virtue that we all should strive for.[22] Indeed it would be absurd to suggest that neutrality on the question of what makes life worth living is in general a good thing or that it is a duty incumbent on everyone in all situations. Not everyone can be neutral on this question without the whole business of evaluating ways of life and making choices between them coming to an end. If the concept of a good life has a *use*, then neutrality cannot be required of everyone, since *good* itself is an evaluating, discriminating concept. Or, even if it is not formally incoherent, a general requirement of neutrality has no place in liberal theory. Of course individual citizens must have ideas of their own about the good life, and they should align and orient their lives to one conception rather than another. If I am deciding which profession to enter, where to live, whom to love and marry, whether to have children, what tastes to cultivate, and so on, my deliberations and decisions will be based on – or will, wholly or partially, reveal – what *I* think makes life worth living. If my account is not the same as that of my neighbour, I may be criticized by her for the content of the particular view I hold ('What a depraved or silly way to lead one's life!'), but it would be quite inappropriate for her to criticize me just for having and acting on a view.

The requirement of neutrality is generally taken to be specific to *political* morality. It is not wrong for someone to favour a particular conception of the good life, but it is wrong for her in her capacity as legislator (and presumably as voter) to favour such a view.[23] Unlike courage or honesty, neutrality is not a virtue whose estimation in the case of political actors is explained as a special case of its estimation in the world at large. It is a specifically political virtue. There is something special about political life that makes us require this of those involved in it.

This special feature need not be something that is confined to legislation. It may characterize certain other types of human action as well, if they share with legislation whatever the characteristic is which, in this regard, distinguishes legislation from other ordinary forms of activity. In defining this characteristic, most liberal theories have concentrated on the relation between legislation and force, or between legislation and coercion. Laws, it is said, bear down on individuals by violence, restraint, and the threat of sanctions; and the suggestion is usually that these are not elements we want operating in the moral sphere or for the pursuit of moralistic purposes.

The underlying argument here may be the view held by John Locke (and perhaps also Immanuel Kant) that force and coercion are simply useless in the realm of morals anyway, because a person's allegiance to a conception of the good life is a matter of her inner commitment, which is not altogether under her control, rather than of her external conduct, which is. If it is not under her control, there is no hope of sanctions or other incentives working to change her mind. So the use of sanctions in the moral sphere is hopeless. On this account, non-neutral action by the legislator is simply irrational: the use of means which are singularly ill-adapted to the end she claims to be pursuing.[24]

Alternatively, the justification may be the more modern point that in our commitment to freedom we attach particular value to a person's autonomous organization of her own life – to her own reflection on desires, plans and projects, and to her own deliberate effort to shape her life into a meaningful whole. On this account, what is wrong with the coercion associated with law is that it usurps and interferes with that process, leaving at best an individual life that has been shaped externally and heteronomously in accordance with someone else's conception of the good, but that has none of the particular value attaching to an autonomously organized life. And there are other ways in which the coercive character of legislation may be thought inappropriate in the moral sphere.

Here, once again, there is a point to be made about the primacy of justification. It is notoriously difficult to draw a sensible line between conduct that counts as coercive and conduct that merely counts as 'persuasive'. Knowing how to draw this line is not a matter of being familiar with the contents of a dictionary. It is a matter of knowing how and why coercion is thought to be a worry, and of working out how far and to what extent the grounds of that worry apply in a particular marginal case. Suppose a government makes no attempt to impose a Christian ethic with sanctions, but its most powerful orators constantly use broadcasting media to preach Christian values. Is this coercion or not? Is it a case that should fall within the ambit of the neutrality constraint? Or suppose the government offers tax incentives to those who organize their family life in what it takes to be a morally respectable way. Is this a mere offer of favour, or is it, too, coercive? We cannot tell, until we know *why* coercion matters and what deep values are reflected in our determination to focus on the coercive aspect in paradigm cases, rather than on some other aspect of the matter. Until we know that, we won't have the evaluative equipment to consider the puzzles at the margin. And similar considerations obviously apply to the way we approach the problem of how far allegedly coercive interactions in private life – in the family or in schools or in the workplace – should be brought within the ambit of the neutrality constraint.

V

The other point was that we will want to know not only who is required to be neutral, but also who or what, exactly, they are required to be neutral between. This is the area in which the liberal doctrine is most commonly misunderstood.

Liberal neutrality is not and cannot be the doctrine that legislation should be neutral in relation to *all* moral values. And it is certainly not the doctrine that legislation should be 'value-free', whatever that might mean. Those ideas are simply incoherent. Neutrality is itself a value: it is a normative position, a doctrine about what legislators and state officials ought to do. It is a doctrine that holds that it is wrong for certain considerations to enter the political arena; it is a doctrine which holds out neutrality in political activity as right and good. At the beginning of his essay 'Against Moral Disestablishment', Neil MacCormick suggests that the liberal may want to get around this point by distinguishing moral theories *about* legislation from the deployment or application of moral value *in* and *through* legislation. Perhaps the liberal holds the moral principle that legislation should never be used to enforce moral values.[25] That would perhaps not be incoherent, but still it would not capture the liberal view, as it has usually been understood. For liberals regard neutrality not only as a value that legislators ought to be constrained by, but also as a value that they ought to enforce (on other people attempting to exercise power in a non-neutral way). Another way of putting this is to say simply: in her own behaviour but also in regard to the behaviour of the people under her, the legislator is not to be neutral about neutrality.

If this is correct, an important consequence about justification follows immediately. The doctrine of liberal neutrality cannot coherently be justified by any general appeal to moral scepticism – that is, by any appeal to emotivism or relativism about values as such. As Ronald Dworkin puts the point, neutrality is required, 'not because there is no right and wrong of the matter, but because that is what is right'.[26] Moral scepticism and moral relativism are usually understood in terms that make them applicable across the board to all value-statements as such. If they apply to any, they apply to all. Emotivist non-cognitivism, for example, is a thesis about all evaluative language: it is the thesis that the characteristically evaluative or normative aspect of a moral judgement is always to be understood in terms of the expression and evocation of attitudes, not in terms of any cognitive aspect that would make it sensible to ask whether such a judgement was true or false. Now, liberal neutralism is undoubtedly an evaluative and normative position: it guides legislative conduct, and it evaluates legislative outcomes or purposes. So, if emotivism, or anything like it, is correct, then liberal neutralism – as much as any *particular* conception of the good life – is to be understood simply as the expression and attempted evocation of certain emotions and attitudes about certain forms of activity. If the non-cognitivist or sceptical aspect of the emotivist theory gives us a reason not to enforce particular conceptions of the good life, then it also gives us a reason not to enforce the doctrine of liberal neutrality; that is, it gives us a reason not to enforce the view that conceptions of the good life ought not to be enforced. (Another way of putting this is to say that we cannot derive an *'ought'* – not even a liberal *'ought'* – from a meta-ethical *'is'*.)

I am not saying, by the way, that liberalism depends on a rejection of emotivism, nor do I want to imply that one can be a liberal only if one believes in the objectivity of liberal values. As a matter of fact, most liberal thinkers (Locke, Kant, Mill, certainly) have believed that both the rectitude of liberal principles and the superiority of certain ways of life over others *could* be objectively established. Few have tried to argue for toleration from a premise of scepticism. (So there is no support for Roberto Unger's suggestion that liberalism, from its inception, 'has

73

been in revolt against objective value'. The only philosopher Unger cites to support his assertion is Hobbes; and of course the significant thing about Hobbes is that his theory became most *il*liberal on those areas of ethics where he was most sceptical, notably in relation to the details of religious faith and worship.[27]) The point to be made is simply that liberal toleration and neutrality cannot be justified on the basis of scepticism. The meta-ethical issue is quite independent of the issue about liberalism.

There is also one other argument against using moral scepticism to justify liberal neutrality. If (which I deny) but *if* moral scepticism were to give the rational legislator no reason to prefer one conception of the good life over another in her legislation, it would presumably also give the rational citizen no reason to favour one conception over another either, even in her private life or her least obtrusive dealings with others. But this violates the constraint we have already noted, that a justification for liberal neutrality should explain why neutrality is a *political* not a universal requirement.

What we seem to be driving towards is that the liberal legislator has to be sensitive to certain discriminations amongst values or principles, or types of values or principles. Some types of values (e.g. liberal values) she *is* prepared to uphold and enforce. Other types she is not. Some values and principles, like the doctrine of neutrality and the liberal theory of justice are the proper concern of the law; while other values and principles are, to use the 'brief and crude terms' of the Wolfenden report, 'not the law's business'.[28] But meta-ethical theories do not make such discriminations among principles or among values; their conclusions, whether they are cognitivist or non-cognitivist, apply across the board. Perhaps P. F. Strawson's discussion in 'Social Morality and Individual Ideal', and R. M. Hare's distinction, in *Freedom and Reason*, between moral views and 'fanatical' ideals, are attempts to challenge this, and to argue for a discriminating meta-ethic; but, even if they work, I am not sure that the discriminations they come up with are the ones the liberal wants.[29]

What sort of principles and values will the liberal legislator *not* want to be neutral between? The principle of neutrality itself is the most obvious example, but it may be worth mentioning one or two others. There may be certain goods which can reliably be said to be regarded as values by everyone, no matter what their conception of the good life. This is the category of what Rawls calls 'primary goods': the examples he gives include health, bodily integrity, wealth, self-respect, negative liberty, some degree of education, and so on.[30] If there are any identifiable goods in this category (and it is, of course, controversial whether there are), the legislator may regard it as her proper function to see that they are provided, on some basis or another, to citizens. Moreover, she will have to formulate a framework of principles and institutions to govern the supply and distribution of these goods. She will have to take care that her formulation of these principles and institutions does not wrongly discriminate between the adherents of various conceptions of the good life. But if a class of these goods can be specified, the attempt to provide principles for their distribution will not in itself be a violation of the doctrine of neutrality for all that those principles fall into the general category of morality. If the importance of having some structure of principles and institutions to perform this task can be established on neutral grounds, then other values may also come into play. That structure will be constituted in part at least by a legal system, and if anything like Lon Fuller's theory of the 'internal morality of law' is correct, then legislators will be committed to certain values, and arguably to their enforcement, simply by the nature of their task.[31]

If these are the values and principles whose enforcement and articulation in the social and legal framework the liberal might be prepared to countenance, what are the sorts of values and so on that are being ruled *out* of consideration by the neutrality doctrine?

In John Locke's theory of toleration, the concern was chiefly about various forms of religious faith. The state was required to be neutral on the question of what constituted the conditions for individual salvation and the question of what beliefs and practices were required of us as conditions for salvation by our almighty creator. In more recent formulations, however, the scope is much wider. According to John Stuart Mill, society should stay neutral as far as possible on the whole question of lifestyle in its dealings with individual citizens. And in the modern formulations with which we are concerned, the term that is used is 'individual conceptions of the good life' (or sometimes just 'individual conceptions of the good'). By this is meant something like individual beliefs about what gives meaning to life, or what it is for a person's life to be meaningful. According to Dworkin, almost everyone has such a conception, though many are far from explicit:

> Each person follows a more or less articulate conception of what gives value to life. The scholar who values a life of contemplation has such a conception; so does the television-watching, beer-drinking

citizen who is fond of saying 'This is the life', though of course he has thought less about the issue and is less able to describe or defend his conception.[32]

On this account, one's conception of the good includes one's aims in life, the goals and values that guide things like career choice, as well as one's tastes and other preferences. Rawls provides a longer account which focuses on the same raw material, but gives a clearer view of the structural elements which go to make an assemblage of tastes, aims, and ideals into a *conception*.[33]

The dominant theme in modern liberalism is that an individual conception of the good life is a plan of life or a strategy for living that an individual uses as a basis for making and reflecting on her more important decisions and for scheduling her enjoyments and setbacks (to the extent that she has any control over them). Her conception, moreover, defines what is to count as a setback or an enjoyment for her; and it defines for her the things that are most, and least, important in her life. The idea of a conception of the good life need not be that of a fully worked out *plan*, in the sense of a detailed career trajectory ('I will be married by 25, vice-president of the company by 35, golf champion by 40' and so on).[34] But it does seem to involve the notion that an individual is in a position to view her life so far and her prospects for the future, at any point, as a whole, so that she can ask herself not just 'What have I done?' and 'What will I do?', but 'What in general – am I doing?'. One's conception of the good life may change from time to time, though it is probably part of the idea that it does not change *too* often (e.g. with every particular decision or choice that one makes), otherwise it would not perform its function. By seeing our lives in this way, we view ourselves as enduring beings, not just in the sense in which our bodies endure, but in the sense that there is a reflective unity of value. We do not see ourselves as successions of agent-slices, each time making decisions on the desires and impulses of the moment without any sense of larger integration between past, present and future.

It is also important to the modern notion, that a conception of the good life should not be seen in purely prudential terms: it is not merely the exercise of scheduling our activities so as to maximize over the course of our lives the satisfaction of the preferences we happen to find ourselves afflicted with. The development of a conception of the good life is seen as a more reflective business than that. It involves a process whereby the individual stands back and distances herself, from time to time, from her occurrent desires, and determines autonomously whether these are the sort of desires she wants to be motivated by. In choosing her motivations, so to speak, rather than regarding them as mere afflictions, the individual associates the business of binding her life into a unity with a process of evaluation: each tries to determine a basis for her action that will be *good* by her own lights.[35]

Now, it is precisely because forming a conception of the good life involves making an *evaluation* that legislators may be tempted to interfere. For who is to say that an individual, acting on her own resources, is going to make a good evaluation? Suppose millions of individuals chose to be motivated by desires for pornography or other morally corrupt tastes. Nothing in the liberal notion of a conception of the good life rules this out. Liberal neutrality is the doctrine that legislators should not interfere with the individual process of making these evaluations; they should not even use their power to try and make it more likely that good evaluations will be made rather than bad ones. And this will seem a crazy and wrongheaded doctrine, unless the liberal can show that there is something important about each individual's making evaluations of this kind for her *own* life which is both independent of, and of a greater order of moral importance than, the moral worth of the particular evaluations she in fact makes. Or, at the very least, she must show that the attempt legislatively to modify these evaluations has itself a certain dis-value which is both independent of, and of a greater order of moral concern than, the dis-value in people's autonomous decision-making that the moralistic legislator may be trying to avoid. There is not space here to discuss the various liberal views that have been put forward in this regard. But the account of why individuals' making their own evaluations is positively important, or of why legislators' interference is negatively important (quite apart from the moral worth of their particular legislative aim), will be the backbone of the liberal justification of neutrality; and by the arguments we have already developed, it will determine the details of what it is to be neutral.

VI

Though we have defined it in a secular way, the notion of a conception of the good life is a very wide one. We can include under it not only an individual's tastes and lifestyle but also her religious faith and ethical ideals. The notion purports to offer a more comprehensive account of the proper objects of liberal solicitude than, say, John Locke's account in *A Letter Concerning Toleration*. It is notorious that in this pamphlet, Locke asserted that toleration was to be confined to the adherents of religions only (and then only *some* religions – Roman Catholicism, for example, was implicitly excluded), and not extended to atheists.[36] Whatever the force of Locke's particular argument for that exclusion, the present account makes no such stipulation. Any attempt to say what is important and unimportant in a human life counts as a conception of the good life; it does not matter particularly what the source of that view may be.

A number of critics, however, have challenged the generality of the liberal theory. As it has been described here, the notion of a conception of the good life seems to involve a very *individualistic* account of the way in which meanings are created in people's lives. The stress has been on an individual planning *her own* life, shaping it into a meaningful whole *for herself*, choosing *for herself* what is to count as a motivating consideration, and so on. Of course, the liberal is not suggesting that this is something individuals do in utter isolation from one another. She recognizes that people acquire their tastes, values and concerns and that they articulate, reflect on, and modify their tastes, values and concerns largely through their interaction with others. One line of criticism to which she must respond challenges her to say why the heteronomy caused by the moralistic legislator differs from the moral heteronomy that flourishes at large in human life, in the various casual or deliberate ways human beings may affect and manipulate one another's values.

But there is a more serious line of objection that goes as follows. As a matter of fact, not all the ethical views (or even religious faiths) held by individuals are individualistic conceptions of the good life of the sort I have described. Not all of them are even life plans *for an individual*, or for giving meaning and coherence to the moments of an *individual* life. (After all, as Derek Parfit has argued, why think there is anything important about the inter-temporal series of experiences that, for us, constitutes an individual life, as opposed to the simultaneous *and* inter-temporal series of experiences that constitutes the life of a group, say, or society?[37]) Some people regard the business of forming a coherent individual life for themselves as secondary to involvement in activities whose meaning is oriented to the coherence of a community or a congregation or a nation. What becomes of these people on the liberal account? It looks as though their ethical views are not treated equally with individualistic ones, for their conception of what makes human life worth living may involve activities of proselytism, regimentation, and perhaps even coercion – in order to get their community into a certain shape – which the liberal theory will condemn. The difficulty is that the reasons the liberal offers for condemning activities of these kinds by these people are reasons that they will see as already non-neutral, already biased towards an individualistic account of human fulfilment.

This objection was put forward forcefully in Thomas Nagel's review of Rawls's book. The liberal principles that Rawls embraces, Nagel argues, the social choice situation that he envisages, and the class of primary goods that he defines, are all oriented towards the pursuit of individual life plans. Far from being neutral, the liberal idea (according to Nagel) presupposes a commitment to a particular individualistic (the term used is sometimes 'Protestant') conception of goodness 'according to which the best that can be wished for someone is the unimpeded pursuit of his own path, provided it does not interfere with ... others'. This presupposition, he says, has the non-neutral effect of 'discounting the claims of those conceptions of the good that depend heavily on the relation between one's own position and that of others'.[38]

On this objection, then, liberal neutrality is bogus neutrality, since the liberal aims to be neutral only between conceptions of the good that are already tailored to fit an individualistic framework. Many conceptions of the good are communitarian in character: they presuppose a structure of civic, social, economic, political, and perhaps religious relations and institutions of various sorts. Since the liberal is committed not to tolerate the determination of social structures by ethical or religious ideals, she necessarily rules these communalistic conceptions out of court. (Indeed, if one wanted to be really charitable, one could put Locke's exclusion of contemporary Roman Catholicism in this category.) This shows, according to the objection, that the doctrine of liberal neutrality is inconsistent and perhaps self-defeating.

I hope I have stated this objection fairly, for it is a common worry, and it is important to understand why it is unjustified. To see why it fails, we need to bear in mind two crucial propositions about neutrality. First, neutrality as a policy is never, in any context, self-justifying: one is always neutral in a particular conflict for a reason, and it is obvious that one cannot then be neutral about the force of that reason. Second, a policy of neutrality in relation to one dispute does not commit a party to a policy of neutrality in all disputes; it does not even commit her to a policy of neutrality in other disputes in which one of the belligerents in the dispute in which she is neutral is involved. (*A* may be neutral in the conflict between *B* and *C*, but not in the conflict between *B* and *D*.) Let us apply these propositions to the doctrine of liberal neutrality.

It is true that the liberal has a decidedly individualistic account of what constitutes a conception of the good life, and of what it is to build and work with such a conception. It is true that this account is quite restrictive, and that, for example, it would exclude (at least certain aspects of) the religious views of Ayatollah Khomeini and his followers, to the extent that those views are intimately bound up with the effort to establish a system of Islamic law. And it is true that the liberal enjoins neutrality only as between conceptions of the good life that fit this highly restrictive specification. But so what? The liberal has not arbitrarily plucked her account of what it is to have a conception of the good life out of the air. She has settled on that view of a subject-matter for her concern because of the fundamental principles and values that underlie her position. She thinks that the shaping of individual lives by the individuals who are living them is a good thing; and she fears for the results if that process is distorted or usurped by externally applied coercion, even the coercion of *gemeinshaft*. On the basis of *these* concerns and *these* fears, she identifies moral views *of this individualistic sort* as those between which legislative neutrality is required.

Now communalistic conceptions of the good – involving as they do an urge by people to implicate themselves in the moral governance of others – are not in that class: that is, they are not in the class of views among which the liberal thinks there is good reason to be neutral. On the contrary, the very reasons that persuade her that it is a good idea to be neutral between individualistic conceptions of the good also persuade her that it would be a bad idea to be neutral between communalistic and individualistic conceptions of the good.

To repeat. On the basis of certain deep concerns, the liberal has identified a certain conflict (let's call it conflict *A*) that she believes the legislator should be neutral in. The fact that a contest of a somewhat different sort can be identified – let's call it contest *B* – need cause her no embarrassment. For contest *B* involves views on moral, political, and religious matters among which the liberal is not prepared to enjoin neutrality, and among which neutrality would be enjoined, if it were enjoined at all, probably for quite different reasons. (That may be too strong: perhaps there are some justifications for liberal neutrality which would also be justifications for neutrality between communalistic and individualistic views; if so, it would be simply inconsistent to enjoin neutrality in one contest and not the other; but the inconsistency does not arise in general – it would centre around the particular justification that was being considered.) One is always neutral in a particular dispute for a particular reason, and one cannot suppose in advance that that consideration gives one a reason to be neutral in a dispute that is different.

The fact, then, that the liberal cannot be neutral in *every* dispute between ethical ideals, and has no reason to be, is certainly not an indictment of liberalism.

Everything therefore depends once more on the particular line of justification that the liberal wants to make out for her position. For the line of argument will determine, not only, as I argued in the first part of this paper, the conception of neutrality we adopt, but also, as I have argued in these last pages, the conception of the contest to which liberal neutrality applies. My parting shot, then, is to stress again the desirability, indeed the inescapability, of articulating the deep concerns that underlie the liberal position. For without that, we will never be sure what the position is, and to what areas of human life it is supposed to apply.

Notes

1 Ronald Dworkin, *A Matter of Principle*, Cambridge, Mass.: Harvard University Press, 1985, pp. 191–204; Bruce Ackerman, *Social Justice in the Liberal State*, New Haven: Yale University Press, 1980, p. 10 ff.; Robert Nozick, *Anarchy, State and Utopia*, Oxford: Basil Blackwell, 1974, p. 33.

2 John Rawls, *A Theory of Justice*, Oxford: Clarendon Press, 1972, pp. 205–16 and 325–32.

3 John Stuart Mill, *On Liberty*, Indianapolis: Bobbs-Merrill, 1956; Immanuel Kant, *The Metaphysical Elements of Justice*, trans. J. Ladd, Indianapolis: Bobbs-Merrill, 1965; John Locke, *The Second Treatise of Government* and *A Letter Concerning Toleration*, ed. J. W. Gough, 3rd edn, Oxford: Basil Blackwell, 1976.

4 Dworkin, *A Matter of Principle*, p. 191.

5 T. S. Eliot, *The Idea of a Christian Society*, London: Faber & Faber, 1939, pp. 9 and 35.

6 For a discussion, see, for example, Charles Taylor, 'Neutrality in political science', in Peter Laslett and W. G. Runciman (eds), *Philosophy, Politics and Society*, 3rd series, Oxford: Basil Blackwell, 1967, pp. 25–57.

7 See, for example, Joseph Raz, 'Liberalism, autonomy and the politics of neutral concern', *Midwest Studies in Philosophy*, 7 (1982), pp. 89–120.

8 For the distinction between *concept* and *conception*, see Ronald Dworkin, *Taking Rights Seriously*, London: Duckworth, 1977, pp. 134–6.

9 There is a good discussion in Julius Stone, *Legal Controls of International Conflict*, New York: Rinehart, 1954, p. 408 ff.

10 Hugo Grotius: 'It is the duty of those who keep out of a war to do nothing whereby he who supports a wicked cause may be rendered more powerful, or whereby the movements of him who wages a just war may be hampered.' Quoted in Roderick Ogley (ed.), *The Theory and Practice of Neutrality in the Twentieth Century*, London: Routledge & Kegan Paul, 1970, p. 34.

11 See Stone, *Legal Controls of International Conflict*, pp. 14–16 and 380–1, for a discussion of Vattel's influence.

12 Alan Montefiore, *Neutrality and Impartiality*, Cambridge: Cambridge University Press, 1975, p. 5; Raz, 'Liberalism, autonomy', p. 91.

13 Mill, *On Liberty*, p. 13: 'the sole *end* for which mankind are warranted ... in interfering ... is self-protection. That the only *purpose* for which power can rightfully be exercised over any member ... is to prevent harm to others. His own good, either physical or moral, is not a sufficient *warrant*. He cannot rightfully be compelled ... *because* it will be better for him to do so, *because* it will make him happier .... These are *good reasons for* remonstrating with him ... but not for compelling him' (my emphasis). See also C. L. Ten, *Mill on Liberty*, Oxford: Clarendon Press, 1980, for an interpretation of Mill along these lines.

14 Locke, *Letter Concerning Toleration*, pp. 147–8.

15 Nozick, *Anarchy, State and Utopia*, pp. 271–3.

16 See for example the discussion of conservation in Dworkin, *A Matter of Principle*, p. 202. But his discussion of the drawbacks of socialist economic decision-making on p. 195 seems to support a more intentionalist approach.

17 The argument for equality in Ackerman's work seems to rely on the consequentialist approach, while his overall orientation to neutral reasons presented in justificatory dialogue suggests a more intentionalist conception. See, e.g., Ackerman, *Social Justice*, pp. 11 and 53–9.

18 For an argument that moral scepticism implies nothing either way on the issue of neutrality, see Geoffrey Harrison, 'Relativism and tolerance', in Peter Laslett and James Fishkin (eds), *Philosophy, Politics and Society*, 5th series, Oxford: Basil Blackwell, 1979, pp. 273–90. See also the text accompanying note 26, below.

19 Ackerman, *Social Justice*, pp. 11–12 and 355–9.

20 Admittedly he is quite candid about this: Dworkin, *A Matter of Principle*, p. 203.

21 I have developed the same point in relation to the concept of 'harm' in Jeremy Waldron, 'Mill and the value of moral distress', *Political Studies*, 35 (1987), pp. 410–23.

22 There is a good discussion of the same point in relation to 'treating people as equals' in Ronald Dworkin, *Law's Empire*, London: Fontana Press, 1986, pp. 173–5.

23 For the issue of whether the requirement applies to voters and citizens acting in a political capacity, see Kent Greenawalt, *Religious Convictions and Political Choice*, New York: Oxford University Press, 1987.

24 Locke, *Letter Concerning Toleration*, p. 129: 'Confiscation of estate, imprisonment, torments, nothing of that nature can have any such efficacy as to make men change the inward judgement that they have framed of things.' See also Jeremy Waldron, 'Locke, toleration and the rationality of persecution', in Susan Mendus (ed.), *Justifying Toleration*, Cambridge: Cambridge University Press, 1988, pp. 61–86. There is a similar sort of view in Kant, *Metaphysical Elements of Justice*, pp. 19–30.

25 Neil MacCormick, *Legal Right and Social Democracy: Essays in Legal and Social Philosophy*, Oxford: Clarendon Press, 1982, pp. 18–38.

26 Dworkin, *A Matter of Principle*, p. 203. See also note 18 above.

27 Roberto Mangabeira Unger, *Knowledge and Politics*, New York: Free Press, 1975, p. 76 and note. For Hobbes's moral scepticism and the consequences he drew from it, see Thomas Hobbes, *Leviathan*, ed. C. B. Macpherson: Harmondsworth, Penguin Books, 1968, pp. 129 and 395 ff.

28 *Report of the Wolfenden Committee on Homosexual Offences and Prostitution*, 1957, Cmnd 247, paragraph 62.

29 See P. F. Strawson, *Freedom and Resentment and Other Essays*, London: Methuen, 1974, pp. 26–44; and R. M. Hare, *Freedom and Reason*, Oxford: Oxford University Press, 1963, pp. 137–85.

30 See Rawls, *A Theory of Justice*, pp. 90–5.

31 Lon Fuller, *The Morality of Law*, New Haven: Yale University Press, 1964, pp. 33–94.

32 Dworkin, *A Matter of Principle*, p. 191.

33 Rawls, *A Theory of Justice*, pp. 395 ff.

34 See Joseph Raz, *The Morality of Freedom*, Oxford: Clarendon Press, 1986, p. 370.

35 See Harry Frankfurt, 'Freedom of the will and the concept of a person', *Journal of Philosophy*, 68 (1971), pp. 5–20.

36 Locke, *Letter Concerning Toleration*, p. 158: 'That church can have no right to be tolerated by the magistrate which is constituted upon such a bottom that all those who enter into it do thereby *ipso facto* deliver themselves up to the protection and service of another prince. ... Lastly those are not at all to be tolerated who deny the being of a God.'

37 Derek Parfit, *Reasons and Persons*, Oxford: Clarendon Press, 1984.

38 Thomas Nagel, 'Rawls on justice', in Norman Daniels (ed.), *Reading Rawls: Critical Studies of 'A Theory of Justice'*, Oxford: Basil Blackwell, 1975, pp. 9–10.

5

Neutrality and the civil service

Adrian Ellis

Introduction

Irrespective of the precise relationship between their executive, judicial and legislative branches, modern liberal democracies require a body of permanent officials to assist the elected leaders of the day in the formulation, presentation and execution of their policies. Excepting the small body of officials, such as ombudsmen, whose permanence is grounded in judicial or quasi-judicial responsibilities, the need for a permanent executive body or civil service stems, of course, from the complexity and size of the tasks undertaken on behalf of elected governments. The greater the complexity and number, the larger the permanent body. The extent of the assistance offered varies between liberal democracies, within them over time and between the spheres of policy formation, presentation and execution.

However, whatever the sphere of their activities, the legitimacy of the standing body depends upon capacity to serve differing administrations both with *maximum* effectiveness in the relevant sphere and with *equal* effectiveness irrespective of the political content of those policies. In the second section of this chapter it is argued that these two requirements constitute the corollaries of permanence, are best understood as encapsulating political loyalty and political neutrality respectively, are only imperfectly realized in any particular set of organizational arrangements, and are themselves contingently in conflict.

In the third section the way in which they are articulated in the British civil service is discussed. The requirements of loyalty are firmly embedded in the constitutional position of the civil service, with its attenuated legal personality, indistinguishable from that of the elected government of the day. Neutrality, on the other hand, has no such constitutional bulwark and is articulated largely through internal codes and conventions which have been developed and sustained by the civil service itself in an attempt to define limits to the constitutionally entrenched demands of the government of the day for loyalty. The mechanisms of neutrality, by constraining certain aspects of these demands, legitimate its permanence.

Four main mechanisms or conventions have traditionally served to protect the neutrality of the civil service: anonymity; the requirement to provide comprehensive and non-partisan advice to ministerial decision-makers; self-regulation; and defined limits to personal and professional involvement in overtly partisan activities. All four of these have been subject to pressure over recent years as a result of changes in the nature of policy formation, presentation and execution. The changes have been incremental and the origins disparate, but they have not been matched by any diminution in the constitutionally-based demands for loyalty or by the introduction of alternative mechanisms such as written codes of practice or explicit demarcation of posts as 'political' (and therefore lapsing with the advent of a new administration). This has compounded the sense of unease the civil service is presently experiencing and which is manifest in, for example, the First Division Association's decision to lobby for a code of ethics and Sir Robert Armstrong's decision to circulate guidance to civil servants on their duties and responsibilities in 1985 and, in a revised version, in 1987. A monocausal explanation of civil service unease, such as an increasing emphasis by the government on loyalty *per se*, does not appear adequate to explain these tensions.

It is perhaps worth adding by way of introduction that a civil service which was completely neutral or completely loyal would of course have the capacity to pursue any potential set of policies irrespective of their nature. It is beyond the scope of this chapter to examine the circumstances in which such moral degeneracy might arise or appropriate responses to it but there are obviously other values and moral imperatives which conflict with the requirements of both loyalty and neutrality (those in which the defence of *Befehlnotstand*, the state of compulsion following an order, is clearly inadequate and where the democratic state has, in some specific context, gone off the rails). Much has been made of these circumstances in, for example, the Ponting and Wright trials and in the Westland debacle, but they are distinct from, and only partially illuminate, the more knotty though less spectacular structural tensions between loyalty and neutrality.

First, then, something more in justification of the definitions of political neutrality and loyalty adopted and of the characterization of these as contingently conflicting 'requirements' which constitute corollaries of permanence in a liberal democracy.

Loyalty and political neutrality defined

The approach taken to what constitutes a good definition is pragmatic: it is one which encapsulates common sense, provided that common sense is itself coherent; which does not of itself generate absurdities or contradictions; and which is sufficiently parsimonious to have some purchase when applied to a context in which it should have relevance.

The definitions proposed here also have another attribute which is relevant in the context of the comments made above: they do not of themselves rely on or derive from constitutional or legal considerations. This is important because *prima facie* one can anticipate that in cases where they conflict, incumbent political leaderships will generally be more concerned with safeguarding or enhancing loyalty than neutrality and that bureaucratic leaders, political oppositions, legislatures and the judiciary will tend to be more interested in championing neutrality or loyalty to some higher moral code than loyalty to the executive. Where the executive is in a strong constitutional position in relation to other branches of government or where the executive below the level of elected or appointed office is constitutionally weak, it follows that the requirements of loyalty will be given greater legal and constitutional emphasis than those of neutrality, even going so far as to define neutrality as a component of it. As F. F. Ridley has observed: 'we [in Britain] turn the word [neutrality] inside out to mean that civil servants will identify with successive political masters'.[1] In states where the formal distribution of powers is struck differently one can reasonably anticipate the opposite.

Definitions of loyalty or neutrality which incorporate reference to the constitutional position of the civil service are therefore likely to contain systematic biases toward the interpretation favoured by the stronger or better articulated branches of the state. The definitions adopted here do not and they are therefore generalizable beyond the circumstances of a particular civil service. In any given case – for example the lengths to which government information officers, who are career civil servants, go in presenting a policy in the best possible light – the assessment of the implications for loyalty and neutrality is essentially a policy-analytic one and the assessment of the desirability of these arrangements a morally evaluative one.

I define political neutrality as *the capacity to serve differing administrations with equal effectiveness.* This definition does not, of itself, carry any implication as to the degree of effectiveness or ineffectiveness, provided that it does not differ between administrations. An objection therefore needs to be addressed: the definition appears to admit the possibility that a civil service which pursued an agenda of its own, or was systematically biased in favour of a particular group, irrespective of the policy of the elected government of the day, could be termed politically neutral (albeit deeply disloyal) as any administrations seeking to impose a contrary view would be equally ineffective. It would certainly be perverse if a civil service which fought consistently and effectively for a particular arrangement of its own internal affairs, or in protection of the interests of a particular group within society, were defined as politically neutral, when extreme bias might be thought a more appropriate label!

However, such behaviour would *not* meet the requirement of political neutrality. If the policy pursued in any way bore upon the policy of *any* potential incumbent, the capacity to serve any administration with an equal degree of effectiveness would be diminished. In other words, the theoretical possibility of an administration whose agenda would be affected by an independently pursued policy vitiates the capacity of the bureaucracy to serve any incumbent with an equal degree of effectiveness. Equally, patterns of recruitment, career management or internal organization which impede or promote, however inadvertently, the policies of potential incumbents are impediments to political neutrality. The definition allows differences of view as to the inevitability of bias and its significance to remain distinct from the establishment of its existence.

In any particular case, one needs to come to a view as to whether lapses from theoretically perfect neutrality are trivial hypotheticals or relevant threats to the legitimacy of the civil service in question and I suggest three criteria bear on this. First, the greater the likelihood of a policy being adopted by a potential incumbent which clashes with or enforces a bias or independently pursued bureaucratic agenda, the more relevant the lapse. Second, the greater the likelihood of the potential incumbent gaining office, the more relevant. For example, the fact that an elected Communist government would find the British civil service an imperfect instrument of its will is both true and irrelevant given the improbability of its election. Third, the more likely it is that the bias or independently pursued policy itself affects the probability of a potential incumbent gaining office, the more relevant the bias. The relevance of any particular instance of bias, for example, a predisposition by Ministry of Defence officials towards multilateralism, will therefore depend on the existence of potential incumbents who differ about its desirability, their likelihood of gaining office, and the extent to which the predisposition of the MoD officials in question towards multilateralism, and actions attributable to it, affect the chances of unilateralists themselves gaining office.

In order to be perfectly politically neutral, a civil service must therefore refrain from pursuing *any* independent agenda and be free from any systemic biases. This conception of neutrality is the same as that which lay behind the Northcote-Trevelyan reforms, which were designed to create a career civil service capable of serving with equal vigour any elected administration.

It is also directly analogous to the concept of the neutral state in liberal-democratic theory,[2] although it is weaker in that it does not of course require that political incumbents themselves should have a neutral agenda, only that its functionaries should. Nevertheless, the ideal of a neutral civil service is extremely demanding: to be able to serve any potential incumbent with an equal degree of effectiveness requires a pliability which is psychologically, sociologically, and organizationally utopian. The value of the concept lies in its use as a standard against which to compare particular arrangements. Consider the following five sets of circumstances:

(i) An individual civil servant publicly declares a belief in either the efficacy of a policy or, if its efficacy is not in question, the desirability of the ends it seeks to achieve.
(ii) There is a deeply and widely held consensus within the senior echelons of the civil service concerning the relevant criteria in assessing whether it is appropriate for an industry to be in the public or private sector.
(iii) Decisions about the management of the economy are informed by a model which postulates a particular set of causal relationships between economic variables and those who operate this model believe it to be a more accurate approximation to the real world than any available alternative.

(iv) The division of responsibilities between government departments and the method of resolving disputes between them when they arise mean that certain outside lobbies or interests have systematically better access to decision-makers and a better chance of affecting the outcome of a particular decision than others.

(v) By virtue of having been elected to three successive terms of office, and by having used opportunities available equally to its predecessors, an administration has directly influenced appointments to key postings across a large part of the public sector, encouraging the advancement of civil servants with a particular management style.

In each example, the political neutrality of the civil service would appear to be in doubt in that its capacity to serve other administrations with equal efficiency is diminished. However, beyond a loose approximation to descriptions of the British civil service during Mrs Thatcher's premiership, that is about all the examples have in common. The origins, relevance and implications of their eradication are widely divergent.

Take the diversity of origins: in the first, for example, it is the absence of anonymity which affects the ability of the individual to plead another case with equal plausibility; in the second, a widely held conviction, rooted in shared values and experience, affects the ability to adopt a new conceptual framework which would lead to different conclusions about the appropriate extent of public ownership; in the third an analytical view held by a group of experts affects their ability to adopt and apply a different causal model with equal facility; in the fourth, a bias stemming from the machinery of government systematically affects the outcome of decision-making; in the fifth, the source lies in the opportunities presented by longevity.

Just as the source of the impediment to perfect theoretical neutrality differs, so too does the *relevance* (that is the extent to which it impedes the agenda of actual or potential incumbents and the likelihood either of potential incumbents whose agenda is affected gaining office or being prevented from doing so by the bias itself). There are also differences in the extent to which the bias could be remedied without threatening other requirements of a civil service (permanence *per se* and loyalty). The point I wish to emphasize at this stage is simply that the merit of the definition of neutrality adopted here is that it approximates to common sense, it is internally coherent, and has a relatively unambiguous leverage in the circumstances which should have relevance.

Loyalty is defined as *the capacity to serve the incumbent administration with maximum efficiency*. It differs in one important respect from the common-sense definition of loyalty as faithful allegiance. It assumes not only the will to pursue the ends of government but the skill too – more the loyalty of the genie of the lamp or a magic wand than that of a sycophantic courtier. Like neutrality it is an ideal, and the assessment of the extent to which a civil service is loyal is again a policy-analytic one. Although the views of civil servants and elected or appointed government are a starting point, they are no more than admissible evidence. Political incumbents will, with honourable exceptions, tend to attribute policy failure more to disloyalty in execution (whether incompetence or bad faith) than to the achievability of the ends. This was so, for example, in the case of the flow of memoirs which followed the 1964–70 Labour administration. Civil servants will tend to the opposite view, though the avenues through which this view is expressed will tend to be more oblique.

The reality, of course, is that administrations come to office with a set of policies of differing degrees of coherence and detail, often differing in the nature, compatibility, and authenticity of stated ends. Some policies are pursued, others dropped, more or less noisily, and still others adopted in response to the circumstances and opportunities which occur following office. Privatization, contracting-out, and wider share ownership, for example, barely got a mention in the Conservatives' 1979 platform.

In the area of policy *formation*, loyalty, from whatever quarter, involves not simply providing facts relevant to an exogenously generated agenda of decisions to be made but also articulating the nature of the objectives which underlie stated preferences; distinguishing between these ends and the means to them to which there is a more contingent attachment; and assessing whether they can be achieved and the social, political and economic costs of success. In the area of policy *presentation*, loyalty involves not just describing a particular policy in the best possible light – the conventional exhortation to civil servants – but often seeking to structure expectations in a way which ensures the most favourable reception of that policy. Loyalty involves news management.

In the area of policy *execution*, it involves managing the pursuit of a policy in a way that ensures that the underlying end is constantly kept to the fore when impediments are encountered. A policy is never perfectly articulated and execution always requires judgement and determination, albeit of a differing nature and degree of generality, depending on whether the civil servant is, for example, giving advice to a small business in a Department of Trade and Industry Regional Office, assessing housing benefits in a claims office, managing the Royal Mint, or privatizing British Gas. Execution is inherently interpretative, iterative, and incremental, and efficiency of execution in public service is much less amenable to the statistical analysis of key ratios which the pursuit of profits affords. The definition is fairly straightforward but the assessment of loyalty takes one to the very heart of policy analysis. General assertions tend to be either banal or easily contradicted.

Neutrality and loyalty legitimate the privileges of power which permanence bestows and, together, amount to political invisibility, metamorphosing the bureaucracy into an instrument which assists the elected leaders of the day in a way which constitutes simply an expert extension of its will. This ideal of a wholly loyal and wholly neutral bureaucracy, in which conflict between the two demands is not admitted, is often proffered as practical and applicable guidance to the civil service in the execution of its duties. Sir Robert Armstrong, who recently retired as Cabinet Secretary and Head of the Home Civil Service, advised civil servants of their responsibilities in the following terms: 'It is of the first importance that civil servants should conduct themselves in such a way as to deserve and retain the confidence of Ministers and to be able to establish the same relationship with future Administrations .... When, having been given all the relevant information and advice, the Minister has taken a decision, it is the duty of civil servants loyally to carry out that decision with precisely the same energy and good will, whether they agree with it or not.'[3] As an ideal its origins lie in Max Weber's model of a bureaucracy in which 'The honour of the civil servant is vested in his ability to execute conscientiously the order of the superior authority, exactly as if the order agreed with his own conviction.'[4] In the real world however the way in which an administration is served can compromise the capacity to serve a future administration, depending on the nature of the tasks it undertakes and the manner in which they are undertaken.

The conflict is a *contingent* one, generated by two differing sets of considerations. The first is that citizens in democracies and their elected representatives tend to exercise their right to change their minds. More precisely, the preferences of electorates change over time, and those changes are often magnified by the infrequency of election and the unsubtle nature of the mechanisms by which electoral preferences are aggregated. If this were not the case – if time were frozen – then a totally loyal executive, publicly and vigorously pursuing the policies of the government of the day, could legitimately regard the requirements of neutrality as relatively undemanding, in the knowledge that future administrations would require them to do the same things in the same way. The trade-off arises from the sociological, organizational, and psychological tensions that a *volte face* and preparedness for it require. The greater the relevant changes of policy, the greater the conflict, and it may be that the apparently low priority given to the implications of a sharpening trade-off by the present Conservative administration stems from its conviction that this contingency is indeed sufficiently remote not to be a relevant consideration.

The second source of contingent conflict stems from the nature of the tasks which the bureaucracy is asked to perform. The less the demands upon permanent officials to involve themselves in areas of policy formulation (which involve both sophisticated causal reasoning and value judgements) and presentation (which requires at least the simulacrum of conviction to be effective), and the less ambiguous and indeterminate the ends to be executed, the easier it is for a civil service to espouse neutrality as a dominating value. In this case it can safely regard the requirements of loyalty as relatively unambiguous and undemanding. Again the tensions arise not from the requirements of democratic theory *per se*, but from the sociological, organizational, psychological, and moral tensions which a *volte face* and preparedness for it create.

One can therefore anticipate that the greater the differences between the policies of potential incumbents, the more deeply involved the civil service is in policy formulation and presentation and the more complex the task, and diffuse the objectives, of execution, then the greater the tensions between loyalty and neutrality and the sharper the trade-off between them.

The trade-off in Britain

British civil servants are servants of the Crown, which means the Queen's ministers, accountable to the Queen's parliament. The position was summarized bluntly in Sir Robert Armstrong's memorandum: 'For all practical purposes, the Crown is represented by the Government of the day ... the Civil Service has no constitutional personality separate from the elected Government of the day.'[5] With the exception of civil servants undertaking certain judicial or audit functions there is therefore no constitutional recognition of the professional responsibility of civil servants to any authority other than the incumbent elected executive. Britain is unique among liberal democracies in this respect. There is no codified constitution or even Act of Parliament defining the nature of civil servants' responsibilities or regulating their relationship with ministers, as is the case in France and Germany; and no code of ethics, such as that which requires federal civil servants in the United States to put loyalty to the highest moral principle and to country above loyalty to persons, party, or government department.

Ministerial demands for loyalty are constitutionally circumscribed only by their own parliamentary accountability and the rule of law. The former, because of the commanding role of the Prime Minister and the cabinet at the pinnacle of both the executive and legislature, is a notoriously weak check and the arguments for and against the description of Britain as an elective dictatorship need not be rehearsed here. The latter is also weak in the context of the demands of neutrality and loyalty because the issues involved are only rarely and co-incidentally justiciable (i.e. ones of legality). In circumstances when civil servants discover ministers breaking the law, or when ministers ask civil servants to do so, the issue is not where the balance is struck between loyalty and neutrality but between rule of law and moral imperatives which might over-rule it; neutrality does not come into it.[6]

In the absence of strong external checks, the civil service has developed internal codes and rules to regulate its own affairs and counterbalance the strictures of loyalty embedded in the constitution. The minutiae of the codes and precedents which encapsulate neutrality can be usefully grouped around four principal identifiable features: objectivity or impartiality of advice, by which is understood the requirement to present all relevant arguments and facts bearing upon a particular decision; self-management, which protects the civil service from the accusation of partisan preferment and the pressure to succumb to it; anonymity, which ensures that civil servants do not become personally identified with particular decisions or policies; and absence of involvement in party politics, either in a professional or personal capacity. These four features together articulate the first corollary of permanence: the capacity to serve a future administration with equal efficiency. However they have nothing comparable to the constitutional backing which loyalty enjoys.

Although there are landmarks in their development such as the Northcote-Trevelyan Report of 1853, the establishment of the Civil Service Commission and the report of the Tomlin Commission of 1931, and although they have been periodically codified in such internal guidance as Estacode and its successor, the Establishment Officers' Guide, these features have developed to a quite extraordinary degree through the accretion of precedent and example rather than through precept. As it was put in Establishment Officers' Guide itself, it has never 'been thought necessary to lay down a precise code of conduct because civil servants jealously maintain their professional standards. In practice, the distinctive character of the British civil service depends on the existence and maintenance of a general code of conduct which, although to some extent intangible and unwritten, is of very real influence.'[7] The process by which these codes have been developed and the mechanisms by which they have been sustained is a subtle and organic one. It is a traditional source of national pride and, on occasion, hubris on the part of the civil service itself.

The process has recently been illuminated in the fascinating study of the career of Edward Bridges, Head of the Civil Service from 1945 to 1956, by Richard Chapman. Taking Bridges as an example, Chapman has shown the extent to which these bulwarks of neutrality have been developed in the absence of constitutional protection through the leadership of individual civil servants and how the recruitment, training and career patterns of the civil service have fostered and disseminated these codes. A similar approach to the leadership of other civil servants would, Chapman argues, doubtless reveal a similar picture of exhortation and example sporadically consolidated into what are to the outside observer often rather delphic injunctions. However, the material upon which to base such studies is extremely meagre, and sources more often than not remain inaccessible to even the most dedicated student.[8]

To illustrate the pressures under which these conventions have come let us briefly examine the nature of the challenges to impartiality of advice, self-management, anonymity, and abstinence from partisan activities.

Impartiality of advice

All policies are informed by particular values and it has never been a requirement that civil servants assisting in the process of policy formation share those values. The role of civil servants is to provide 'impartial and honest advice, without fear or favour, and whether the advice accords with the Minister's view or not'.[9] The ability to provide an accurate analysis of the facts bearing upon a decision is not impeded by the need to provide an equally competent analysis to successive governments of differing political outlook. (The one caveat to this is the convention that ministers do not have access to the papers of previous administrations, generated as much by the civil service to protect its neutrality against the potential depredations of loyalty as by defunct administrations anxious to cover their tracks.)

This familiar abstraction glosses over both the nature of 'relevant facts' and the nature of 'decisions' in all but the most humdrum and apolitical of circumstances. Specifically, what constitute relevant facts has become more difficult to ascertain as a result of the increasingly ideological nature of policy formation. By 'ideological' I do not mean that policies are informed by particular values – all policies are – or that those values are in some normative sense extreme, but that policies are premissed upon contested, untested or untestable hypotheses about causal relationships. Consider first those civil servants whose profess-ional *raison d'être* in policy formation is grounded in their ability to furnish factual analysis – i.e. specialists. The British civil service, like most, has specialists organized into separately managed cadres. As part of their career development they may be placed in more generally administrative posts, as a way of broadening their understanding of the pressures which inform policy formation. Above middle management in the 'Open Structure', there is, at least in theory, a much broader interchange between postings in the professional and the administrative cadres. There is also debate about the extent to which professional expertise ought to be recognized as distinctive in such areas as personnel and financial management, where functional expertise is honoured more in the breach. Notwithstanding these grey areas, there is currently recognition of the professional expertise of scientists, accountants, economists and statisticians and in the area of policy formation and advice their professional expertise lies in their understanding of the causal relationships which pertain in their disciplines.

The more contested these relationships, the greater the necessary element of ideology in any policy impinging on their professional competence. If consensus on causal relationships breaks down (as it has in economic policy), is unestablished (as in, for example, such areas as penal reform), or if new areas of policy emerge where no consensus has formed (as, for example, over the method or extent of control required in privatized natural monopolies), then the ideological component of a policy is necessarily high and an administration wishing to avoid its taint would effectively be paralysed.

One result of this is that those employed to offer expert analysis are either marginalized – their contribution being confined to uncontested areas or to gathering data which might reduce the area of controversy – or they become implicitly politicized in that their advice is premissed upon ideological assumptions, whether shared by or conflicting with the recipient administration. This tension between loyalty and neutrality may be exacerbated by a government adopting what might be called 'gratuitously' ideological premisses (i.e. ignoring relevant causal evidence where it does exist) but it is inherent even where this is not the case.

In Britain, as in most liberal democracies, there has been a decline or failure to establish a causal consensus across a wide range of disciplines which inform policy-making and this has inevitably made life uncomfortable for those employed for their professional skills in these areas. This government's tendency to by-pass the advice of professional civil servants has been the focus of critical comment, but the replacement of the Central Policy Review Staff with a more partisan Policy Unit at No. 10 (although significantly still staffed partially by civil servants), the reliance on think-tanks with an ideologically sympathetic predisposition – like the Adam Smith Institute or the Institute of Economic Affairs – and the importation of policy advisers to give professional rather than political advice would all appear to be appropriate responses to the paralysis of professional cadres in an innately political predicament. Value-free advice on causal relations is only one component of policy advice but willingness to provide advice containing a fair amount of ideological suspension of disbelief is problematic if one's professional *raison d'être* is thereby threatened.

This is not the case for administrative civil servants – 'generalists' – whose skills are recognized to be more pragmatically based. They have tended to find this pressure correspondingly less acute, as have those in such disciplines as accountancy where there has been no such decline in professional consensus. Indeed the 'specialist versus generalist' debate which used to exercise students of public administration has largely been overtaken by the crisis of professional self-confidence which has afflicted social and economic scientists whose specialisms were felt to be neglected in the governance of Britain ten or fifteen years ago.

For administrators, the tension manifests itself in a slightly different form: unencumbered by the professional fastidiousness of the expert the dangers are, in the words of Lord Bancroft, a Head of the Civil Service who retired early in 1981, that civil servants 'seeing that the advice which Ministers want to hear falls with a joyous note on their ears...will tend to make officials trim, make their advice what Ministers want to hear rather than what they need to know'.[10] If ministers are not to become the wilful instruments of their own ignorance, there is little which can check this other than the self-discipline, self-confidence, and integrity of the political and administrative leadership.

Self-management

Incoming administrations often busy themselves with honing the administrative machine they have inherited to achieve their own differing policy goals and the usual focus has been the machinery of government. The Wilson Government created new departments including the Ministry of Technology and the Department of Economic Affairs and, later, the Civil Service Department to reflect, articulate, and implement their agenda. The Heath Government amalgamated existing departments into super-departments such as the Department of the Environment. However, with the exception of the abolition of the Civil Service Department in 1981 and a certain amount of redistribution of responsibilities between, for example, the Departments of Employment, Environment, and Industry (which was amalgamated with Trade) and the recent separation of Health and Social Security, Mrs Thatcher's administration has been much more circumspect in its 'shuffling of the pack'. It has, instead, taken a deep interest in the internal management and efficiency of the civil service and, over a period of nine years, has profoundly and deliberately changed the managerial principles upon which the civil service is run. This process began with the appointment of (then) Sir Derek Rayner, borrowed from the department store Marks and Spencer, to oversee management and efficiency reviews, building on his experience in an earlier secondment to the Ministry of Defence in Edward Heath's administration. The lessons gleaned from the short, sharp examinations of the purpose and cost-effectiveness of executive operations and support services were more broadly disseminated through the development of management and budgeting systems closely modelled on private sector practice under the general rubric of the Financial Management Initiative. Simultaneously, the government pursued extensive privatization and contracting out of executive functions and the initiatives have culminated in current plans to hive-off large (but as yet mainly undetermined) executive areas into autonomous managerial units, still within the public sector and still politically responsible to departmental ministers.

In parallel the government has pursued a clearly stated and promulgated preference for a more entrepreneurial, less procedurally formal management style on the part of senior civil servants (often characterized as 'can-doism'). Nine years has been long enough to influence the appointment of most of the top two or three levels of the service. This has involved the accelerated promotion of officials who would not necessarily have been the first choice of the civil service itself, if for no other reason than that promotion to the highest ranks at a relatively young age (forties and early fifties) has short-circuited the careers of some of the preceding cohort.

The management of the civil service has as a result become an object of policy and of political controversy. It is higher on the national agenda than at any time since the war. Over the same period civil service pay has dropped behind its traditional private sector analogues by about 30 per cent, pay comparability has been abandoned and merit pay introduced, civil service numbers have been cut by about 20 per cent and some civil servants have been compulsorily de-unionized (testing the loyalty of some individual civil servants to their employers and making further inroads into self-management).

There is an important distinction to be made here between vulnerability to politicization and politicization *per se*. A recent review of the evidence by the Royal Institute of Public Administration concluded that increased political interest taken in senior appointments has not been used for partisan ends. Recent statements on hiving-off have suggested that the government is aware that senior civil servants rather than ministers should take the lead in the management of the civil service; recruitment remains firmly in the hands of the Civil Service Commissioners. But whilst the efficiency of the civil service in implementing the ends of the government continues to be a focus of political attention and monitoring and information systems are sharpened-up, the opportunity to use them for partisan ends remains.

As significant is this consideration. Suppose those officials whose accelerated promotion is perceived as stemming, at least in part, from their working relationships with cabinet ministers and the particular managerial styles associated with them prove unacceptable to future incumbents, then the civil service will have difficulty occupying its present position, with the security of tenure which a career service implies, without unsustainable friction between the demands of loyalty and neutrality. In the short term the frictions may be partially accommodated by 'natural wastage', as senior civil servants gracefully retire or move across to posts in industry or international organizations when their faces no longer fit. But in the longer term, unless governments only change at the same speed and time as cohorts move through senior posts into retirement, the one-way movement will become an unsustainable burden. The pool will need to be replenished by recruitment and, whatever the formal mechanisms of appointment, ministers will take an understandably close interest, as they have with the few senior appointments made from outside the career civil service in recent years.

Anonymity

The convention of political anonymity entails the willing suspension of disbelief when confronted with the proposition that the elected leaders of the day are responsible not just for the strategic direction of policy but equally for the small print of its formulation and execution. The purpose of the myth is not to present ministers as superhuman polymaths but to keep responsibility firmly pinned to those who are politically accountable. There are minor constitutional caveats to this, such as the responsibility of Permanent Secretaries as accounting officers for their departmental budgets, but the convention covers the vast majority engaged in policy formation and execution. It has always been a cumbersome artifice with costs to all parties: ministers brought down by maladministration implausibly attributed to the political leadership; parliamentary and public frustration when unable to unravel the true dynamics of decision-making or to attribute decisions to individuals in any meaningful sense; and bureaucrats reduced to platitudinous circumspection in their attempts to tread the line between the political and the factual. Two new pressures have, however, made the suspension of disbelief both more implausible and more reluctant.

First, the scrutiny of the executive by the legislature has grown more detailed and with it the individuation of responsibilities more readily apparent. The present system of select committees, created in 1979, shadowing individual departments and empowered to summon witnesses and papers, has given determined groups of backbenchers a means to examine executive action not available when the executive was answerable primarily on the floor of the House of Commons. Persistent questioning of ministers and officials, as for example in the defence committee's examination of the Westland affair, does not reveal every detail of policy-making and execution and the prospects of action or censure stemming directly from such scrutiny remain limited by the sanctions of the whips' office. However the select committee system undoubtedly reduces the seamless anonymity which the convention requires to sustain it. Similarly, the work of the National Audit Office and the Public Accounts Committee, the activities of the Parliamentary Commissioner or Ombudsman, and the increasing recourse to judicial review of ministerial decisions by those who take issue with them, have all made the mysteries of the executive less opaque to other branches of government and to the interested public.

In parallel to parliamentary and judicial scrutiny, academics and journalists, weaving more or less delicately around the provisions of the Official Secrets Act, have increased the attention paid to decision making in the executive. Most 'quality' dailies and weeklies run regular features tracking managerial and administrative issues and the personalities behind them. The paraphernalia of official secrecy and the reliance upon unattributable briefing this necessitates makes such features on occasion little more than conduits for Whitehall propaganda battles, but undoubtedly more is known and greater interest evinced in the work of civil servants than ever before.

Second, part of the shift in management style under Mrs Thatcher's administration has itself involved individuation of responsibility through delegation of managerial authority and the encouragement of a more entreprenurial management style. This is a matter of degree rather than a sea-change but there is an inherent tension between political answerability at the top and managerial discretion down the line which remains unresolved. It was not unheard-of before 1979 for senior civil servants to be associated publicly with certain policy options. (William Armstrong, when Cabinet Secretary during the period of industrial unrest in 1972–74, is the most frequently cited example.) But there is undoubtedly a growing acceptance that civil servants can, and should, publicly articulate, defend, and rally support for particular policies. This does not necessarily mean prime-time television – politicians would be reluctant to give up this sort of exposure – but it does mean presenting cases to professional lobbies, the press, and adjacent institutions.[11]

At the sharp end of this predicament are government information officers: Bernard Ingham, the head of the Prime Minister's press office, and a career civil servant, clearly embraces news management as an integral and legitimate activity for career civil servants. At the other extreme however is the information officer who was recently quoted as calling at his union's annual conference for 'a code of ethics ... to protect those members who are expected to expound untruths on behalf of government, produce dodgy material or leak documents in the Government's interest'.[12]

As with self-management, the extent to which these developments compromise the capacity to serve future administrations depends upon the attitude adopted by those administrations. Given the fluidity of political opposition in Britain today, this is very much a moot question. It may be that the political culture of Britain is sufficiently mature to obviate the need for the myth of ministerial omniscience which underlies anonymity and indeed that the convention itself has retarded the development of that culture. If this transpires to be the case, then neutrality can withstand the passing of the convention.

Partisan involvement

The fourth convention protecting the neutrality of the civil service is that civil servants should not take part in overtly partisan activities in either a professional or a personal capacity. The rules concerning personal involvement remain largely unaltered: passive membership, behind the scenes support and limited involvement in local politics are acceptable for those in less sensitive posts or grades. If anything, there may be some tightening-up in the interests of equity in parallel with proposals aimed at limiting the involvement of council officials in the electoral politics of adjacent boroughs.

However, the involvement of officials in what might be termed partisan activities as a result of their professional functions has undoubtedly increased. This is not only because of the increase in the areas which might be considered 'partisan' which has resulted from the decline in political consensus discussed above. It stems equally from the way in which lines between policy formulation and presentation have become blurred. One of the many changes in British politics of the past decade has been in the extent to which the ends of government have been achieved through direct impact upon the expectations and assumptions of the electorate itself. The extent to which the success of policies is dependent upon preparing their reception by the electorate, financial markets, the international political community and the media is a permanent feature of the political landscape and consideration of that reception necessarily takes place at the earliest stages of policy formation and permeates its execution. One cannot disentangle the politics from anything beyond the most basic executive action. The extension of share ownership, or capital ownership through council house sales, the downward revision of assumptions concerning sustainable levels of employment, changes in assumptions about acceptable differences of income distribution or public ownership and about sustainable levels of public expenditure all involve political judgements by civil servants at every stage, and existing conventions on partisan involvement – such as the requirement that civil servants do not assist ministers in constituency work or party political speeches – offer little guidance in these circumstances.

Given the diffuse and organic ways in which the conventions protecting neutrality have grown up, any change in the nature of the leadership or the values which inform it impact directly upon its capacity and determination to withstand the imperatives of loyalty embedded in its constitutional position. When the leadership of the civil service collectively or individually attempts to articulate or refine the mechanisms it is done without much constitutional 'cover'. The apparent reluctance of the top management of the civil service to address these issues is therefore understandable. Without the acceptance, tacit or otherwise, that the deontological requirements of neutrality may need to be met at a cost to the short-term consequentialist demands of efficiency, such activity lays itself open to the accusation of disloyalty or of using neutrality as a guise for inefficiency. Richard Wilding, a career civil servant, then in the Civil Service Department, wrote in 1979 that 'it is absolutely necessary to pursue today's policy with energy; it is almost equally necessary, in order to survive, to withhold from it the last ounce of commitment ... and to invest that commitment in our particular institution, the Civil Service itself, with all its manifold imperfections'.[13] Mrs Thatcher's administration took a different view and 'commitment', 'enthusiasm' and 'energy' are now standard exhortations in management documents and the civil servant who expresses concern for the legitimacy of his or her profession in the face of these exhortations does so at their own peril.

It may be that the protective mechanisms discussed were generated by a mandarin concept of national interest or they may have had their origins in a functional imperative on the part of the civil service to preserve its legitimacy and long-term survival through protecting its capacity to serve future administrations. Either way, they have hitherto enabled the career civil service to operate in the highest and most politicized areas of public life under successive administrations. However, an incoming administration of a differing political composition will inherit many individual civil servants publicly associated with either the style or the substance of the present administration and an administrative machine finely tuned to a particular set of managerial and political demands. It is unclear how future administrations will react to the legacy they will inherit.

Conclusion

Political loyalty and political neutrality are both requirements of a permanent civil service in a liberal democracy and although the requirements of loyalty are more strongly articulated in the British constitution, the claims for both have equally firm grounding in democratic thought. The demands of loyalty have increased whilst the traditional bulwarks of neutrality have, for unrelated reasons, been eroded and have not been replaced by alternative mechanisms. The area of conflict between them has increased as a result of, *inter alia*, a decline in the consensus within the society whose politicians the bureaucracy exists to serve, at least as articulated by its political leadership; the increasing complexity of the policy formulation/presentation nexus; a decline in the monolithic appearance of the policy machine which has individuated functional responsibilities; and the explicit pursuit by the present administration of policies and arrangements which themselves reward loyalty more than neutrality. The reluctance of both the bureaucratic and political leadership to address this steepening trade-off risks undermining the legitimacy of the permanent civil service as it does the splits over the chasm which is slowly opening up between the diverging demands placed upon it by neutrality and loyalty.

The trends which have given rise to these tensions are not unique to Britain: the collapse of the postwar political consensus; the increased demands by legislatures, the media and pressure-groups for information about bureaucratic decision-making; and the increasingly close links between presentation, formulation, and execution of policies are common to most liberal democracies. Some of these pressures might diminish, if party systems realign or electoral systems were adopted which dampened the amplitude of the effect of voting changes upon election results. Others pressures are, however, unlikely to slacken off. In particular, it is unlikely that demands by legislatures, the media and ombudsmen for greater knowledge of the mechanics of bureaucratic decision-making will diminish. Once a threshold of access has been passed – for example the right to examine advice to ministers, or to call certain witnesses before legislative committees for examination – only the most determined government can overturn precedent and only at a high political cost. National security is accepted by even the most ardent campaigners for greater access to decision-making as a reason for withholding certain information, releasing it retrospectively or at a high degree of generality, or only to intermediate bodies such as commissions or, in Britain, groups of Privy Councillors. But if the justification for withholding information rests solely on the conventions of ministerial responsibility and anonymity which are required for the operation of a permanent civil service at all but the very top level of political decision-making, then inevitably the costs of permanence itself will be scrutinized with increasing hostility.

Similarly, once the channels are established by which criteria for senior posts can be laid down by that government, and short-lists are influenced and appointments vetoed as a matter of course, it would be a timid administration that renounced the opportunities which this presents. Again, it is most unlikely that the concern with presentational aspects of policy increasingly evident at all stages of formation and execution is likely to diminish. One may see this as a maturing of the political culture of liberal democracies – in that decision-making is increasingly open to, and determined by, the reactions of a wider range of citizens and institutions to a wider range of issues. Alternatively one may see it as regression: the entrenchment of a political culture increasingly driven by trivial plebscitary considerations. Either way, 'politics' will continue to permeate and infuse 'administration' and a safe delineation of the two will require the line to be drawn much further down the executive than it is at present.

The contingent conflict between neutrality and loyalty is therefore more likely to grow in liberal democracies than to recede, and neutrality is more likely to bear the pressure than loyalty. In some liberal democracies – particularly those with a clear separation of powers, like the United States – the pressure is alleviated by conceding permanence itself and with it the apparatus that neutrality requires to sustain it. The cost is conventionally measured in terms of the sacrifice of professional standards and skills at the higher levels, of the calibre of the executive at the lower levels – the pinnacles of whose professional careers are correspondingly lower – and of the problems associated with the co-ordination of business through the wider and more ragged interface between career civil servants and appointees. The benefit is, in effect, the ability to legitimate the activities which the executive undertakes on behalf of the citizens and, with its legitimacy established, to allow an understanding of the executive which the distortions and conventions of neutrality necessarily impede.

Notes

1 F. F. Ridley, 'Political neutrality and the British civil service', in *Politics, Ethics and Public Service*, London: RIPA 1985, p. 37.
2 Peter Jones's contribution to this volume, Chapter 2.
3 Sir Robert Armstrong, *Duties and Responsibilities of Civil Servants in Relation to Ministers*, circulated to all civil servants in February 1985, revised and re-circulated in December 1987, pp. 3–4.
4 Max Weber, quoted in Dennis F. Thompson, *Political Ethics and Public Office*, Cambridge, Mass.: Harvard University Press, 1987, p. 42.
5 Armstrong, *Duties and Responsibilities*, p. 2.
6 For an illuminating discussion of this issue, see Thomas Nagel, 'Ruthlessness in public life', in Stuart Hampshire (ed.), *Public and Private Morality*, Cambridge: Cambridge University Press, 1978, pp. 75–91.
7 Quoted in Richard A. Chapman, *Ethics in the British Civil Service*, London: Routledge, 1988, p. 305.
8 Chapman, *Ethics in the British Civil Service*, pp. xii–xviii.
9 Armstrong, *Duties and Responsibilities*, p. 4.
10 Quoted by Peter Hennessey in 'Mrs Thatcher's poodle?', *Contemporary Record*, 2(2), p. 3.
11 See for example David Walker's analysis of Geoffrey Holland's 'barnstorming' speeches on youth training whilst at the MSC, in *Contemporary Record*, 2(2), p. 15.
12 Quoted in *The Observer*, 5 June 1988, p. 15.
13 Richard Wilding, 'The professional ethic of the administrator', *Public Administration Bulletin*, 1979.

6

Neutrality in education

Peter Gardner

Most enquiries into neutrality in education, like most recommendations for neutrality in education, have been concerned with neutral teaching, and this paper will follow this trend. No doubt to many people neutral teaching may seem a surprising topic for an inquiry, for they may think that the idea of the neutral teacher belongs to the same group of self-contradictory ideas as 'married spinster', 'survivor of fatal injuries' and, possibly, 'straight gay'. Others with a more robust appreciation of what teaching can involve may see the idea of the neutral teacher as belonging to that group which includes such ideas as 'pacifist army' and 'promiscuous celibate', the group whose members, though not contradictory, nevertheless tax the imagination for a consistent reading. For my part, I neither regard the notions of neutral teaching or the neutral teacher as contradictory nor find them conceptually taxing, but what I do find and what I will argue for in this paper is that many of the cases for neutral teaching are flawed. In particular I want to argue that one of the most popular cases for teacher neutrality, this being what we can call the sceptical case, involves irreconcilable tensions. But more of this later. My immediate concern is to give some indication of the scope of our topic and this I will attempt to do by looking at different cases for neutrality in education. These, I will suggest, may be divided into the sceptical and the non-sceptical, though, as I will show, some which at first sight look to be non-sceptical cases, may be found to contain sceptical elements. Thereafter I will explore what teacher neutrality requires of the teacher before returning finally to the problem of the tensions that are housed within sceptical cases for neutral teaching.

Some sceptical cases for teacher neutrality

The usual and limiting focus of attention for inquiries into teacher neutrality is the set of recommendations put forward by the Schools Council Humanities Project team in the 1970s.[1] In fact it was these recommendations that introduced many teachers and educationalists to the notion of neutral teaching. Yet what I want to point out is that not only are there other recent endorsements of teacher neutrality but that the history of education reveals various prescriptions to teachers to be neutral. Terms such as 'neutral teaching' and 'neutrality' may not have figured in these early recommendations, but, as we shall see, their message was clearly neutralist; it was that teachers should be neutral in their dealings with certain issues and in their treatment of certain areas. Still, it might be profitable for us to begin by considering the recommendations of the Humanities Project.

Under the directorship of Lawrence Stenhouse, the Humanities Project team was responsible for compiling what many teachers regarded as a trail-blazing set of prescriptions.[2] One of the team's recommendations was that pupils in secondary schools consider what were called controversial issues, these being issues such as war and peace, relations between the sexes, and race relations; issues on which people, including parents, pupils and teachers, were thought of as holding conflicting views.[3] The team also recommended that 'discussion, rather than instruction' should form the core of such considerations and that in these discussions teachers were to submit their teaching to 'the criterion of neutrality'.[4] Satisfying this criterion, however, did not result in the teacher playing no part in discussions. Instead, the teacher was to play the part of a chairman (the team used the term 'chairman') who was to be 'procedurally neutral', and, contrary to what the label might suggest, procedural neutrality required the teacher to ensure that in discussions pupils followed certain general principles and formal procedures, such as those concerning respect for persons and evidence.[5] What was proscribed in all of this was teachers instructing and saying what they thought was right on those issues labelled controversial.

But why did the project team recommend that teachers abandon their traditional instructional role, their position as authorities? Well, the team claimed that 'the inescapable authority position of the teacher in the classroom is such that his view will be given an undue emphasis and regard which will seriously limit the readiness of students to consider other views'.[6] Now this claim may look like nothing more than part of an argument for a pedagogic technique that would aid discussion and reflection, and, as such, it would seem independent of any particular concern for the controversial. But to see the Project's case in this light is to misunderstand it; for the Project's argument for neutrality is about handling a certain type of material in the teaching situation and that argument is that in the realm of the controversial it would be wrong for the teacher to present his own views and have them treated as authoritative. In fact Stenhouse and his team argued against the teacher being 'an arbiter of truth or warranter of knowledge' in the area of the controversial and for a 'relaxation ... in the teacher's claim to be *an* authority by virtue of his knowledge'.[7] And the reason why they argued this way is to be found if we consider what they meant by 'a controversial issue', for as far as they were concerned such an issue is 'one which divides students, parents and teachers because it involves an element of value judgement which prevents the issue's being settled by evidence and experiment'.[8]

R. F. Dearden has criticized this account on the grounds that what is controversial need not be a matter of evaluation,[9] and surely he was right to do so. Whether a certain member of a British intelligence service was a Soviet agent may be a matter of controversy though whether he was or was not is not itself an evaluative matter. But whatever the blemishes of its account what I want to draw attention to is that the Project team regarded controversial issues as being those that cannot be settled by evidence and experiment. Of course, it might be claimed that no issue, not even a scientific one, can be settled by evidence or experiment, but all this would seem to mean is that no amount of evidence and no number of experiments can ever settle something conclusively, which is why this claim is not a very interesting one. It is also why we may suggest that those who maintained that controversial issues involve judgements which cannot be settled by evidence and experiment were seeking to make a stronger and more specific claim than one concerned with the impossibility of settling contingent matters conclusively. This stronger claim I take to be something to the effect that even if we lower our sights from the impossible demands of conclusive settlability and simply concern ourselves with being able to establish with some degree of certainty and confidence what judgements are correct, we would still be employing a criterion that is too demanding for the realm of the controversial.

Given this view we can clearly see why the Project team did not want teachers' views on controversial issues to be given particular emphasis and regard and why the team argued against teachers being arbiters of truth or warranters of knowledge in the realm of the controversial. If controversial issues are as the team believed them to be, no stance on such an issue is worth the kind of regard one would pay to the view of someone on a topic on which one took her to be an authority. For if views on controversial issues cannot be established with any degree of certainty or confidence, then, I take it, the realm of the controversial is one where there cannot be authoritative views or authorities in virtue of their knowledge. And the prescription that emerged from this was that on controversial issues teachers should keep their views to themselves lest those views were treated as authoritative.

Someone who in the 1970s expressed support for the type of neutrality favoured by the Humanities Project team, albeit in connection with morality as a whole, rather than with certain specified issues, was R. M. Hare.[10] Hare advocated that teachers should teach the procedures, what he regarded as the formal or logical aspects, of morality, that is, the universalizability and prescriptivity of moral discourse, but this should constitute the limit of instruction. 'As in mathematics', advised Hare, 'having taught them [our pupils] the language, we can leave them to do the sums.'[11] By 'the language' Hare presumably meant something like 'the formal or logical nature of the discourse' which is why his advice may strike us as most odd; for how can one teach the logic of mathematics without teaching sums? Equally, how can one teach the logic of 'ought' except to those who have some rudimentary grasp of the concept through being taught that they ought to do certain things? Still, we may take it that Hare was concerned to draw a line of demarcation: given that teachers are dealing with those who have moral concepts in some rudimentary form or other, they should ensure that their pupils reason and formulate principles in accordance with the logic of moral discourse, but this is as far as teachers should go in terms of instruction or in trying to ensure compliance. Teachers may, of course, encourage children to formulate their own universal and prescriptive principles, and Hare wanted teachers to encourage pupils in this direction, but what they must not do is to teach pupils that particular judgements are correct or encourage children to treat certain moral views as authoritative. What we should remember, Hare maintained, is that 'there are not authorities on moral questions',[12] to which he should, perhaps, have added: 'except at the formal level'.

Another recent neutralist, or so I would contend, is J. P. White, though White's interest in neutrality stems not from a belief that teachers are not moral authorities, but from the view that they are not authorities on what will be good for their pupils.[13] Unconvinced by the efforts of various philosophers and educationalists to show what the good life consists of, White has argued that those involved in education should abandon the idea that they know what is good for people and the type of education that ensues from the assumption of such knowledge. Teachers and curriculum planners, White has insisted, should cease imposing their views about self-regarding goods on pupils. Instead, pupils should be put in a position to make an informed choice about what is good for themselves and they should be encouraged to make such a choice. This requires teachers to ensure that pupils come to understand about the options they may wish to pursue at some stage of their lives and that pupils acquire the wherewithal and receive encouragement to make reflective choices about those options.[14] But teachers should not cultivate favourable views of any of those options. They should develop and encourage what is necessary for informed and reflective choice, but they should not advertise or impose or have their views treated as authoritative. Teachers, White has maintained, should not use their positions of influence to determine what is best left to subjective preference. It is the individual, not philosophers and not his teachers or curriculum-planners, insists White, who 'is in the best position to know what is intrinsically worthwhile for him[self]' because he, not they, 'is the final authority on what his reflective desires are'.[15]

So far we have looked at some contemporary neutralists. Let us now consider some earlier advocates of teacher neutrality. The idea of philosophers, such as Hare and White, questioning the existence of moral authorities and authorities on the good life may call to mind the type of activity engaged in by the early Socrates, and, indeed, we may argue that the early Socrates should be seen as a neutralist. In support of our case we can note that the early Socrates cast doubt on the existence of authorities on matters of value and he espoused the doctrine that whereof people are ignorant or confused and are manifestly not authorities, they should not impose or instruct. Socrates can also be seen supporting a feature of teacher neutrality which our contemporary examples display. This particular feature we may call the positive aspect of neutrality and it is that pupils and students should be encouraged to investigate, reason and explore those matters on which, or so it seems, no one can speak with authority. In fact it was this very encouragement that led to Socrates' downfall. In addition a case can be made for claiming that the early Socrates was a procedural neutralist for he can be seen as insisting that if we are to investigate and explore questions about values, then we should follow certain procedures and principles. We should, for example, follow the dialectical route and we should search for universal definitions.

Another early neutralist that we might mention is Peter Abelard whose *Sic et Non* listed over one hundred and sixty issues, most of which were theological, on which contradictory or apparently contradictory statements and positions, both Biblical and patristic, could be found.[16] Teaching about such issues, many of which were controversial, could not proceed by the customary practice of appealing to authorities and authoritative texts, for on these issues there seemed no authoritative view. Nevertheless, despite this or, rather, because of it, Abelard wanted students to investigate these issues and he advocated discussion and disputation, what he called *inquisitio*, not instruction, as the proper means of investigation.[17] In keeping with the demands of *inquisitio* teachers were to ensure that students followed certain procedures and strategies in their exploration of the designated issues. Were we to look for a contemporary educationalist whose recommend- ations might be thought to resemble Abelard's most closely, we might well turn to Lawrence Stenhouse. Such a comparison, we can observe, is not only encouraged by various references to Abelard in Stenhouse's writings, but also by similarities between the presentation of ideas in *Sic et Non* and in the packages of material on 'controversial issues' prepared by the Humanities Project team for schools.[18]

While Abelard favoured a neutralist approach to certain specific issues, some early neutralists have prescribed neutral teaching for whole areas of thought. John Stuart Mill for instance, recommended that religion be treated in this way. Thus, in his inaugural address to the University of St Andrews, Mill argued against the legitimacy of authoritative pronouncements in this field and advocated a neutralist approach. He reasoned that the

> diversity of opinion among men of equal ability, and who have taken equal pains to arrive at the truth ... should of itself be a warning to a conscientious teacher that he has no right to impose his opinion authoritatively upon a youthful mind .... The pupil should not be addressed as if his religion had been chosen for him, but as one who will have to choose it for himself.[19]

Rousseau might also be mentioned in this context for on the subject of Emile's religious upbringing Rousseau opposed authoritative imposition and attachment to a 'sect'. Instead he prescribed an approach which would allow Emile 'to choose for himself'.[20]

Schoolteachers who would support these sorts of recommendations have of late found a curricular home in what has been called 'the New RE', this being a label for a range of educational activities that shun religious particularism and evangelism, but which aim to make pupils aware of different faiths and creeds and even of non-theistic perspectives, and which encourage pupils to make their own reflective decisions about these matters.[21]

One other early neutralist that might be mentioned is Matthew Arnold. In an important passage in his *Culture and Anarchy* Arnold first presents the kind of sceptical view concerning the absence of authorities which the preceding cases have led us to expect in prescriptions for neutral teaching. He proceeds to proscribe telling or instructing or 'lending a hand' but recommends the encouragement of reflection and inquiry. Arnold writes:

> If we look at the world outside us we find a disquieting absence of sure authority .... And ... when we are accused of preaching up a spirit of cultivated inaction ... of refusing to lend a hand at uprooting certain definite evils .... We shall say boldly that we do not at all despair of finding some lasting truth to minister to the diseased spirit of our time; but we have discovered the best way of finding this to be not so much by lending a hand to our friends and countrymen in their actual operations for the removal of certain definite evils, but rather in getting our friends and countrymen to seek culture, to let their consciousness play freely round their present operations and the stock notions on which they are founded, show what these are like, and how related to the intelligible law of things, and auxiliary to true human perfection.[22]

The cases we have outlined, though few in number, show that not only should we not confine enquiries into contemporary cases for neutral teaching to the recommendations of the Humanities Project, but that neutrality is not a new issue in education. We may also suggest that while the cases we have mentioned cover a variety of issues and topics, they follow a certain pattern. First, they involve a sceptical foundation or base which points to or makes claims about the absence of authorities in an area or which questions our right to be sure or certain in that area.

This is why the cases outlined above can be called sceptical cases for teacher neutrality. Second, they have a negative aspect or side which proscribes teachers acting as if they were authorities in the areas in question and which forbids teachers from instructing and advancing their own views in those areas. Third, these cases have a positive aspect or side concerned with encouraging reasoning, searching, discussion and inquiry. Fourth, many have a procedural dimension concerned with ensuring that those who are encouraged in the ways just mentioned abide by certain rules and procedures.

Some other cases for teacher neutrality

It could be claimed that so far we have only looked at one group of cases for teacher neutrality, at sceptical cases, and that there are other types of case. It might be maintained, for example, that one type of case that we have not examined rests on the view that while traditional styles of teaching and instructing pave the way for docile and authority-dependent children, teacher neutrality fosters self-reliance, independence, initiative and personal autonomy.[23] Opposition to this approach might come from those who, like Plato, have grave doubts about the desirability of encouraging independent judgement and autonomy amongst the masses, from those who, like James Fitzjames Stephen, subscribe to the doctrine that 'close and continuous discipline' is the most likely way to develop people with vigour and originality,[24] or from those who, fearing excesses, would urge that autonomy without regard for moral standards or the proper canons of reasoning is valueless.[25] No doubt we could become embroiled in these disputes, though all we need note for our purposes is that the central argument here does not seem to be a sceptical argument for neutrality, for it does not appear to rely upon a sceptical assessment of a certain range of material, but concentrates on the efficacy of neutrality in developing certain personal qualities and dispositions, which is why this argument could be employed even when teachers are handling material that is highly resistant to the sceptic's probings. Nevertheless, I would contend that sceptical arguments are not too far away from these concerns. The fact is that educational recommendations for the development of personal autonomy are often associated with and give rise to proscriptions against indoctrination. Furthermore, in educational writings indoctrination is frequently seen as involving the teaching of a particular type of content, a content made up of doctrines of a religious, political, or even moral nature which, or so it is claimed, are not the sorts of things we can be sure or certain about.[26] The inference to be drawn here seems to be that if doctrinal material is to be handled at all in the teaching situation, it should be handled neutrally. All of which means that even in this area sceptical cases for neutrality can be found.

A second type of argument that we could consider as being non-sceptical is based on the grounds that non-neutral teaching may, at best, get pupils to accept pieces of information and equip them with beliefs, but not leave them with knowledge, since knowledge requires the personal involvement of 'seeing' or grasping or discovering or what some would call 'the act of knowing'.[27] In this respect it might be maintained that Plato was correct in claiming that we can no more give someone knowledge than we can put sight into blind eyes, for knowledge cannot be given or transmitted, but is something learners may achieve when teachers adopt a neutral, non-interventionist role. Contemporary supporters of this line of reasoning might be found in some branches of the child-centred movement, amongst those who insist that knowledge is personal, amongst those who stand alongside Paulo Freire and oppose the banking model of education,[28] amongst those who reject the empiricist model of the knower as passive receiver and, in the moral sphere, amongst those who see moral knowledge as the product of intuition or *a priori* insight. Several responses to this type of cognitive case for neutrality can be suggested. It could be argued, for instance, that in order that learners can progress towards the appropriate 'seeing' and grasping, then, as in the *Republic*, they will need to follow routes and employ techniques dictated by their teachers, which means that this case for neutrality may presuppose a great deal of instruction and non-neutral teaching. Second, if this case is concerned with the acquisition of knowledge involving public concepts, the knower cannot be as independent from others as this cognitive case might be thought to assume. Third, we can point out that while knowing may be personal in that, unlike parroting or recitation, it requires an agent's understanding and commitment, accepting, agreeing and believing can be said to be similarly personal. Now if it is conceded that accepting, agreeing and believing can be the products of instruction, then we may wonder why the fact that knowledge is personal means that it cannot have a similar pedagogical antecedent. No doubt other criticisms of this cognitive case for neutrality could be advanced, but whatever their strengths, one thing we need concede here is that in so far as this case is concerned with the possibility and acquisition of knowledge, it should not be classified as sceptical.

A third case for neutrality that may also seem to be non-sceptical is another that might be associated with the child-centred movement, and with growth theories in particular.[29] Central to this case is the idea that teachers should not impose or mould or force or try to graft-on what they see as missing abilities, or implant preferences. Instead, educational environments should be sources of nutrition and sustenance and provide the educational equivalent of April's sweet showers, enabling children to grow and develop in some 'natural' and spontaneous way. But even if we were to go along with much of this optimistic and simplistic picture, why should we not accept, in the terms of the analogy, that teachers know best about what talents need bringing on, what abilities need feeding and what should be left to fade and wilt? And if they do know and use such knowledge, aren't they being far from neutral? Such questions may be greeted with the rejoinder that teachers do not and cannot know these things, but nature knows and should have its way, which means that even here a sceptical base may be lurking in the undergrowth. As for letting nature have its way, such advice will only be useful to teachers if they know what is natural and what isn't, that is, if they know what should be encouraged to bloom and flourish and what should be nipped in the bud. But this, it seems, is the very information they cannot have, which, needless to say, does not bode well for the usefulness of this advice.

Three more cases for teacher neutrality might be mentioned all of which may look non-sceptical. The first might be called the case from pluralism. It involves the prescription that where pupils come from different cultural and religious backgrounds, the teacher should not indicate that he supports the cultural and religious preferences of some of his pupils and not those of others. But, then, is the teacher to allow anything to be practised and go unchallenged providing it is part of a pupil's cultural or religious inheritance? Should racism, sexism and religious bigotry be allowed to go unchecked and unquestioned just because they are part of some pupil's upbringing?[30] And should a teacher do nothing to combat the kind of untenable ethical relativism that deference to cultures and sects may well engender? Of course, supporters of the case from pluralism might insist that it would be unfair and unjust as well as incompatible with the respect that is required in this area for a teacher to indicate that he thinks that some of his pupils' cultural preferences or religious beliefs are mistaken. But what of those preferences and beliefs which might promote unfairness and injustice? There again, it might be worth noting that, contrary to what often seems to be assumed, 'all cultures are worthy of respect' is not tautologous and our believing that a person's religion or culture or life-stance embodies numerous mistaken propositions is quite compatible with our respecting both that person and their beliefs and attitudes.[31] Indeed, if we could only respect those people, cultures and sets of ideas with which we agreed totally, then there would be even less respect in the world than there is, though, on the credit side, respecting people and their views might not be too taxing. This concern with moral values such as justice and fairness could prompt defenders of the case from pluralism to argue that moral values together with the differing metaphysics which provide the foundations of different forms of life do not belong to areas of inquiry in which one can claim the right to be sure or to be an authority and, therefore, these are matters on which teachers should be neutral, and this, it is clear, is a sceptical case for neutrality.

The next case I want to mention, which is not unconnected with the case for pluralism, involves parental rights, the supporting and, or so it may appear, non-sceptical argument here being that failure by teachers to be neutral on certain issues could involve their encroaching on the moral right that parents have to determine what their children believe in certain areas. Many might oppose this case by arguing that there can be no such moral right since it would conflict with such fundamental moral concerns as respect for persons and self-determination.[32] In addition, we might ask whether it is being proposed that teachers should desist from teaching certain aspects of physics or geography just because the parents of some of their pupils believe in a flat earth. In reply it might be suggested that appeals to parental rights in support of teacher neutrality will be found most frequently in areas where, unlike geography or physics, one cannot be justified in claiming that one's way of arriving at a conclusion is *the* proper way or that one's view is correct, which means, if this suggestion is true, that underpinning appeals to parental rights we will frequently find sceptical bases.

The final case for teacher neutrality I will mention could be called the liberal case, and this, unlike the former, is specifically concerned with the right of self-determination, with the individual's right to choose and pursue the good as he sees it. From this foundation it can be argued that teachers should not impose views about the good life, but should be neutral on this matter. In fact it may be argued that instead of trying to influence pupils' views about the good life, teachers should simply be part of a service that equips the learner with information and the like so the learner can make some kind of informed choice for himself about what he prefers, though deschoolers and free-schoolers may wish to add that the learner has the right to determine whether he wishes to avail himself of this service.[33] Were we to take some contemporary views of the liberal state or, we might contend, some of the political views from Mill's *On Liberty* and extend them into education, then this type of liberal case for teacher neutrality might emerge.[34] Moreover, we can note that unlike the line of reasoning pursued by J. P. White which we outlined earlier, this type of case in its pure form does not involve a sceptical base. Being founded on the right of self-determination the liberal case is quite compatible with the view that teachers know best or are better judges than pupils on matters relating to the good life. This, of course, does not mean that the liberal case is usually found on its own; as in the political domain the underpinning concern for self-determination is frequently found in the company of other influential ideas, such as the belief that paternalistic encroachments are rarely effective or that the individual is the best judge of what his own good life will involve or that interference is not needed because individuals will achieve the good for themselves.[35] This latter view, I take it, being what A. S. Neill had in mind when he claimed: 'If left to himself without adult suggestion of any kind, he [the child] will develop as far as he is capable of developing'.[36]

Although I make no claim for completeness any more than I want to claim that each of the cases I have identified is always to be found isolated from other cases, nevertheless, I hope this survey has shown that there is a variety of cases for teacher neutrality and that, while not immediately obvious, several of these cases may involve sceptical bases or elements. The sceptical case for neutrality is, it seems, influential and ubiquitous. But what precisely does such a case and what do other cases for neutrality require from the teacher? And does the sceptical case involve particular problems or tensions? These are matters to which I now turn.

On the nature of neutral teaching and tensions within the sceptical case

According to Leszek Kolakowski and Alan Montefiore being neutral is always a matter of acting with a certain intention.[37] As for what this intention is the following attempt by Kolakowski to account for

117

neutrality provides an answer: '*I am neutral in relation to a conflict when I purposely behave in such a way so as not to influence its outcome.*'[38] Such an approach to neutrality is, I believe, open to various criticisms. Consider a headteacher confiding to her diary: 'On the subject of parental involvement in curriculum planning I'm quite neutral. I've no strong views either way. But for the sake of an easy life I always say I wholeheartedly support my local authority's view that parents should be involved.' Now however we would describe this headteacher's behaviour, we might say that she is epistemically neutral on the subject in question, and we might point out that the state of being epistemically neutral is something that is rarely, if ever, intentional; it is a destination one may find that one has arrived at after thinking about a dispute or conflict, but not a state one would normally, if ever, reach intentionally.[39]

Still, even if accounts of neutrality as being intentional are not exhaustive, it might be maintained that when we consider neutral teaching, we need to concentrate on intentional accounts; after all, recommendations to teachers to be neutral in certain lessons would be most odd if they were understood as recommendations to teachers to cease to hold certain beliefs for certain periods of time, whereas there is nothing odd in instructing teachers to act in a certain way in certain lessons.

Should we, therefore, accept an account of neutrality of the kind advanced by Kolakowski when we consider neutral teaching? Faced with this question we may point to another problem with Kolakowski's account, for we may argue that the type of intention outlined by Kolakowski is not necessary. Having the intention not to influence the outcome of a conflict presumably requires the agent to believe that she could be influential in this way. But surely the fact that a physics teacher believes or even recognizes that she will not influence the outcome of a contemporary scientific controversy, such as that concerning the intensity and duration of a nuclear winter, does not mean that she cannot endeavour to be neutral on this matter when her pupils discuss it. In addition we may argue that neutrality does not require conflicts. A person may be neutral, we can insist, on any matter on which contrary views are possible, irrespective of whether the matter is one that would generate sufficient heat to warrant the label 'conflict'. From this we may infer that the intention involved in neutral teaching is more modest than a writer like Kolakowski would lead us to believe; it is something along the lines of not intending to indicate or reveal support for a standpoint on an issue.

A further problem with Kolakowski's account is its ambiguity. Under what we can regard as a task interpretation Kolakowski is saying that being neutral is just a matter of acting with a certain intention, whether one is successful or not, whereas under an achievement interpretation his account would have us treat being neutral as acting with a certain intention and being successful because one has so acted. With regard to the task interpretation, we may observe that in discussions about neutrality with teachers one often hears the claim that in 'the New RE', for instance, teachers who have a particular religious commitment cannot be neutral because in the course of a series of lessons their own beliefs are bound to come through even though they may try to hide them. One could criticize those who advance these views on the grounds that teachers may be more successful at hiding their beliefs than is being suggested, though to concentrate on this criticism is to overlook the important issue these views emphasize, that being neutral in the teaching situation, but no doubt not only there, involves being successful, which means that Kolakowski's account under a task interpretation is wanting.

Turning to the achievement interpretation of his account, this suffers from the fact that it assumes that we can only be neutral when we can influence a conflict's outcome. Yet, concerning influence, and here we develop our earlier criticisms, surely a science teacher could intend to be and be neutral on some contemporary scientific controversy but be in no position to influence the outcome of that controversy, and surely a teacher could intend to be neutral on an issue which would fail to satisfy the emotional demand of being a conflict. It seems, therefore, that if Kolakowski meant to advance an achievement account, he should have concentrated on more modest achievements, and, as far as teaching is concerned, we may suggest that these involve teachers not indicating or revealing support for a standpoint on an issue.

Our suggestion focuses on non-indication and non-revelation rather than on teachers not influencing their pupils. Of course, subscribers to the Humanities Project's insistence that 'the inescapable authority position of the teacher ... is such that his view will be given an undue emphasis and regard' may maintain that the distinction between indication or revelation and influence in the context of teaching is scarcely worth drawing. Against this I would say there could be cases when, as John Kleinig observes, a teacher's taking a stand on an issue 'may be ineffectual ... it may be a breath of wind, possessing no power to advance the prospects of a particular view point'.[40] And if a teacher took a stand and even if his doing so was 'like a breath of wind', we clearly could not describe him as having been neutral. This is why in accounting for neutrality in teaching we should focus on non-indication and non-revelation. But, then, the important question arises as to whether the non-neutral teacher we have described, who is also uninfluential, need worry those who favour teacher neutrality. Bearing in mind that there can be various cases for neutrality, let me rephrase this. Would the teacher we have described worry those who favour a sceptical case for neutrality if that teacher advanced a view in an area that they had identified as one in which teachers should be neutral? We may feel justified in replying that while these neutralists might query the possibility of such a teacher and claim we could never be sure about any teacher's lack of influence, the fact is that the teacher under consideration would not be a source of anxiety to them because what they are concerned to guard against is influence. Alternatively, the neutralists we have mentioned might reply that there is something worrying about the teacher in our example because even if his pupils do not take his view as authoritative, his behaviour might suggest to his pupils that the area in which he advances his view is one where authoritative pronouncements are possible.

Now I grant these answers are only speculative, but they do, I believe, get to the heart of the matter, for I would contend that it is not neutrality as such that many neutralists are concerned with, but influence; they fear that teachers' views will be taken as authoritative in domains where, or so they would argue, there are or can be no authorities, and this is why those same neutralists might object to the teacher we have described on the grounds that his behaviour might be suggestive of the possibility of authorities and authoritative pronouncements in areas where, they would claim, scepticism should be the order of the day. In brief, it is not neutrality as such, non-indication or non-revelation, that is important to those who favour sceptical cases; their concern is that teachers do not influence pupils in ways which, they would claim, are irreconcilable with the epistemic character of certain domains and issues. All of which brings us to what I regard as one of the major problems in this much troubled area, a problem that is also concerned with irreconcilability.

There are, as we have seen, many sceptical cases for neutrality, cases which identify certain subjects and topics as in need of neutral teaching. We have also seen that these cases involve a positive side or aspect; they involve, either explicitly or implicitly, the prescription that pupils should be encouraged to reason, to argue, to consider the evidence, to judge, to form their own views. This means that pupils will come to believe that they have the correct answers supported by sound reasons or that their evidence and reasons are overriding and that they are operating in an area where epistemic progress is being or, at the very least, can be made. So what the positive aspect encourages is a sense of epistemic optimism, a commitment to the idea that in the areas in question one can have the right to be sure and that epistemic gains are possible, and such encouragement is likely to be reinforced where there is concern for procedural neutrality, for then pupils will feel there are procedures, rules and routes to follow in order to arrive at what is secure and above suspicion. But aren't these attitudes the very ones that sceptical cases for neutrality would have us regard as mistaken? Surely if the case for the teacher being excluded from advancing opinions in certain areas stems from what we have identified as sceptical bases, then from those same bases it should be argued that pupils are to be discouraged from feeling sure, from believing that their views are correct and that their reasons and evidence are decisive.

It seems, then, there are serious tensions in sceptical cases for neutrality between the sceptical foundations of such cases and those attitudes that the positive dimension of such cases is likely to promote, tensions that will be compounded if a concern for procedures further encourages a sense of epistemic optimism. Moreover, if teachers were to discourage such attitudes, they would surely be threatening the very point of inquiry, judgement, and argument. All of which raises the question of whether such epistemic optimism can be reconciled with the foundations of sceptical cases for teacher neutrality.

At least two lines of reconciliation suggest themselves here. First of all it might be argued the tensions we have described are not present in some cases because some areas of inquiry are such that while scepticism is in order from the teacher's point of view, this is quite consistent with the pupil reasoning, forming judgements, being confident and proceeding with a sense of epistemic optimism, the reason being that in some areas the pupil has what can be called privileged access. J. P. White, I believe, is one who would support this type of defence as far as his particular commitment to neutrality is concerned, for White would claim that the pupil, but not his teachers, has privileged access to decisions about what is good for him. This claim rests on the view that what is good for an individual is dependent on that individual's informed and reflective preferences, and the individual, White insists, is *the* authority on his own preferences.[41] However, what supports this latter idea seems to be nothing more than some thesis about the privacy of feelings and preferences.[42] If this is so, then even if we accept both White's view of what is good for people[43] and the thesis that preferences are private, we could still argue that this does not avoid some of the difficulties that are to be found in his particular case. The point is that accepting White's ideas need not prevent us from insisting that teachers are better informed about and better able to reflect on the future and even that they could be better able to judge what their pupil's future preferences will be. After all, if the idea that pupils have privileged and private access to their preferences is to be defensible, it must surely be understood as excluding the view that at any present moment pupils have privileged and private access to their future mental states and desires. But whatever the success or otherwise of this particular argument about privileged access, such arguments are scarcely going to be pressed into service in defence of many sceptical cases for teacher neutrality. No one, I take it, is seriously going to argue that pupils, but not their teachers, have private access to the truths of morals, the solutions of controversial issues, the verities of theology, or the mysteries of the universe.

The second line of reconciliation that might be advanced involves the argument that epistemic optimism is reconcilable with sceptical cases because the underpinning scepticism of those cases is merely of a temporal variety. According to this argument the sceptical foundations in question simply assert that as things stand at present there is, to borrow from Arnold, 'a disquieting absence of sure authority', and such assertions are clearly compatible with the view that things may or will or are likely to change if learners inquire and speculate and follow the proper procedures. But how many neutralists fit this model? Here it might be contended that the type of restricted sceptical case just outlined describes the positions of the early Socrates and Abelard and that it also describes how Arnold was able to reconcile what he saw as 'a disquieting absence' with his recommendation about 'the best way' of proceeding and why he was able to suggest that although as things stood instruction was out of the question, nevertheless, 'in his own breast ... every man' has 'a possible Socrates'.[44]

Yet, even if we were to support this contention, we could also claim that many sceptical cases do not fit this model because many cases rest upon scepticism of a timeless or unhistoric variety, that is, they rest on the foundation that in certain areas progress can never or will never be made, issues can never or will never be settled and there cannot be epistemic gains or authorities. This, it seems, is how the Humanities Project viewed controversial issues, it may be how Mill intended religion to be regarded when he delivered his inaugural address at St Andrews, it may be how many supporters of 'the New RE' view religion and it is likely that this is how Hare regarded morals when he prescribed a neutralist approach in moral education.[45] Moreover, we may suggest that what these exemplify is the common sceptical position that where there can be no authorities or certainties, pupils should be encouraged to enquire and speculate and form their own ideas. In short, this second line of reconciliation does not appear to fit several important and common cases for teacher neutrality.

As for the restricted kind of sceptical case involved in this line of reconciliation, we may note with interest that any case for neutral teaching of this type could contain the seeds of its own redundancy. If epistemic gains are possible in certain areas, then, presumably, the way is open for there to be authorities and authoritative pronouncements in those areas, and, hence, the way is open for there to be instruction. Looked at in this light Abelard's *inquisitio* might be seen as paving the way for the formal teaching prescribed by Peter Lombard.

Another matter worth noting is that the restricted kind of sceptical case we have been considering might still house a certain tension. One might accept, for example, that epistemic optimism is in order in an area where thus far no one has been able to speak authoritatively, but be disinclined to support the idea that children and youngsters should be encouraged to speculate in that area or to feel optimistic about their speculations. Progress, it might be insisted, if it is to be made, will be made by those experienced in the area, not by novices. In fact it might be added that to encourage optimism amongst novices would be both pointless and cruel. Bearing this in mind, we could consider the position of Socrates and Abelard. If they did favour some restricted kind of scepticism, why were they so concerned to get the young or those Abelard called 'tender readers' to follow their procedures?[46] Did they think that those who are not so tender will have face and positions to save and, like Protagoras, will marshall their forces to defend their views, whereas youngsters, as in the *Lysis*, will not feel aggrieved even if their inquiries lead to their looking 'rather ridiculous'? And did Socrates and Abelard accept that those of experience will be less inclined to examine the ideas of people who occupy positions of esteem? Clearly there is no room here for further inquiry.

Still the significant issues to arise from these considerations as far as our inquiry is concerned are that many sceptical cases do not involve foundations of a restricted variety and that even in those that do there might be a tension between pupil speculation and optimism and the view that progress is possible. Now we saw earlier that the tensions we have highlighted in sceptical cases do not seem to be avoidable by arguing in terms of privileged access and we have just seen that the tensions in many sceptical cases are not avoided by arguments concerned with restricted scepticism. What, then, is to be done? Well, we may suggest a policy of openness; we may suggest that if an area of thought is one where some kind of scepticism is in order, teachers should endeavour to explain to their pupils what the area is like and why it is one where scepticism is apposite and they should encourage their pupils to adopt the kind of attitudes appropriate to such an area. If, for example, the area is one where it seems one cannot have the right to be sure, teachers should explain why this is so and discourage their pupils from feeling certain or confident in that area. If an area is one where a restricted kind of scepticism seems in order, again we may suggest that teachers should endeavour to encourage the kinds of attitudes that are appropriate to such an area, such as, for example, not feeling sure or confident but not being entirely pessimistic about the possibility of progress being made, especially by experts.

Were teachers to proceed in this way, they could provoke a strong reaction amongst parents, particularly if they were to treat religion as warranting such an approach. 'Better neutral than sceptical' might be the slogan of many parents, and some might well appeal to parental rights. But at least the policy of openness just sketched out would mean that the tensions we have highlighted would be avoided. Such a policy might also prompt inquiries into whether certain areas, as, say, morality, the realm of the controversial, and religion, are as vulnerable to scepticism as various neutralists proclaim. Inquiries of this type would clearly be of relevance here, but this, we may insist, does not detract from the case for openness; for if some areas are ones where scepticism is in order, then surely pupils ought to be informed about this and not encouraged to have attitudes and expectations which are incompatible with such scepticism. Yet even the case for openness may house an unacceptable tension if an attempt is made to employ it in the realm of morals; for there is surely something paradoxical in insisting on scepticism in morals while maintaining that teachers *ought* to tell pupils certain things and *ought* not to act in certain ways, though this paradox, we can note, is also to be found in sceptical cases for neutrality in morals since these also prescribe what teachers *ought* to do.[47]

Let us now take stock of our line of reasoning. Sceptical cases for neutrality can be seen as encouraging attitudes which seem irreconcilable with the sceptical foundations of such cases. Claims about privileged access and even restricted scepticism may do little to remove all of these tensions. We may, therefore, recommend a policy of openness; whereof we cannot speak with confidence, we should not encourage children to think they can. Instead we should inform pupils about why certain areas are ones where the proper attitude is one of scepticism. In fact, we might amend Mill's recommendation: where there is diversity of opinion amongst able and informed people who have taken equal and great pains to arrive at the truth, we should be wary of encouraging optimism and confidence. We might even entertain the idea that if an area is one where scepticism is in order, there will not be diversity of opinion amongst people of ability; for such people would not have opinions in such an area. Of course, the case for openness may not be employed in morals, but, then, the sceptical case for neutrality in morals is similarly paradoxical. If moral advice is never justified, then even the prescription that we ought not to give such advice is not justified. In brief, the case for openness may be argued for in some areas, and by following this type of procedure, teachers can clearly avoid the tensions we have identified in sceptical cases. Morality, however, raises its own particular problem; if we are to see ourselves as justified in recommending certain courses of action, we cannot embrace or operate from a meta-ethic that conflicts with such a perception.

Some concluding observations

Recommendations to teachers to be neutral are neither novel nor follow one particular pattern and many are not unblemished. Indeed, as we have seen, what is perhaps the commonest type of case for teacher neutrality, the sceptical case, seems markedly flawed. But in addition to the various blemishes that we have highlighted there is another source of anxiety that is worthy of attention. It is that many cases for neutrality are concerned to keep pupils ignorant of the opinions of those in positions of status and authority. But can this be justified as a long-term educational goal? Or, rather, do we want an education that is concerned that pupils should examine and assess such opinions? If we support this latter picture of education, then we may suggest that eventually we want learners to confront and examine their teachers' beliefs, and this means that neutral teaching is at best an interim device. If in the long run we want learners to consider, evaluate and even criticize their teachers' views, then neutral teaching has to give way to interchange, discussion and dialogue where the recommendation that teachers do not advance their ideas is replaced by a willingness by all parties to reveal, defend, discuss and inquire into what they believe. Of course, if, as some neutralists believe, there are areas where such inquiries are pointless, then let this dictate and inform how we proceed in those areas. Let us not encourage the young to go where the wise will not.

Notes

I would like to thank Dr Andrew Barker, Dr Keith Hoskin, Professor David Jenkins, Professor Gwynne Lewis, Mr Terry McLaughlin, and Dr Andrew Reeve for their encouragement and comments on several of the ideas raised in this paper. I would also like to thank members of the Cambridge, West Midlands, and Bristol branches of the Philosophy of Education Society of Great Britain for their comments on earlier drafts of parts of this paper.

1 See The Schools Council/Nuffield Foundation, *The Humanities Project: An Introduction*, London: Heinemann, 1970.
2 See *The Humanities Project: An Introduction*, pp. 1–36.
3 *The Humanities Project*, p. 6.
4 *The Humanities Project*, p. 1.
5 See, for example, *The Humanities Project*, pp. 17–21. See also L. Stenhouse, 'The humanities curriculum project', in L. Stenhouse, *Authority, Education and Emancipation*, London: Heinemann, 1983, pp. 73–89; L. Stenhouse, 'The humanities project and the problem of motivation', in *Authority, Education and Emancipation*, pp. 119–32; and J. Elliott, 'The values of the neutral teacher', in D. Bridges and P. Scrimshaw (eds), *Values and Authority in Schools*, London: Hodder & Stoughton, 1975, pp. 103–20.
6 *The Humanities Project*, p. 7.
7 L. Stenhouse, 'Towards a vernacular humanism', in L. Stenhouse, *Authority, Education and Emancipation*, p. 168. Stenhouse's italics.
8 *The Humanities Project*, p. 6.
9 See R. F. Dearden, 'Controversial issues and the curriculum', *Journal of Curriculum Studies*, 13 (1), pp. 39–40. See also P. Gardner, 'Another look at controversial issues and the curriculum', *Journal of Curriculum Studies*, 16 (4), p. 380.
10 See R. M. Hare, 'Value education in a pluralist society', *Proceedings of the Philosophy of Education Society of Great Britain*, 10, pp. 7–23.

However, given the substantive nature of the principles involved in what
the Humanities Project regarded as procedural neutrality, and given
Hare's limited and non-substantive view of the formal or procedural
requirements of morality, we may suggest that there is a difference
between what Hare favoured as procedural neutrality and what the
Project team supported.

11 R. M. Hare, 'Platonism in moral education: two varieties', *Monist*, 58
    (4), p. 577.
12 Hare, 'Value education in a pluralist society', p. 12.
13 See J. P. White, *Towards a Compulsory Curriculum*, London:
    Routledge & Kegan Paul, 1973, pp. 8–24. See also J. P. White, *The
    Aims of Education Restated*, London: Routledge & Kegan Paul, 1982,
    pp. 9–60.
14 See White, *Towards a Compulsory Curriculum*, pp. 17–24.
15 J. P. White, 'The compulsory curriculum and beyond: a reply to Peter
    Gardner', *Journal of Philosophy of Education*, 19 (1), p. 131.
16 See J. G. Sikes, *Peter Abailard*, New York: Collier-Macmillan, 1965,
    pp. 77–87.
17 See B. Smalley, 'Prima clavis sapientiae: Augustine and Abelard', in
    D. J. Gordon (ed.), *Essays in Honour of Fritz Saxl*, London: Thomas
    Nelson, 1957, pp. 95–6; and K. W. Hoskin, 'The professional in
    educational history', in J. Wilkes (ed.), *The Professional Teacher*,
    *Proceedings of the 1985 Annual Conference of the History of Education
    Society*, London: History of Education Society, 1986, pp. 4–5. See also
    Abelard, *Sic et Non*, Prologue, in J-P. Migne (ed.), *Patrologia Latina*,
    Paris, 1844–1864, 178, cols 1949A–B.
18 Concerning Stenhouse's references to Abelard, see, for instance,
    Stenhouse's 'Research as a basis for teaching', in L. Stenhouse,
    Authority, Education and Emancipation, pp. 177–95. Concerning
    similarities in presentation, *Sic et Non* presents conflicting or apparently
    conflicting statements from Biblical and patristic sources on 168 topics.
    On each 'controversial issue' selected by the Humanities Project team
    packs of material were prepared which contained extracts from
    speeches, poems, newspaper articles and more besides, and frequently
    the views advanced in one extract conflicted with those advanced in
    another. For example, the material on 'Relations Between the Sexes'
    contains extracts from Roman Catholic literature on sexual relations and
    contraception as well as some contemporary and radical views on sexual
    relations.
19 J. S. Mill, 'Inaugural address', in J. B. Schneewind (ed.), *Mill's Essays
    on Literature and Society*, New York: Collier-Macmillan, 1965, p. 399.
20 J.-J. Rousseau, *Emile*, London: Dent, 1911, p. 223.
21 See Editors' Preface in R. N. Smart and D. N. Horder (eds), *New
    Movements in Religious Education*, London: Temple Smith, 1975, p. i;
    and J. M. Hull, 'Agreed syllabuses, past, present and future', in *New
    Movements in Religious Education*, pp. 114–17.
22 M. Arnold, *Culture and Anarchy*, Cambridge: Cambridge University
    Press, 1932, pp. 162–4.

23 See, for example, C. Mason, *An Essay Towards a Philosophy of Education*, London: Dent, 1931, chs. 4 and 5. See also R. F. Dearden, 'Autonomy and education', in R. F. Dearden, P. H. Hirst and R. S. Peters (eds), *Education and the Development of Reason*, London: Routledge & Kegan Paul, 1972, pp. 448–65.

24 J. F. Stephen, *Liberty, Equality, Fraternity*, Cambridge: Cambridge University Press, 1967, p. 81.

25 See, for example, R. G. Woods and R. St C. Barrow, *An Introduction to Philosophy of Education*, London: Methuen, 1975, pp. 108–10.

26 See, for example, A. G. N. Flew, 'Indoctrination and doctrines', in I. A. Snook (ed.), *Concepts of Indoctrination*, London: Routledge & Kegan Paul, 1972, pp. 67–92; J. Gribble, *Introduction to Philosophy of Education*, Boston: Allyn and Bacon, 1969, pp. 29–40; and R. F. Atkinson, 'Instruction and indoctrination', in R. D. Archambault (ed.), *Philosophical Analysis and Education*, London: Routledge & Kegan Paul, 1965, pp. 171–83.

27 See, for example, C. Mason, *An Essay Towards a Philosophy of Education*, pp. 99 and 271.

28 See P. Freire, *Pedagogy of the Oppressed*, New York: Seabury, 1970, ch.2.

29 See R. F. Dearden, *The Philosophy of Primary Education*, London: Routledge & Kegan Paul, ch.3.

30 See P. H. Walkling and C. Brannigan, 'Anti-sexist/anti-racist education: a possible dilemma', *The Journal of Moral Education*, 15 (1), pp. 16–25.

31 See P. Gardner, 'Believing other people are mistaken: a rational consequence of multicultural education', *Wolverhampton Educational Bulletin*, 4, forthcoming.

32 On questions relating to the conflict or compatibility of upbringing and autonomy see T. H. McLaughlin, 'Parental rights and the religious upbringing of children', *Journal of Philosophy of Education.*, 18 (1), pp. 75–83; E. Callan, 'McLaughlin on parental rights', *Journal of Philosophy of Education.*, 19 (1), pp. 111–18; T. H. McLaughlin, 'Religion, upbringing and liberal values: a rejoinder to Eamonn Callan', *Journal of Philosophy of Education.*, 19 (1), pp. 119–27; and P. Gardner, 'Religious upbringing and the liberal ideal of religious autonomy', *Journal of Philosophy of Education.*, 22 (1), pp. 89–105.

33 See R. Barrow, *Radical Education*, London: Martin Robertson, 1978.

34 See P. Gardner, 'Liberty and Compulsory Education', in A. Phillips Griffiths (ed.), *Of Liberty*, Cambridge: Cambridge University Press, 1983, pp. 109–29.

35 It has been argued that Mill had this unrealistic and optimistic view of people. See, for example, H. L. A. Hart, *Law, Liberty, and Morality*, London: Oxford University Press, 1963, p. 33.

36 A. S. Neill, *Summerhill*, Harmondsworth: Penguin, 1968, p. 20.

37 See L. Kolakowski, 'Neutrality and academic values', in A. Montefiore (ed.), *Neutrality and Impartiality*, London: Cambridge University Press, 1975, p. 72; and A. Montefiore, 'Neutrality, indifference and detachment', in *Neutrality and Impartiality*, p. 5.

38 L. Kolakowski, p. 72. Kolakowski's italics.
39 One of the issues involved here is the question of whether belief and disbelief can be a matter of choice. Some would argue that these states of mind cannot be chosen. See, for example, R. S. Downie and E. Telfer, 'Autonomy', *Philosophy*, 46 (178), pp. 293–301. My own view is that it is possible for a person to choose a belief, since a person may choose to be indoctrinated. However, I would suggest that most of our beliefs are not chosen and that most of us who are epistemically neutral about certain issues have not chosen to be so.
40 J. Kleinig, 'Principles of neutrality in education', *Educational Philosophy and Theory*, 8 (2), p. 3.
41 See White, 'The compulsory curriculum and beyond: a reply to Peter Gardner', p. 131.
42 See White, 'The compulsory curriculum and beyond: a reply to Peter Gardner'. See also P. Gardner, 'The compulsory curriculum and beyond: a rejoinder to John White', *Journal of Philosophy of Education*, 21 (2), pp. 273–5.
43 I have, however, argued that we should have reservations about such a thesis. See P. Gardner, 'The compulsory curriculum and beyond: a rejoinder to John White', pp. 275–7.
44 M. Arnold, *Culture and Anarchy*, p. 2ll.
45 In 'Value education in a pluralist society' Hare accepts that there are 'determinate answers' to moral questions, but argues that 'in practice we shall never have gone on discussing long enough, or familiarized ourselves with all the relevant evidence'. By which, I take it, he means that we can never know or be sure or certain what those answers are. See R. M. Hare, 'Value education in a pluralist society', p. 19.
46 See K. W. Hoskin, 'The professional in educational history', pp. 4–5.
47 A similar type of paradox is to be found in several criticisms of moral education. See P. Gardner, 'Defending moral education', *The Journal of Moral Education*, 13 (2), pp. 75–82.

7

Neutrality and the media

Ken Newton

Freedom of the press is guaranteed only to those who own one.

A. J. Liebling

The whole country is littered with papers pushing every political line from anarchy to Zen ... it's the very free-for-all which guarantees the freedom of each. You see, you don't have to be a millionaire to contradict one .... The *Flat Earth News* is free to sell a million copies. What it lacks is the capability of finding a million people with four pence and a conviction that the world is flat. You see, people don't buy rich men's papers because the men are rich: the men are rich because people buy their newspapers ... freedom is neutral.

Tom Stoppard, *Night and Day*

Theory

What is news media neutrality?

Let us start with the simplest approach to the question of what media neutrality is, and see where this leads. Let us further simplify by limiting the task to a discussion of news reporting and current affairs programmes. It is well recognized that all media content carries a political message of one sort or another, but to extend the discussion to soap operas and advertising would complicate the task inordinately, and is best left for another time. This paper will deal only with hard news and commentary.

From this admittedly artificial starting point, a simple and common sense approach to news media neutrality might treat it as a matter of telling the truth, the whole truth, and nothing but the truth. The news media should, in other words, stick to a straightforward account of the facts. The opposite would be news which is biased, ideological, or partisan in the sense that it ignores or suppresses important facts, or else presents facts in a way which influences (intentionally or unintentionally) an evaluation of them. In short, this sort of approach to the definition of media neutrality treats it as a matter of accurate treatment of facts, without omission or commission. A neutral media will present a full and fair account of the facts.

Unfortunately, this is not just a simple view but also a simple-minded one, for there are practical and theoretical reasons why the role of a neutral news media cannot be described so easily. The practical reasons are those of economics, politics, and time. The neutrality of some occupations such as judges, civil servants, and sports referees, is institutionally protected by removal from the political arena and the economic market place. News agencies are in a completely different situation: most are businesses; some are active participants in politics;[1] and even the radio and TV channels which are publicly funded or regulated are not free of the need to watch audience ratings. The third practical difficulty of time makes it more difficult to achieve balance and neutrality. News is a perishable commodity and must be very hastily assembled. A great many neutral tasks are undertaken quickly, but few mix the extreme complexity of news reporting with the daily rush to meet deadlines.

The problems of achieving political neutrality are also caused by more abstract difficulties to do with facts and objectivity in handling them. These are the standard problems which any social scientist should be aware of, and they will not be discussed in any great detail here. It is enough to say that facts are neither equal nor colourless, that they cannot speak for themselves, nor are they mute, and that they are never pure and simple. Even the most trivial news story has an infinite number of facts associated with it, and reporting them all is neither possible nor desirable. Nonetheless, selecting the important and interesting ones necessarily involves subjective judgement and interpretation, and the supposedly simple act of communicating facts necessarily involves colouring them, and placing them in a context which encourages one sort of interpretation rather than others. Besides, the journalist's job is to make the news story interesting, and this involves more interpretation and colouring than the dry-as-dust recounting of one fact after another.

To this extent the news is not merely a matter of reporting facts. In any case, the well informed citizen wants not just the news, but also interpretation and commentary. We commonly link the words 'news' and 'commentary' and quite rightly so, for they are different sides of the same coin, and a systematic presentation of both is the proper function of the news media. There is no such thing as news without comment, and without comment the news makes little sense. A neutral media, therefore, is one which presents not only a full and fair account of the facts, but also a wide range of opinion and interpretation.

However, the claim that reporting cannot be perfectly neutral does not lead to the conclusion that reporters are entitled to be as biased as they please. Like the social scientist, the reporter's job is to recognize the limits of neutrality, while trying to push as close to them as humanly possible. This is why the best newspapers present commentary as well as news, but try to keep the two quite separate. The fact that they are part and parcel of the same thing does not mean that they should be confused or confounded.

This, in turn leads to a second point. It would be unrealistic to expect anything like a complete range of opinion to appear in each and every organ of the media – every newspaper, journal, or radio or TV station. Given the wide range of views on almost all important matters, as well as the complexity of many issues and interpretations of them, we must expect something different – namely that the media as a whole should present the public with a full range of news and commentary. In this sense the neutrality of the media does not mean the elimination of all forms of ideological bias, but on the contrary, the presentation of all forms of ideological bias. If neutrality in the first simple-minded sense is impossible, then perhaps it is possible to achieve neutrality by doing the reverse – by airing all opinions, including those which are unpopular, eccentric, or supported only by small minorities. After all the editor of a good features page will cover a wide mixture of opinions, including those which are likely to be at odds with the prevailing view of the paper and its readers. The features editor cannot be impartial himself, but he can treat the partiality of others with impartiality.

By the same token, the neutrality of the media as a whole consists of a range and diversity of news and opinion – a range of different and conflicting views. In this case the hallmark of news media neutrality is not a monotone (or monotonous) uniformity, but a variety and diversity, with the news being treated from an assortment of cultural and political perspectives.

The point is that the citizen should choose and judge, not the reporter. That is, neutrality requires presenting as full an account of the news, and as wide a range of opinion as possible, leaving citizens to make up their own minds. This is no easy task, for the media cannot possibly avoid choice and judgement, but must nevertheless minimize its own selections and evaluations in order to maximize those of the citizen. The application of the principles is difficult and subjective, but the principles themselves are reasonably clear: the media should be broadly not narrowly selective; judgements should be open, not doctrinaire or party political; the emphasis should be on inclusion rather than exclusion, and in presenting all sides they should take no side.

At this point it is worth mentioning that although the question of news media neutrality is theoretically separate from that of the freedom of the press, the two converge on the need for diversity of expression. In analysing the philosophical foundations of the freedom of the press, Judith Lichtenberg argues that the liberal goal of individual autonomy and development cannot be achieved in a vacuum, but requires freedom of speech and expression to present a wide diversity of views and opinion. She concludes: 'All the arguments, with the possible exception of the arguments from self-expression, demonstrate the centrality not of speech simply but of discussion, debate, diversity of ideas and sources of information. They point to the multiplicity of voices as their central and unifying theme.'[2] In discussing the idea of the neutrality of the media we reach the same conclusion by way of a different route.

This approach to media neutrality rests upon a clear distinction between news and commentary with a full and fair account of the news which minimizes the errors of omission and commission, being complemented by a diversity of commentary and opinion. However, there is an important distinction to be made between a national news system which is neutral in this sense, and any part of it which may be highly partisan and biased. This distinction is important in the modern world of mass media, and we will return to it later.

How do we achieve news media neutrality?

The question obviously arises of how we can best achieve a satisfactory degree of news media neutrality. The classic answer is that of the liberal theorist who argues that it is best achieved through free-market competition, not because the end result is perfect or guaranteed, but because the system is less imperfect and less dangerous than the alternatives which involve public regulation or control of the media in one form or another. The outstanding advantage of free-market competition, it is argued, is that it neatly resolves two problems at the same time: freedom of speech and expression, and freedom of choice and consumption. The beauty of the free-market system is that it allows people to write and say what they want (within the limits of public safety, state security, and the libel laws), and it allows the public to hear, see, and read what it wants.

Market competition is at its fiercest during times of technological change and innovation, for new technology, it is claimed, helps to prevent any trends towards monopoly or oligopoly. Big producers are forced to stay on their toes by market rivals, especially new and small firms which are likely to be better able to exploit new methods of production, new products, and new demands. This certainly appears to have been the case with the media over the past few decades. The print media is currently undergoing one of its biggest upheavals since Guttenberg, with direct input by journalists, computer-driven production, new methods of colour printing, quicker ways of transmitting information around the globe, and smaller and more local changes, such as free sheets, disturbing the older and more established local papers. Meanwhile, print as a whole has had to give way first to the radio, and then to television, and the 'free' television channels, in their turn, are facing stiff competition from pay channels, and terrestrial broadcasting from satellite and cable. Moreover, new technologies make it possible to satisfy ever smaller and more specialist markets. In short, it is claimed that the effect of market competition will be to increase the diversity and plurality of the media.

Liberal theory does not rely exclusively on the market, however. It has a set of fall-back mechanisms to ensure that the free market does operate (market regulation) and to curb any programme excesses (content regulation). Most liberal democracies are conscious of the dangers of media monopolies and give the state powers to prevent them. Some, particularly in Scandinavia, provide substantial amounts of money to fund opinions which tend to be overlooked in a market system. In addition, liberal theory also provides for regulatory or self-regulatory bodies, and most Western nations have a Press Council or similar agency to keep a watch on the press. Besides, it is said, the professional training and ethos of editors and reporters help to ensure that reasonable standards are maintained.

Despite all this, liberal theory makes a clear exception of some parts of the industry. The reason is simple. Since anyone may set up a printing press and go into the newspaper or magazine business, there are no limits in theory to the number and variety of publications. Broadcasting, however, is characterized by 'spectrum scarcity' because radio and TV wavelengths are in scare supply. Consequently in the earliest days of broadcasting the state licensed the use of the wavelengths and, in the absence of the hidden hand of the market, maintained the public interest by regulating the content of radio programmes, particularly their political content. In Britain, the BBC was set up to be formally free of the government, and although it was not in the earlier days,[3] eventually it was able to gain a measure of independence,[4] and develop a code of conduct which satisfied at least some of the requirements of news media neutrality.[5] In the United States, the 1934 Communications Act (following the Radio Act of 1927) licensed the use of the airwaves, and required broadcasters to serve 'the public interest, convenience, and necessity'. To this end, the Federal Communications Commission was empowered to impose rules governing political fairness.[6]

Television is no different from radio in respect of spectrum scarcity, so it too was brought under public regulation in both Britain and the USA. In the absence of an equivalent of the BBC, the Americans established the point that broadcasting space was in the public domain, and that broadcasting operators should obtain a license to use it, provided they used it for the public interest.

Consequently, two different systems work within the media business. In the first, the print media, the basic idea is to minimize restrictions on the operation of the free market, and to use regulation or self-regulation only in the case of market failure, or when the market fails to satisfy the public interest. In the second, which relates to radio and television where the free market cannot operate, the state regulates who can broadcast, and to a certain extent what they can broadcast. In the future, cable and satellite transmission may allow many producers to operate in the market, in which case there will be no difference in principle between the print and electronic media, and both can then be united under the same market conditions.[7] Meanwhile, the two operate according to different models.

There is, of course, a considerable debate about the relative merits of these two models. The economist R. H. Coase comments on the general view that 'in the market for goods, government regulation is desirable whereas in the market for ideas, government regulation is undesirable and should be strictly limited ... intellectuals have shown a tendency to exalt the market for ideas and to depreciate [sic] the market for goods.'[8] He observes that the position of the intellectuals might not be altogether devoid of self-interest, but, more important, goes on to say that he does not believe that the distinction between the market for goods and ideas is valid, and that we should make decisions about the market for ideas on the same basis as the market for goods.

Coase forgets, however, that there are two models for the market for ideas, not one, and that we can compare and contrast the workings of both in order to see which is the better. This will be the task of the second part of this paper which will compare and contrast the workings of the two models in Britain and the United States.

Some difficulties with the theory

Before examining the operation of the two models in practice we should take note of some important difficulties with market theory: the first concerns the nature of property rights and their relationship to freedom of speech; the second concerns the market for goods and the market for ideas, and whether free market competition has anything to do with media neutrality; the third is about the assumptions which liberal theory makes about the consumers of the media; and the fourth concerns the differences between a media system which is pluralist, and the use which any given individual may make of this system or parts of it.

In some versions of liberal theory the right of property owners to do what they like with their property is extended to the right of media owners to publish or broadcast what they like. The theory has special appeal, of course, to those who own the media, particularly when they are threatened with regulation or control. Since the principle of freedom of speech is an enormously important and strong one, and since any infringement of it requires convincing defence, the argument is often enough to carry the day. But it is not water-tight by any means. In the first place, no right is absolute; all are qualified by other rights: nor are even the strongest rights of any given person absolute; they are also qualified by the rights of others. Property rights are no different. They are qualified in all sorts of ways in ordinary life, and there is no reason in principle why the property rights of those who own the media should not be qualified in the same way.

Moreover, we must be particularly careful not to confuse the matter of freedom of speech with the matter of property rights, and we certainly need not accept the argument that owning a paper or a broadcasting station gives the owners the right to print or say what they want. Liberal free-market theory makes it easy to slide from property rights to freedom of speech rights, and although this has suited the political interests of media owners, the argument is a weak one. The reason is simple. I am free to own a radio and to play rock music on it, but I am not free to play it full volume at night and disturb my neighbours. The issue is one of noise, not of property. By the same token, I am free to set up a newspaper, but I am not free to publish lies and distortions. The issue is about lies and distortions, not about property ownership.

The point was clearly made in the *Red Lion* decision of the Supreme Court of the USA. The case was brought over the matter of a journalist, Fred Cook, who had been criticized as a liar and a left-winger in a programme broadcast on WCGB AM–FM in Red Lion, Pennsylvania in 1964. Cook asked for time to reply but was refused, although he was offered advertising time at the usual rates. The FCC ruled that the Fairness Doctrine gave him the right of reply, and eventually the case went to the Supreme Court which affirmed that 'It is the right of viewers and listeners, not the right of broadcasters, which is paramount. It is the purpose of the First Amendment to preserve an uninhibited marketplace of ideas in which truth will ultimately prevail, rather than to countenance monopolization of the market, whether it be by the government itself or a private licensee .... It is the right of the public to receive suitable access to social, political, aesthetic, moral and other ideas and experiences which is crucial here.'[9]

This ruling is important in the context of the present discussion for several reasons: it is grounded in argument about freedom of speech and not in property rights; nevertheless it uses the language of the market place for ideas; it underlines the importance of diversity in media messages; and it argues that freedom of speech is not just about the rights of journalists, editors, or newspaper owners, but also about the rights of audiences and readers.

There is another and very different problem with liberal free-market theory. In the classic case of the supermarket, free competition is presented as the best way of satisfying public demand at the lowest possible price. When this model is used to justify freedom of speech or media neutrality, however, an additional and very important element is smuggled into the argument – free-market competition is not only supposed to be the most efficient and effective way of satisfying consumer demand, but market competition is also the only way in which neutrality and truth will emerge.

There seem to be two questionable assumptions behind this argument. The first is that truth is relatively robust, and untruth is relatively frail. In fact the reverse may also be true: complex and subtle truth may fall foul of simple but appealing falsehood. In any case, whereas supermarket shoppers take their goods home and put them to the first hand test of experience, how do they find out if their news is unreliable? Most of us do not have first-hand experience of most news events, and the only way to evaluate the accuracy of any one report is to compare it with another, which leads us into an infinite regress. There is no market test of news content.

In this sense Coase merely confuses things by talking about the market for ideas, for there is no such thing. Ideas are not goods or commodities. We cannot draw supply and demand curves for them, or calculate their marginal utility or marginal costs, nor can they be put to the same kind of test as consumer durables or commodities.

The second assumption is that the market for news can do far more than was ever claimed for the market for groceries. Supermarket competition is a way of providing the consumers with what they want at prices they are willing to pay, and if they want junk food and are willing to pay for it, then that is exactly what they will get. The supermarket system does not guarantee wholesome food. By the same token, a free market for ideas might be the best way of providing consumers with what they want and are willing to buy, and if they want junk news – bigotry, racism, prejudice, xenophobia, sexism, or reassuring lies and gossip – then that is what they will get. Neutrality or a respect for the truth has nothing to do with it, necessarily. To combine free-market competition with the triumph of truth, beauty, honesty, fairness, and neutrality is to insinuate into the argument something which it was never designed to handle in the first place.

Another way of making this point is to say that the difficulty with liberal market theory when applied to media neutrality is that it is concerned almost exclusively with the producer side of the equation – how to ensure a plurality of news sources – but there is an equally important range of concerns about the consumer, and the theory seems to make some extremely questionable assumptions about them.

First, it assumes that the ordinary citizen is serious and intelligent, and sufficiently concerned about politics to be willing to spend a fair amount of time and money to keep up with the news and opinion. In other words, liberal theory assumes that citizens are rather like the individuals who developed the theory in the first place – clones of Herbert Spencer or John Stuart Mill.

Even if it were conceded, the theory then assumes that the citizen is a rational actor who recognizes the truth for what it is. In the battle of ideas faulty products will fall by the wayside, and the truth will go marching on. Since the days of Spencer and Mill, however, we have learned more about the irrational and non-rational aspects of human behaviour, and in the studies of the impact of the media, in particular, we have discovered how the human mind selects, distorts, forgets, and subverts what it does not wish to know. All of this is the stock-in-trade of (some) journalists who know well enough how to exploit weakness and prejudices, hopes, and fears.

Moreover, the world has changed enormously since the heyday of liberal-market theory in the late nineteenth century. Not only have political issues themselves become considerably more complex technically (though not morally, necessarily), but the worldwide scope of the news has expanded, and with it the total amount of news and interpretations of it. More important, the mass media have developed far beyond anything envisaged by the classical Victorian theorists.

This raises two issues: the first concerns the practical problem of how the average citizen can possibly keep abreast of world events; the second concerns the question raised earlier of the difference between a neutral news system, and the bias of any one part of it. The first matter is a commonly understood and experienced problem which does not need labouring, but the second calls for closer examination.

Even the most pluralist news system will not produce a balanced picture for any particular individual, if that individual is limited to one biased section of it. And yet most people, even in the educated Western world, where access to most of the media is not particularly expensive, do exactly this. To use our supermarket analogy again: the shops may have the full range of food necessary for a balanced and healthy diet, but individual shoppers may be encouraged in all sorts of ways to live on the junk. And if it is easier, more convenient, and cheaper to live on the junk, then this is likely to be the outcome. In modern Britain and the United States it is indeed the outcome.

This problem is greatly increased by the emergence of the modern mass media which have transformed the classical liberal conditions in which a relatively large number of publications competed for the attention of a relatively small class of educated people. The modern media system is dominated by relatively few news sources which compete for mass markets by adopting a lowest-common-denominator approach to news and commentary. This combination of mass media and mass standards makes a diet of junk news readily available, and not surprisingly a majority of people depend heavily upon it. The rest of the media system may be of much higher quality, and display all the virtues of pluralist diversity, but this does not affect the majority which makes little or no use of it.

This is a way of saying that liberal-market theory tends to assume what it wants to achieve. Democracy requires a politically educated and informed electorate, and it is the job of the media to supply high quality information and education. But in a free market the mass media will only do its job if there is a mass demand for a high quality media in the first place. If there is not, then the mass media is likely to be of poor quality. Moreover, if the media is not up to its informing and educating task, then the population is likely to remain in ignorance and prejudice, and to be insufficiently aware or disturbed to want to do anything about it. Of course, the mass media are not the only, or even the main agents of mass education in modern society, but this observation does not help market theory much since the main agents are outside the market altogether – particularly free and compulsory education.

The argument, therefore, is that liberal-market theory is mainly concerned with producer issues, and rests its case very largely on the claim that free competition will generate a large number of news sources, and consequently a diverse and pluralist news system. Liberal theory cannot, however, ignore the consumer side of the equation, simply because the theory states that market competition is consumer driven, in that it is bound to produce what consumers want. The assumption that consumers want a fair and neutral account of the news is unwarranted, at least for the majority of the population in the mass media era. As a result, though a diverse and varied range of news may be available in the modern free-market system, the news diet of the great majority of people who consume the mass media may be anything but neutral and balanced, varied and pluralist. Even in a perfectly competitive system, individuals may restrict themselves to a narrow and biased range of news sources, but in a mass-media system in which the masses do not value neutrality particularly highly, the chances of a majority of the population doing so are greatly increased.

To conclude: there are very serious difficulties with liberal-market theory so far as it is claimed that it sustains media neutrality, or any other quality to do with balance, fairness, truth, or diversity of approaches to news and commentary. Indeed, it may even be that market failure is not just likely but inevitable because a fairly high degree of market competition is necessary to sustain the pluralist diversity of news sources required by liberal theory. This may be found in some areas of the economy, but there are good reasons for believing that it is unlikely to characterize the media market where the need for great speed, increasingly expensive capital equipment, extensive news gathering networks, and distribution networks for newspapers, are all likely to create a smaller and smaller number of producers. Moreover, the market for national news (as opposed to international news) within any given country is a local one which is unlikely to be opened up to foreign competition: newspapers and news programmes are not like consumer durables, or even like soap operas, which can be imported from the other side of the world.

Although a certain degree of oligopoly may not be sufficient to destroy market theory in some areas of production, the liberal-market theory of the press requires such an open and highly competitive market to guarantee pluralist diversity that the normal degree of concentration of ownership and control in the modern world is unlikely to satisfy its basic conditions. It might also be argued that the mass media are of such strategic importance politically that those with wealth and power will want to control them, and given present levels of inequality of wealth in most Western societies, will not find it difficult to do so.

For all these reasons it might be argued that the unregulated model of media neutrality will inevitably fail, if not totally then at least in some crucially important respects. The second part of this paper will examine the evidence.

The practice

Free market competition and media diversity

The first and most obvious deficiency of liberal theory is that the market has not sustained an adequate degree of competition to produce a pluralist diversity of news sources. On the contrary the ownership and control of the media has generally become more and more concentrated, and the range and diversity of the mass media has become narrower. A few figures illustrate the trend. Between 1921 and 1983 the number of British national daily papers fell from fourteen to ten, and the number of national Sundays fell from fourteen to eight. Since then both daily and Sunday titles have been added, but those with the biggest circulation have come from the existing producers of mass-circulation papers. The number of provincial and local papers has also declined from 134 in 1921 to 99 in 1983.[10] By 1975 only 18 per cent of British towns had competing papers run by different owners, half the figure of 1921.[11]

At the same time, ownership and control of the papers that remained has become more concentrated, although it was hardly fragmented in the first place. By 1983, three owners (Maxwell, Murdoch, and Matthews) controlled three quarters of national daily circulation, over 80 per cent of national Sunday circulation, and almost two thirds of combined national daily and Sunday circulation. Five companies accounted for 84 per cent of national daily and 96 per cent of national Sunday sales. The biggest five companies have also strengthened their position in the provinces, taking a 54 per cent share of evening papers, and a 72 per cent share of morning ones, compared with 44 per cent and 65 per cent in 1947. They increased their proportion of the local weekly market from 8 per cent to 29 per cent in the same period.[12]

At the same time, the newspaper business has become increasingly integrated into a few multi-media, multi-national conglomerate corporations. Maxwell's Pergamon Group has newspaper sales of around 12 million, and interests in TV and cable, as well as book, magazine, journal, and computer software publishing; the Pearson Group with national and local papers also controls Penguin and Longman books, as well as TV and film companies. Rupert Murdoch owns newspapers on three continents (he has a circulation of over 10 million in Britain alone), plus interest in TV, cable, books, magazines, transport, oil, gas, and property. According to Curran and Seaton, 'The cultural domination of big business is reinforced by the high degree of concentration that has developed within the media business as a whole. Just under half of commercial TV programmes, over half of rented video films, paperback and recording sales, over three-quarters of women's magazine circulation and cinemas admissions, and over nine-tenths of national newspapers are controlled by the five leading companies in each sector.'[13]

The British newspaper market is noted for its centralization among a few London companies, but the same trend is apparent in the USA where, by the late 1970s, ten companies owned nearly half the nation's 1800 daily papers, and four accounted for 22 per cent of sales.[14] Gannet owns seventy-eight papers in thirty states. In 1923, 500 cities in the USA had competing papers; in 1979 there were thirty-six. Only New York and Philadelphia had a choice of three. Increasingly, different papers are printing the same or similar material because a large proportion of copy is syndicated, or else compiled from reports provided by a few news agencies.

Television is more concentrated than newspapers. The three major networks cover 38 per cent of all TV owning households, and a further 550 stations are affiliated to them and give two thirds of their time to network programmes. Even the ninety independent stations show a large amount of network material, including the evening news.[15]

Overall, the US shows the same strong trend towards the formation of multi-media companies which, in their turn, are part of giant conglomerate corporations. Capital City's takeover of ABC for $3.5 billion produced a company owning 12 TV stations, 23 radio stations, and 55 cable systems covering 16 states, plus 6 publishing companies, and a range of entertainment and leisure industries. CBS controls a TV network, 5 TV stations, 14 radio stations, 22 magazines, Columbia records, and several major publishing houses. Finally, three-quarters of the major stockholders of the three national networks are big banks like Chase Manhattan, Citibank, Morgan Guaranty, and Bank of America.[16] Network analysis shows that tight links exist between the media business and the highest reaches of the American corporate economy.[17] One recent book concludes that 'The concentration of ownership and control in the communication industry raises serious questions about the quality and diversity of public discourse.'[18]

Technical innovation and diversity

Why has technical change and innovation not produced competition and diversity? The answer is that the theory which links them together is wrong, at least for the media industry.[19] The initial stages of technical innovation do tend to generate competition, it is true, for small and new firms are often able to exploit changes; but these often get overtaken by other small and new firms which pioneer the second generation changes, and so on. The biggest producers know this well enough, and avoid the new markets until they have stabilized, but then they enter and use their economies of scale and their financial resources to establish themselves as market leaders once again, leaving the small firms to find their own specialized niches. One example of this process is the typewriter/word processor revolution. Olivetti never made an electronic typewriter because the market was changing too rapidly for a large producer, so it waited and jumped to the word processor market when the time was right. IBM used the same strategy in the desktop computer market.

In Fleet Street the same pattern is repeated. Eddie Shah, a small, provincial independent newspaper publisher set out to use the very latest technology to break into the national market. Amid tremendous publicity which heralded him as exactly the type of giant-killing newcomer of classical market theory, Shah launched *Today*, the first new national daily for decades. Within weeks of the first issue he was in financial trouble, and within months he had sold out to Tiny Rowland's Lonrho group, one of the larger multi-media, multinational conglomerates. On the other hand, it is also true that the *Independent*, with only £18 million capital, has established itself among the quality papers, but even so, with a circulation of around a third of a million, it has about $2\frac{1}{2}$ per cent of national circulation, and it has scarcely disturbed the mass circulation oligopolies. It has added to diversity and variety, but only in a small way, and certainly not enough to undermine conclusions about growing concentration of ownership and control.[20]

The consolidation of the newspaper business, however, is only part of the story, the other part involving changes in the more volatile magazine market. Here there are three trends evident in Britain. First, sales of the leading magazines of opinion (except the *Economist*) have fallen substantially, mainly because the market has been transferred to the serious Sunday papers and their special sections. Second, as with the national papers, a few large companies have gained control of most of the mass circulation magazines, the largest being the International Publishing Corporation with 200 titles.[21] These two trends add up to a further concentration of the media business, but the third suggests fragmentation. The magazine business is notoriously changeable, and a rapid turnover of titles, new production technology, and new markets has produced a proliferation of small circulation magazines of opinion covering educational, political, literary, and minority group interests. There seems to be a polarization, therefore, between mass circulation publications, which are increasingly centralized in a few giant companies, and the fragmented, specialist market for journals and magazines, which is more diverse and competitive.

Regulating the media – the question of ownership and control

Liberal theory's fallback position, in the case of market failure, is to invoke state powers of anti-trust and anti-monopoly laws. This has not worked in Britain. Successive Royal Commissions on the Press (1949,

1962, 1977) have been anxious about monopolistic tendencies and eventually something was done in 1965, when large companies were required to obtain the assent of the Secretary of State before they could acquire further press holdings. Between 1965 and 1977, fifty companies applied and all were accepted either by the Secretary or by the Monopolies Commission.[22] When the machinery was put to a crucial and well-publicised test in 1981, Rupert Murdoch was allowed to buy *The Times* and *The Sunday Times*, giving him slightly less than a third of the national daily, and slightly more than a third of the Sunday, circulation.[23]

Similar recommendations of the Royal Commission on the Press to keep ownership of the press and broadcasting separate have also been ignored, with the result that publishing houses have gained significant holdings in Independent TV and commercial radio. However, there were a few victories such as the Independent Broadcasting Authority's ruling that Lord Thomson should reduce his holdings in Scottish TV, and the government's decision to prevent joint holdings of cable and local papers. This does not prevent either publishers of the national press or TV owners having cable interests. The prospect in Britain for the continued growth of multi-media giants looks favourable.

Although American legislation has not worked as it was supposed to, it has been far more effective than Britain's, at least until Reagan started his programme of deregulation. The Federal Communications Commission forced RCA to divest itself of one of its networks, although the outcome of this was the growth of the divested part, ABC, into a third network giant. More important, in 1953 it passed the 7–7–7 rule which limited a single company to seven AM radio stations, seven FM radio stations, and seven TV stations. In the mid-1970s it also prevented the acquisition of different media in the same location (though existing holdings were not affected), and barred network TV from cable TV. Consequently the networks have begun to face serious competition from cable, although this, in its turn, has started to develop the same old oligopolistic trends, led by Ted Turner's Cable News Network. By 1984 about a third of all TV owning households in the USA were hooked up to cable.[24]

However, in 1980 both ABC and CBS took advantage of a new ruling which allowed the networks into cable, and in 1984 Capital Cities used the change from the 7–7–7 to a new 12–12–12 rule to take over ABC, going close to the new limits and thus forming a larger multi-media company than ever before. Nonetheless, it is still fair to say that the

American system is more fragmented and diverse in terms of ownership and control than the British, and that this is, in part, due to anti-trust legislation. There is nothing in Britain to force Rupert Murdoch to sell one of his newspapers because he owned a TV station in the same city, as he has recently had to do in Boston.

Regulating the media – the question of content

The second fallback position provides for state regulation of the content of radio and television, on the grounds that since the airwaves are public property, they should be used in the public interest. In the USA this goal has been heavily qualified by the First Amendment guarantee of freedom of speech. In Britain, the state is not constrained by any such limits to its power, and has thus been able to impose quite clear and strict regulations on radio and TV reporting of news and current events.

In the USA the FCC has the power to rescind licenses, or to refuse renewal to any company which has failed to act in the public interest. To this end it required stations to devote a minimum percentage of their time to local affairs, news, and non-entertainment programmes (the 5–5–10 rule). But the FCC's authority is limited by the fact that it has no power over the networks whatsoever, and it has only ever refused a licence renewal to one station, a decision that provoked such strong reaction in the industry that the law was subsequently amended. In any case the 5–5–10 rule was effectively abandoned for radio in 1981, and for TV in 1984.

The FCC also has the duty to apply the Equal Time Provision which requires stations to sell time to all election candidates on the same basis. The loophole in the rule is that it excludes news programmes (which are held to include special news programmes and Presidential press conferences), leaving broadcasters to do pretty much what they want within news-time and, it is said, encouraging them to avoid controversial matters outside it.[25] To this extent, some argue, the effect has been the reverse of that intended.[26] In any case no station ever lost its licence for failing to observe the rule.

Another provision, the Fairness Rule, requires broadcasters to give 'reasonable time' to those who wish to reply to programmes, but since 'reasonable' was not defined – a thirty minute programme might be given two or three minutes rebuttal time – and since even this short period could be at the most unfavourable broadcasting hour, the doctrine has not been notably successful.[27] Moreover a series of court decisions left the broadcasters generally free to decide for themselves how best to comply with the Fairness Doctrine and Equal Time Provision,[28] and this, together with deregulation in the 1980s, has progressively whittled away such power as the FCC had in the first place.

Though never as effective as they were intended to be, it should not be assumed that the Equal Time Provision, the Fairness Rule, and the 5–5–10 rule were worthless. It has been claimed that their unintended effects included a tendency for broadcasters to play safe and avoid controversy outside the safety of news programmes, as well as a somewhat ritualistic compliance with the Fairness Rule, but one legal opinion questions these arguments on the grounds that they are largely speculative (they are inevitably based on counterfactual arguments) and lacking hard evidence.[29] Another work claims that the 5–5–10 rule 'has certainly encouraged stations to take their responsibility for airing public affairs programming more seriously'.[30] There are also examples of groups opposing nuclear power making effective use of the Fairness Doctrine to put their case.[31] In these instances, broadcasters did not avoid what were subsequently deemed to be controversial matters, in spite of their claim that the legislation encourages them to do so, and they were also forced to give time to views which they would not otherwise have represented.

In Britain the regulation of the broadcasting media in the interests of fairness and impartiality is both more complete and more successful. By law the BBC is subject to few legally binding conditions,[32] but in practice it subscribes to the long and elaborate code of conduct imposed upon Independent television by the Act of 1954, and updated in 1981. The same code applies to local radio. The code places a complete and effective ban on political advertising, and on editorializing, so that the broadcasting media are limited to news alone. Moreover, programmes have a duty to maintain 'proper balance ... accuracy and impartiality'. In the technical sense of the strict rationing of time to parties and candidates, TV and radio stations have faithfully followed these rules, as well as a further set of regulations requiring the neutral treatment of particular candidates. Lastly, party political programmes, made and financed by the parties themselves, are broadcast free with time allotted primarily according to voting strength and number of candidates.[33]

So far as anything is ever generally agreed to be fair in politics, British broadcasting seems to be so, certainly in the narrow, stop-watch sense, but also in a broader and more substantive sense. There is, of course a fierce debate about bias in television news,[34] but the point here is not whether television news is as neutral as it can be, but more practically, whether it is more neutral as a result of its regulation, than the unregulated, free-market media, most notably the newspapers – a point to be considered shortly.

Self regulation of the media

The third form of non-market control involves self regulation by the media itself, or, since radio and TV are publicly regulated, by the newspaper industry. However, because it is thought to interfere with the freedom of the press, self-denying ordinances by the press are almost wholly ineffectual, so far as they exist at all. Consequently, as many politicians have discovered, the press is pretty much free to say what it likes, with or without regard to neutrality or truth or any other standard, save only the observation of the libel laws which are concerned mainly with personal rather than political reputations. Formal rights of redress are available, but politicians are well advised to forget them; as the saying goes, a controversy with the press is the controversy of the fly with the spider.

The press's regulation of itself is unsatisfactory. The American Society of Newspaper Editors has a code of conduct – 'A Statement of Principle' – but it is entirely voluntary, and so vague as to be practically meaningless. Sanctions are seldom imposed, and yet anything more rigorous would probably fail the first court case. In Britain the Press Council has a very limited remit, is founded upon voluntary self-regulation, and is meagrely funded by the main press trade associations. Its procedures are slow, its code of conduct vague, and it is widely believed to be biased towards the interests of the press rather than the public.[35] The Council is often described as 'toothless' but actually it has neither bite nor bark.

Professional standards

The fifth source of neutrality in the media is said to be the professional standards of reporters and editors. It is clear, however, that they are not professionals in the sense that the term is applied to doctors, lawyers or teachers; they do not have the same sort of training or qualifications, nor do they have an equivalent professional ethic. Journalists are not responsible to the public or its good, but to the people who employ them, and most newspaper proprietors from James Gordon Bennett Snr to

Murdoch have made the responsibilities of their employees absolutely plain. Faced with a choice between the standards of good, neutral reporting and their job, most reporters will naturally choose the latter.

Some research has suggested that in order to evade blame, and to cope with the intense pressures of deadlines, news reporters often adopt a set of rituals which allow them to claim accuracy and objectivity.[36] This is not to say that journalists are without standards, for this is clearly not true, but it does suggests that, in the last analysis, little reliance should be placed on professional standards as a guarantor of neutrality in political reporting.

The implications for media neutrality

It is clear from the preceding account that the unregulated media market does not operate as liberal, free-market theory says it should. But it does not follow from this that the media will inevitably fail the test of political neutrality. A last and crucial step is necessary to the argument – to show that the unregulated media are systematically biased in their coverage of political news, and that the regulated media are more satisfactory in this respect.

This is not difficult to do. Many observers have commented on the decreasing diversity of news and opinion covered by the press in Britain and the USA. The national press in Britain has increasingly taken on a uniform political complexion. In 1945 Conservative national dailies took 52 per cent of the market, and Labour ones 17 per cent; in 1983 Conservative papers took 74 per cent, and Labour ones 22 per cent.[37] The Liberal/SDP Alliance had no newspaper of its own to express its point of view. Four of the five mass circulation tabloids (excluding the newcomer *Today*) are strongly Conservative, and three of them, far from providing diversity and variety, are virtual clones of one another.[38]

This has become a cause of concern, not to say alarm, among many writers. According to Hugo Young: 'Taken as a whole the press is massively biased in one direction. In the last three years it has become distinctly more so. Not only has detachment been devalued and politic-isation increased, but the process is all one way .... At the very time when politics is becoming more open, fissiparous and diverse, the press becomes more narrow, monolithic and doctrinaire .... It fails to reflect and assist in the debate about the future of the British left – that is anything to the left of Mrs Thatcher. It is generally so preoccupied with reinforcing anything that the government it trying to do that all activity is assessed by its helpfulness to that enterprise. Most press criticism of Mrs Thatcher, indeed, comes from the right not the left of her.'[39]

Another distinguished Fleet Street journalist puts it this way: 'I have been sceptical of the constitutional claims made for Britain's fourth estate. Far from acting as the watchdog of the body politic, Fleet Street has so often served as its lapdog. However proprietorially independent, it has integrated itself into the political establishment rather than stood over against it.'[40] A third writer, Neal Ascherson, claims that 'Press bullying today arises from the dogmas of "consensus" ... Scargill, Benn, Ken Livingstone, even the pathetic Peter Tatchell, are harassed and hounded with a venom and persistence which have no justification and no precedent.'[41] A recent book provides over 250 pages of detailed evidence for this charge.[42]

As in Britain, most American papers lean towards conservative political positions, although it must immediately be said that they are not so clearly partisan. Perhaps as predominantly local papers they have to appeal to a wide spectrum of local readers, and therefore have to take a more moderate political line. However, one survey of 450 daily papers in the USA found that 86 per cent supported Reagan in the 1984 Presidential campaign.[43] Another review of eighty-four separate studies of political bias in American papers in the 1960s found 'a very high correlation between editorial policy and news bias. Of the 84 studies of bias, 74 found pro-Republican bias in the news in papers with pro-Republican editorial policies ... so where political bias in the news is found, it is overwhelmingly pro-Republican and pro-conservative ... the real question is how liberal electoral politics survives at all with the overwhelming opposition of the conservative press.'[44]

Doubts about the neutrality and trustworthiness of the unregulated media are reinforced by surveys of consumer opinion. Views vary between different sub-groups who use the different media for their own purposes, and they also vary over time, but in the United States, television news has been judged consistently and appreciably more believable than newspapers. Throughout the 1960s and 1970s, about 20 per cent of Americans believed a newspaper rather than a television report if the two conflicted or differed, whereas somewhere between 40 per cent and 50 per cent trusted the television.[45] While reporters and journalists in general are deemed more honest and ethical than lawyers, stockbrokers, politicians, or businessmen, TV reporters had a rather higher rating than newspaper reporters (36 per cent compared with 30 per cent).[46]

Social surveys also show that television is believed to be more trustworthy and impartial than newspapers as a source of political information in Britain.[47] In the 1979 general election campaign, 70 per cent and 71 per cent thought the BBC and ITV were unbiased, compared with 35 per cent who took the same view of the papers. On the other side of the same coin, over a third thought the newspapers showed a Conservative or Labour bias, compared with 13 per cent and 8 per cent who made the same judgement of the BBC and ITV.[48] Three-quarters of those asked said that television was a useful way of following the election campaign, compared with 53 per cent who found the papers useful.[49] In 1983, fewer than one in ten thought press coverage of the election campaign was the most complete, compared with a figure of 60 per cent for television.[50]

Conclusions

This chapter has argued that there are serious flaws in the unregulated liberal-market model of media neutrality. On purely theoretical grounds, there is no reason to believe that free-market competition will necessarily result in a full and fair coverage of the news, or in a diverse range of opinion about it. Free-market theory argues only that consumers will get what they want and are prepared to pay for, but it is silent about what they will or should want – fairness, balance, honesty, or neutrality, or anything else. There is no free-market guarantee that the truth will be printed or broadcast, and if it is, there is no guarantee that it will win the day amid the welter of truth, half-truth, untruth, and irrelevance.

The theory also assumes what it wants to demonstrate: that the general public will be informed and educated enough to want a mass media which informs and educates. The way around this circular argument is to go beyond market theory and call upon non-market forces, particularly free and compulsory education, and hence in this respect the market cannot sustain itself. In any case, the market for news and commentary is not like the market for goods, because they are neither amenable to objective and comparative tests – such as testing engines to destruction – and nor are they purely a matter of subjective taste, like chocolate ice cream. More generally, there is no such thing as a market for ideas, and economic theories which work with this assumption are bound to fail.

There are practical and empirical problems as well. The theory specifies a high degree of market competition to sustain the necessary variety and diversity of sources of news and opinion. These conditions may have held for the newspaper industry in Victorian times, but the modern mass media market shows strong oligopolistic features in both Britain and the United States. Far from promoting competition and diversity, technical innovation has encouraged the concentration of ownership and control of the mass media. Self-regulation of the industry has proved largely ineffectual on both sides of the Atlantic.

For these theoretical and empirical reasons it seems that the unregulated media market it bound to fail to produce a diverse and varied range of sources for news and commentary, certainly so far as the mass media are concerned, and this is all that matters for the great majority of the population. But how does the regulated media market – radio and television – measure up to the requirements of balance and fairness? The answer is much better, though in rather different ways in the two countries. Market regulation in the USA has been more effective than in the UK in restraining oligopolistic tendencies, and Britain has a lot to learn from the United States, although in neither place has the state actively promoted a competitive market, as it has done with the help of public funds in Scandinavia.

So far as content regulation is concerned, the British record is more satisfactory than the American, where the power and effectiveness of the FCC has been limited by a tendency to confuse the property rights of media owners with the right of freedom of speech, and by a narrow conception of the First Amendment (the Supreme Court's *Red Lion* decision notwithstanding), which has been applied more rigorously for media owners than for the general public. This reinforces the view that liberal-market theory is rather too much concerned with the producers of the media, and rather too little concerned with consumers. It may also be the product of a political system which places supreme importance on property rights, and then confuses property rights with rights to freedom of speech.

Although regulation of the media has not been entirely effective, and has not always had the intended results, there is reason to believe that the electronic media in both countries are less systematically biased than most (but not all) newspapers, and have a better record for balance, fairness, and neutrality. The general public in both countries is of this opinion.

If this analysis is on the right tracks, the prognosis for the immediate and mid-term future must be rather gloomy. In both Britain and the United States a policy of deregulation and privatization is being pursued, and although it may not be developed in the USA after Reagan, it seems unlikely that even the rather mild controls of the mid-1970s will be restored. In both countries, therefore, we are likely to see a greater concentration of ownership and control, and also a greater degree of systematic bias in the mass media. Ironically, these reforms are being undertaken, in the name of market competition and freedom.

Indeed, it is increasingly asserted in some circles in the US that it is paradoxical to leave a local monopoly newspaper unregulated, while the increasingly competitive electronic media continue to be regulated.[51] However, if the various arguments of the present paper are accepted then the paradox dissolves, and it becomes difficult to avoid the conclusion that the regulated model has served the public interest for a neutral and balanced mass media system of news coverage better than the unregulated model in both Britain and the USA. The market model has failed in both countries, as it is bound to do for both theoretical and practical reasons, and a degree of both market and content regulation is justified not only because the free-market model is inappropriate for news and commentary, but also because the regulated model more adequately meets the public interest requirement for a neutral and balanced coverage of current affairs. Besides, the special features of the modern mass media require a degree of public regulation in order to ensure that they provide a balanced news diet for the great majority of the population who are almost wholly dependent upon them for political news and opinion, and irrespective of whether the minority media are marked by a high degree of competitive and pluralist diversity. What matters most is not the overall character of the total system of mass and minority media, although this is certainly highly important, but the ethos of balance and neutrality which should pervade the mass media, but which betrays a marked tendency towards oligopoly and systematic bias if it is not regulated.

Notes

I am most grateful to Bob Goodin whose prompt, detailed, and copious notes on earlier drafts of this chapter have improved it enormously.

1   Simon Jenkins argues that Fleet Street proprietors may be more interested in politics than profits – Simon Jenkins, *The Market for Glory*, London: Faber, 1986. See also Peiers Brenden, *The Life and Death of the Press Barons*, New York: Atheneum, 1982.

2 Judith Lichtenberg, 'Foundations and Limits of Freedom of the Press', *Philosophy and Public Affairs*, 16 (4), p. 348.
3 See Asa Briggs, *The Birth of Broadcasting*, vol. 1 *The History of Broadcasting in the United Kingdom*, London: Oxford University Press, 1961, pp. 360–72; W. A. Robson, 'The BBC as an institution', *The Political Quarterly*, 6 (1935), p. 470.
4 Krishan Kumar, 'Holding the middle ground: the BBC, the public and the professional broadcaster', in James Curran *et al.* (eds), *Mass Communication and Society*, London: Arnold in Association with the Open University Press, 1977, pp. 231–48.
5 Jean Seaton and Ben Pimlott, 'The struggle for "balance"', in Jean Seaton and Ben Pimlott (eds), *The Media in British Politics*, Aldershot: Avebury, 1987, pp. 133–53.
6 Erwin G. Krasnow and Lawrence D. Longley, *The Politics of Broadcast Regulation*, 2nd edn, New York: St Martin's Press, 1978, pp. 8–13.
7 See, for example, *Report of the Committee on Financing the BBC* (Peacock Committee), Cmnd 9824, London: HMSO, 1986, p. 124.
8 R. H. Coase, 'The market for goods and the market for ideas', *American Economic Review*, 64 (1974), pp. 384–91, at p. 385.
9 Quoted in Kenneth S. Devol, *The Mass Media and the Supreme Court*, New York: Hastings House, 1976, p. 327.
10 James Curran and Jean Seaton, *Power Without Responsibility*, 2nd edn, London: Methuen, 1985, p. 288.
11 Nicholas Hartley *et al.*, *Concentration of Ownership in the Provincial Press*, Royal Commission on the Press, 1974–7, Research Series 5, London: HMSO, 1977.
12 Curran and Seaton, *Power Without Responsibility*, pp. 92–3.
13 Curran and Seaton, *Power Without Responsibility*, p. 101.
14 Benjamin M. Compaine, 'Newspaper', in Benjamin M. Compaine (ed.), *Who Owns the Media?*, New York: Harmony Books, 1979, p. 18.
15 See Thomas R. Dye and Harmon Zeigler, *American Politics in the Media Age*, 2nd edn, Monterey, Calif: Brooks/Cole, 1986, pp. 97–102.
16 Michael Parenti, *Inventing Reality*, New York: St Martin's Press, 1986, p. 27.
17 Peter Dreier, 'The position of the press in the US power structure', *Social Research*, 29 (3), p. 302.
18 Ronald Berkman and Laura W. Kitch, *Politics in the Media Age*, New York: McGraw-Hill, 1986, p. 45.
19 See the essay by Hugh Ward in this volume.
20 See Linda Melvern, *The End of the Street*, London: Methuen, 1986.
21 Jeremy Tunstall, *The Media in Britain*, London: Constable, 1983, pp. 90–1.
22 Curran and Seaton, *Power Without Responsibility*, p. 293.
23 For an account of these events see Harold Evans, *Goods Times, Bad Times*, London: Weidenfeld & Nicolson, 1983.
24 Dye and Zeigler, *American Politics in the Media Age*, p. 101.

25 The argument is presented in Doris Graber, *Mass Media and American Politics*, Washington: Congressional Quarterly Press, 1980, p. 95.
26 See Thomas Emerson, *The System of Free Expression*, New York: Vintage Books, 1970, pp. 660–1.
27 See Devol, *The Mass Media and the Supreme Court*, p. 332.
28 Berkman and Kitch, *Politics in the Media Age*, p. 57.
29 The view is Justice White's and is quoted in Emerson, *The System of Free Expression*, p. 660.
30 Berkman and Kitch, *Politics in the Media Age*, p. 52.
31 See Randy M. Mastro, *et al.*, *Taking the Initiative*, Washington, DC: Media Access Project, 1980, pp. 14–22.
32 Representation of the People Act, 1983.
33 For a general account of the legal constraints see Colin Munro, 'Legal controls on election broadcasting', in Ivor Crewe and Martin Harrop, (eds), *Political Communications: The General Election Campaign of 1983*, Cambridge: Cambridge University Press, 1986, pp. 294–305.
34 See, for example, the controversy surrounding the publications of the Glasgow Media Group, *Bad News* (1976), *More Bad News* (1980), *Really Bad News* (1981) and *War and Peace News* (1985) and the criticisms of these works by Martin Harrison, *TV News: Whose Bias?*, Hermitage, Berks: Policy Journals, 1985 and Alastair Hetherington, *News, Newspapers and Television*, London: Macmillan, 1985.
35 Geoffrey Robertson, *People Against the Press*, London: Quartet Books, 1983.
36 Gaye Tuchman, 'Objectivity as a strategic ritual: an examination of newsmens' notions of objectivity', *American Journal of Sociology*, 77 (4), pp. 660–79.
37 Tunstall, *The Media in Britain*, p. 12.
38 Jenkins, *The Market for Glory*, p. 223.
39 *Sunday Times*, 18 March 1984.
40 Jenkins, *The Market for Glory*, p. 223.
41 *London Review of Books*, 21 February 1985.
42 Mark Hollingsworth, *The Press and Political Dissent*, London: Pluto Press, 1986.
43 Parenti, *Inventing Reality*, p. 13.
44 Ben Bagdikian, *The Effete Conspiracy*, New York: Harper & Row, 1974, pp. 146, 148.
45 Dye and Zeigler, *American Politics in the Media Age*.
46 Gallup Opinion Index, September, 1981.
47 Barrie Gunter, *et al.*, *Television Coverage of the 1983 General Election*, Aldershot, Hants: Gower, 1986, p. 77.
48 Peter Kellner and Robert M. Worcester, 'Electoral perceptions of media stance', in Robert M. Worcester and Martin Harrop (eds), *Political Communications: The General Election Campaign of 1979*, London: Allen & Unwin, 1982.
49 Kellner and Worcester, 'Electoral perceptions', p. 63.
50 Martin Harrop, 'The press and post-war elections', in Crewe and Harrop (eds), *Political Communications*, p. 144.

51 See, for example, William F. Baxter, 'Regulation and diversity in communications media', *American Economic Review*, 64 (1974), pp. 392–402.

8

The neutrality of science and technology

Hugh Ward

Introduction

During the 1950s and 1960s a critical movement began to develop among scientists and technologists. This can be linked to the growing connections between science and the military as exemplified by the Manhattan Project, individual pressures on scientists working in large, bureaucratic research organizations, and growing awareness of the links between recently introduced products of science and environmental degradation. Besides becoming active in nuclear disarmament and the nascent environmental movement, some scientists began to examine the established dogma about the social implications of science.[1]

The dominant view sees science and technology as being inherently benign and progressive. Although there may be problems arising from science and technology, these are the result of the way in which knowledge is applied. Science and technology are *neutral tools open to use or abuse*. Science and technology are also self-healing; where a problem arises a technical fix may often be found to overcome it.[2]

There are two important variants of this underlying position. The first is most closely associated with the work of liberal industrial and post-industrial society theorists.[3] Within this perspective the direction taken by scientific research is governed by the internal culture of the scientific profession even though more applied research and technology may be partially conditioned by other social forces. It is this relatively autonomous development of fundamental science together with growing preference for services which will propel society into a post-industrial phase characterized by the decline of old class-based antagonisms, the dominance of the service sector, and the crucial importance of theoretical knowledge as a power resource. There may be social, environmental or political problems associated with technology and science. 'Yet none of this has to be. The mechanisms of control are available .... Technology assessment is feasible. What is required is a political mechanism that will allow such studies to be made and set up criteria for the regulation of new technologies.'[4]

A different variant of the neutrality thesis has also been held by many orthodox Marxists, particularly among the Moscow-orientated European communist parties and in the Soviet Bloc.[5] Marx separated the consequences which flow from the forces of production themselves from those which stem of capitalist relations of production:

> The life long speciality of handling one and the same tool, now becomes [with the introduction of machinery] the life long speciality of serving one and the same machine. *Machinery is put to the wrong use*, with the object of transforming the workman, from his very childhood, into part of a detail-machine .... *Here as everywhere else, we must distinguish between the increased productiveness due to the development of the social process of production and that due to capitalist exploitation of that process.* (my emphasis)[6]

Under socialism, and eventually communism, the full emancipatory potential of capitalist science and technology will be unfettered: the historical role of capitalism being to develop those forces. Although Marx believed that economic interests might condition the rate and the direction of scientific research, the content of scientific knowledge was seen as set by the constitution of the natural world itself.[7]

Many authors have questioned the idea of progress which underlies the liberal industrial society and orthodox Marxist positions. What was new to the neutrality debate was the idea that scientific and technical change might *necessarily favour some groups and harm others* – that it might be biased.

In Britain at least, the problem of neutrality was first raised to prominence within the British Society for Social Responsibility in Science, and particularly in the written work of Hilary and Stephen Rose.[8] Their central claim is that in capitalist and state socialist societies science no longer develops autonomously. Drawing heavily on the work of the critical theorists of the Frankfurt School, they argue that science is controlled by existing economic and political elites who are able to build their values and interests into its very constitution, so that capitalist science may be distorted and ideological. The radical science movement argues that in capitalist and state socialist societies science and technology function to meet the most important needs of elites, furthering the process of accumulation and ensuring legitimacy and social control, and in so doing harming the interests of the working class. (Any particular technologies or scientific paradigm may of course have contradictory or dysfunctional effects.) Capitalist science would need to be replaced by socialist science, and capitalist technology by some socialist alternative technology to achieve emancipation. As one recent statement of the radical position puts it:

> The myth of a neutral science and technology carried out in pristine social settings by morally neutral, objective scientists is one of the last sacred cows of capitalist society. Art, music, schooling, health care, have all been criticised for their domination by powerful monetary interests, and for being laced with class, racial and sexual biases. As we have tried to show, the same is true of science and technology.[9]

This paper will criticize both the liberal and the Marxist versions of the use–abuse argument, but at the same time, it will reject the radical science movement's claim that the most important forms of capitalist technics are not neutral. Clearly there are many technologies which are not distributionally neutral and cannot be made to be so by any form of social planning: even if fossil fuels are not finite in any economic sense, existing methods of extracting and burning them make access to these resources less easy for future generations. Besides distributing well-being in favour of certain classes, technics may favour a certain sex, certain generations, nations, or groups. However, the distributional implications of technics need not be determinate.

The first four parts of this chapter examine four types of abstract, high level argument about the neutrality question:

(a) That all technics are either neutral or can be made so through technical fixes or planning;
(b) That science itself must be neutral because facts about how the world works cannot alone imply anything about what ought to be done.
(c) That technics are not neutral because they are forged within the context of class based society – they are 'socially constructed'.
(d) That technics are not neutral because, even if in principle they have some degree of flexibility, in practice they will be deployed in ways that favour existing elites.

I will argue that none of these positions for or against the neutrality of technics is adequate. We will be forced back upon a case-by-case analysis of *particular* technics.

The planning and fixing of technics

The non-Marxian variant of the use–abuse argument has been summarized very well by Lipscombe and Williams:

> Any beneficial or harmful effects arise out of the motives of the people applying a particular piece of technology and the end to which it is used. Where a particular application, chosen for its beneficial results, produces harmful side effects these are blamed either on inadequate social policies or on lack of sophistication in the control of the effects of the technology. Whichever is the whipping boy, the technology itself remains 'neutral' (or blameless) .... The progress of technical innovation is seen as inevitable and unrelated to any consideration outside the state of scientific and technical knowledge.[10]

There are a number of problems with this approach. Firstly, it is largely blind to the ways in which science and technology distribute values between social classes, sexes, generations, and nations. By concentrating on the way in which technology and scientific knowledge are *used*, the conventional approach ignores many of the distributional effects of the way in which science and technology are produced in the first place. For example, there is a good case for believing that the micro-processor itself is a neutral tool open to an enormous range of applications, not all of which favour existing elites.[11] Be that as it may, some would argue that the production of micro-processors has inevitably biased distributional effects. It is technically possible to remedy some of the present abuses: chip packaging processes carried out in South Asia could probably be organized so as not to damage the health and eyesight of the women who work in the industry.[12] But more generally the international division of labour ties less-developed nations into the world economic system in exploitative ways which perpetuate their relative underdevelopment. This might be seen as merely an abuse of a monopoly of a certain kind of knowledge, not inherent in the technology itself and destined to disappear as access to the relevant information becomes easier to achieve.[13] Although this might be true in some areas, chip manufacture is, and is certain to remain, a highly capital intensive process requiring esoteric knowledge easily monopolized by and within a particular nation or small group of nations. Chip production is also open to the sort of radical monopoly discussed by Ivan Illich in which a tool upon which we have come to depend is controlled by an elite. This possibility would exist in a socialist as well as a capitalist society because of the ease with which technicians or professionals can control knowledge.[14]

This argument would be undercut if we are moving towards a post-industrial future of the sort Bell and others envisage. There we can plan technical change, choose research programmes, and divest ourselves of older technologies, so as to ensure that all social groups are better off. However, there are obvious problems with this argument.[15] Since Bell wrote, methodologies like technology assessment and environmental impact analysis have proven extremely problematic.[16] They suffer from the usual defect of applied cost-benefit analysis; placing a value on incommensurable items, many of which are not traded in the market. There is enormous controversy about which values to consider and the relative weight to give each of them, and as Bell realizes, such conflicts will continue even in a post-industrial world. Finally it is extraordinarily difficult to foresee future impacts, even though, as my argument here implies, non-deterministic forecasts of impacts can sometimes be constructed.

Even if it was possible to plan technical change and scientific research, there must be a question about whether we can use such techniques to make choices about which forms of technics to put back in Pandora's Box. As Collingridge has argued, technologies become entrenched within societies; vested interests build up around them, the social costs of the transition to some alternative increase as the technology is more and more widely used, and alternative lines of research are snuffed out the more any possibility succeeds. The dilemma of control is that we may not know what the distributional effects of a technology are until it is too late to act.[17]

There remains to be considered the argument that some technical fixes can be found. These would have to correct the adverse effects of technics we cannot choose to do away with, those fixes leaving our habits and social and institutional forms intact. The radical science movement shows how particular technologies and scientific methodologies have definite distributional implications which are not amenable to fixes. Some methodologies for IQ research led to results which were inevitably biased against blacks and other minorities.[18]

Given the social inequalities characterizing most Third World countries, it was inevitable that the Green Revolution should harm poorer farmers.[19] Such examples can be multiplied at will. Often technical fixes themselves fail because of unanticipated second-order effects.[20]

Can 'is' imply 'ought'? The value-neutrality of natural science

Although it is easy to reject the claim that science and technology never have in-built distributional effects, there are authors who would claim that science at least is blameless. The argument, which goes back at least as far as Hume, is that factual statements cannot logically yield value statements. There is a radical disjunction between facts and values: as it is often put, 'is' cannot imply 'ought'. Thus, science is value-neutral and any distributional effects result from an injection of values from elsewhere, or from the way in which the natural world itself is constituted which makes certain biases physically unavoidable. I will briefly review two ways in which this argument has commonly been criticized and then discuss another argument which is less commonly heard in relation to the neutrality of natural science (although it has been used in relation to political science by Charles Taylor).[21]

Scientific research obviously concentrates on some areas at the expense of others. The distribution of research may have implications for the distribution of values even if the facts do not speak directly about what should be done. Although many scientists and social scientists would resist the argument that their values or political and economic pressures influence the *content* of their work, they will often admit that such values influence the choice of research area. This means that science as a social institution has some responsibility for the distributional implications of what is known and is not known. For example, it has been argued that the relative concentration on surgical intervention and chemotherapy in cancer research is partially the result of the higher professional prestige of these areas of work compared with work in environmental medicine.[22] I will argue below that the fact that the values of some groups affect their research does not *always* imply that distributional bias will result. Nevertheless, scientists sometimes have responsibility for what is and is not researched and its distributional effects.

Hard-core positivists might construe this argument as relating to the neutrality of what scientists do, not to the neutrality of scientific statements. A more radical approach would be to deny the validity of the fact-value distinction which is one of the central tenets of positivism. There has been considerable debate in philosophy over the question of whether is can imply ought. Ethical naturalism argues that there are objective moral facts which, either alone or in combination with facts about how the natural world works, can lead to valid logical inferences about what ought to be the case. Also some concepts in common use within science (such as pathology, high yield reaction, or equilibrium) secrete a notion of what is good and bad into the conceptual framework of science.[23] To say something is 'pathological' is to say that *ceteris paribus* it should be cured. These sorts of arguments have been related to the neutrality debate by Black to show that,[24] very often, scientific research has obvious implications for what ought to be done.

While I accept this point, it carries us only a short way in relation to science because value conflict rather than value consensus underlies most major social problems of science. There are often no obvious, strong moral facts to appeal to. Nevertheless there is a weak version of ethical naturalism that has critical bite in some contexts.

Let us accept for the moment the common view of what science is – a body of as yet unrefuted laws about the natural world rather than a social institution. If this is so, science must contain statements about what is, and is not, physically feasible. Although science thus defined might have no implications for which of a feasible set of options should be chosen by society, it will also have implications for what is feasible and what is not. A very weak universal value premise is that society should not pursue the impossible.

There would be nothing disturbing about this if science were always right; it would just be the way of the world. But philosophers of science now accept the eternal openness of scientific hypotheses to falsification and the provisional nature of knowledge. Thus, with the addition of only a very weak value premise, what are currently held to be facts about how the world works may result in distributional effects which are not, in fact, built into the constitution of the physical world.

While some of the arguments of the radical science movement about the non-neutrality of technics have great force, I am far less happy with their claims that science and technology *as a whole* are not neutral. Obviously there is a degree of rhetorical exaggeration in such statements. (The radical science movement does not wish to condemn modern science and technology and all its works, although it has often enough been accused of being anti-scientific and Luddite.) Nevertheless, if the general arguments of the radical science movement have any force they ought to apply to such important developments as, for example, information technology. But I hope to establish that it is not obviously the case that information technology is biased.

My argument here falls into several parts. Firstly, I will argue that between the intentions of elites and distributional outcomes as mediated by technics many other variables intervene, so that it is by no means clear that intentions will be fulfilled. Secondly, it is difficult to see how some invisible hand will inevitably lead technical change to benefit elites. Thirdly even if science and technology are part of a superstructure resting upon a base of economic and class relations, this does not necessarily imply they are non-neutral.

Elite intentions and the form of technics

The radical science movement often makes use of the argument that technics cannot be neutral because elites design them to further their interests. Thus Hilary and Stephen Rose, writing about the development of CS riot-control gas, said that the work was done for a specific objective, it was not value-free; by definition not neutral.[25] But, although we might accept that CS gas is a biased technology, the objectives of researchers or designers provide no definitional guarantees about *distributional* non-neutrality i.e. who uses it against whom.

Consider the design of machine tools. A standard argument in the Marxian literature on the labour process in the wake of Braverman's seminal work, is that while Taylorism and Fordism may have been intended to control the workforce, class struggle in the workplace intervenes between intention and outcome.[26] For example, earlier generations of numerically controlled machine tools were intended by their designers to reduce the power of highly skilled workers by replacing them with a combination of less skilled operatives on the shop floor and relatively malleable, white collar programmers in the office. However, the technology never operated as anticipated. Relatively skilled labour was needed to use such machinery at all efficiently.[27] Similarly, workers on modern computerized numerically controlled machine tools have been able to protect their skills and autonomy by learning how to programme the machines themselves (even though this is difficult given that it necessitates the awkward use of editing facilities on the machine).[28] It is questionable whether the sort of monitoring devices which can now be built into micro-electronically controlled machines will eliminate worker autonomy.

The radical science movement argues, further, that elite intentions translate directly into desirable research in the natural sciences through funding policies. For example, Rose and Rose write,

One way of illustrating the non-neutral nature of science is to examine the constraints which operate on science within the present system. Thus, if we recognise that *big science is state financed*, and that there is always more possible science than actual science, more ideas about what to do than men or money to do them, the debate is, in a sense, shortcircuited .... Whoever makes these choices about what to finance, by definition, they cannot be ideology or value free.[29] (my emphasis)

Does elite control of research funds always select out the best ideas for further development? Besides understating the autonomy of big science to put money into projects of interest largely to the scientific profession concerned, this argument ignores evidence that outcomes do not always conform to funders' intentions. For example, it is often claimed that the enormous funding of particle physics relative to other lines of research was based on the anticipation of military spinoffs, but that such beliefs were mistaken and particle physics (of the last twenty years, at least) is unlikely to have such spinoffs. Science policy has notably failed to make research more closely match (immediate) industrial and state needs.[30]

There is a more important theoretical point here. As the quotations above show, the Roses along with many other members of the radical science movement operate with an extremely crude reductionist theory of the state. If the idea of the autonomy of the state is taken seriously, which it is not in most Marxian writing, the possibility is opened that political elites will act in ways having little connection *if any* with the interest of capital. Science funding reflecting the bureaucratic, electoral, and above all military interests of state managers might result, and sometimes wider social interests may be promoted.[31]

The most important scientific and technical developments are usually emergent, unanticipated consequences of individual decisions made by large numbers of decision makers. In the next two sections I turn from the micro to the macro level to examine such emergent consequences and structural effects.

Market selection and the functions of technics – the workings of the invisible hand

It has been argued that, without any design or elite conspiracy, a judicious mixture of technics adapted to further the accumulation process and to ensure legitimacy will be selected by the market mechanism.[32] The argument, which strongly echoes the work of Sidney Winter and his co-workers on the evolutionary theory of the firm, is that the market mechanism will select out the efficient technical innovations.[33] Different firms try different innovations; the most successful will make higher profits, grow faster, and be more likely to survive the rigours of competition. Gradually firms using less efficient practices will be eliminated, and the more successful methods will also spread through the population by emulation. Without any firm having the information needed (or, in the first instance at least, the intention) to seek the best methods, the invisible hand of the market will select them out. In this way, functional technics arise without design.

This extremely interesting argument suffers from a number of problems. First, as Elster has shown, local rather than global optima are all that can be attained by such mechanisms.[34] Second, it is doubtful whether competitive pressures in the crucial monopoly sector of business are always so tight that the adoption of the best technical practices are a necessary condition for short run survival though they may be in the competitive sector. In any case motivational questions are crucial to short run productivity.[35]

Finally, and most importantly, it is far from clear that market pressures will ensure the selection of technics functional for capital as a whole.[36] I shall use the debate on the employment implications of information technology to illustrate this point, and will pursue the issue further at the end of this essay.

Many authors on the left see information technology as a functional response to the low rates of profit which they argue underlie the present world economic crisis.[37] The new technology cheapens capital, increases productivity, and increases the reserve army of labour. Each of these should increase the rate of profit *in the short run*, other things being equal. Although it may be individually rational for each capitalist to introduce the new technology no matter how many others have already done so, the long term emergent consequence may be that the rate of profit is further depressed.[38] It may be extremely difficult to realize profits with the sustained levels of technological unemployment which many authors see arising. Along with the problem of chronic underconsumption might go the problems of legitimizing an economic system in which the time freed by the new technology is being squandered by massive unemployment.[39] Finally, in the long run, increases in productivity may be stifled if workers are intensively supervised, threatened by redundancy or deskilled: their consent, and hence their creativity, may be lost.

There has been much detailed empirical work done on the first-order effects on employment in particular industries of introducing the new technologies. Both the manufacturing sector and the service have been covered, and white-collar work in the manufacturing sector has been analysed.[40] The key issues in this debate seem to me to be:

(a) how fast will the new technologies be introduced?
(b) are there compensating increases in demand which might result when the price of existing products and services are reduced as productivity increases?
(c) is the new technology being introduced as a defensive strategy to cut costs and service competition, or with a view to expanding production and a bigger national or international market share?
(d) are there new products or new services which will create new markets rather than substituting for an existing product using new, more productive, techniques?

The answers to questions (a), (c) and (d), at least, must depend upon political developments. Whether investment is defensive or offensive and how fast it proceeds surely depends upon the broader macro-economic climate, which can presumably be influenced by the state. It is unlikely that either micro-electronic consumer products or capital investment in new production techniques for existing markets are capable of generating a long term upswing in growth in the world economy. Only if there is strong growth in markets catering for 'post-material' needs like education, health, leisure, and security will the unemployment ensuing from the new technologies be absorbed.[41] Despite some room for private provision in these markets, many would argue that increased state involvement would be necessary.

Some neo-classical economists argue that if the wage rates fall enough any technological unemployment will be mopped up. 'Low tech or no tech' jobs in the direct service sector are often seen as substituting for manufacturing losses if wages fall.[42] Nevertheless, the neo-classical model still advocates government intervention to reduce frictional unemployment: retraining, youth training schemes, help with relocation, and so on.

A third argument emphasizes export-led growth as a compensating mechanism. Through the ruthless expansion of the use of information technology nationally costs may be cut and, although employment in the export-orientated sector of the economy would be reduced, such an economic expansion would be generated nationally that compensatory growth in employment in the labour intensive state sector would be possible.[43] This is a pious hope, for as long as one country (such as Japan) does not expand its state sector and welfare payments and is able to undercut its international competitors, there will be no room for such an expansion elsewhere. The logic of the situation forces states to pursue strategies which lead to sub-optimal results: clearly not every nation can succeed in gaining the technological lead, and countries like Britain are poorly placed relative to the USA and Japan. As Mandel has argued, only a co-ordinated expansion of the economies of the North contingent upon reform of the world monetary system, reduction of barriers to trade, an expansion of demand in the communist world, and real growth in the less developed countries, could lead to successful export-led growth through the North.[44] Also, in order to create new markets for technically sophisticated products produced in the North full rein would need to be given to the 'new international economic order'. Rather than protecting their basic industries, countries in the North would import standardized mass produced products from the newly industrialized countries.

The implications of this for the market selection argument are clear. Without political intervention, both nationally and internationally, the long-term consequences for unemployment of information technology may be adverse; and there may be resulting accumulation and legitimacy crises. While that might most naturally lead toward authoritarian state forms, it may be possible to envisage a more corporatist, interventionist strategy in some states. This may enable capitalism to avoid these problems. But given the real autonomy of the state, there can be no guarantee that the implications of such a settlement would favour capital.

Science as superstructure

In a reversal of the basic tenets of historical materialism, some members of the radical science movement now claim that technics are part of the superstructure rather than the base of society, part of a system of overall structural determination powered by conflict between classes. In the first part of this section I will draw together some underlying themes from this literature at the risk of overstressing its unity.[45]

The key to the superstructural nature of science is the idea that science is a social product, not merely a reflection of the natural world. Science is produced in the laboratories of big business and the state in a manner analogous to the production of commodities. However it is also a social construct in a wider sense. Rather than being inductively derived from sense data, scientific laws are worked up by scientists from existing conceptual, methodological, and theoretical resources to produce new knowledge. Besides this, the process whereby knowledge is legitimized is also social and cannot rely on observations in some theory-neutral observation language to mediate conflicts.

For Marxists a commodity is not a thing – it is a crystal of dead human labour, the condensation of the social relations of dominance and exploitation which have gone into its production. To perceive a commodity as natural object is to reify it. There is a similar reification in seeing a scientific law as merely a naturally given fact. Scientific laws are a reflection of the base of society: they are imbued through-and-through with class interests and provide a distorted, ideological, view of the natural world.[46] As Young puts it, 'science is social relations'.[47]

Science is also ideological because the ideas of the ruling class are the ruling ideas of society. In contrast to those philosophers and historians who have seen internal influences within science itself as being crucial to paradigm formation, it is argued that science often uses resources drawn from elite ideology. For example, Sahlins has argued that sociobiology has come to rely on ideas drawn directly from micro-economics.[48] In the same way that micro-economics puts up a particular ahistorical model of economic man, sociobiology erects a view of human nature based on the idea of the maximization by genes of their self propagation. Sohn-Rethel has gone as far as to claim that the emergence of the forms of abstract thought used in the physical science is linked with the emergence of commodity production and the 'exchange abstraction' whereby two dissimilar commodities are bought into equivalence by a divisible and timeless abstract commodity, money.[49]

Moving directly from the superstructural nature of science to its non-neutrality between classes, Ciccotti, Cini, and de Maria argue that, although a certain degree of relative autonomy can be given to pure science,

> Science [is therefore] a particular socially determined growth of the productive forces, destined to extend to a maximum the surplus value which can be extracted from the masses .... This clearly shows the inadequacy of all theories of the neutrality of science.[50]

It is easy to see how physical commodities may come to embody market relations, either by design or selection. For example, Edison's decisions about the voltage at which to run his domestic lighting system, and indeed his whole engineering strategy, were conditioned by the desire to minimize the use of expensive copper. The system reflected the *social relations* lying behind copper prices.[51] But it would be wrong to see this as having anything useful to say about the neutrality or social construction of technics.[52] For example, a green socialist society might have come to just the same decision because of the wish to minimize the *environmental impact* of copper production and to maximize the access of future generations to this non-renewable resource.

The radical science movement has been greatly influenced by structuralist Marxism. Different 'levels' of the structural totality – the economic, the political, the ideological, class-struggle – form an interacting system or 'structure in dominance' in which the form taken by the interactions and their relative strengths are determined by one 'level', in this case class struggle. Critics of structural Marxism argue that no internally consistent account has been offered of what the notion of structural causality means. Certainly those members of the radical science movement who use these ideas offer no account of how the structure 'finally determines' the form of technics.[53]

One implication of the structuralist approach is that individuals (or small social groups) are merely bearers of structural relations, so that their actions have no independent impact on social outcomes. There is ample evidence that this perspective is inadequate. Studies of scientific research carried out from an ethnomethodological perspective amply illustrate both that individuals matter, and why they matter. The meaning of concepts, what is to count as experimental evidence, and which new ideas should be accepted are all determined through processes of negotiation of shared meaning between individuals.[54] Presumably those outcomes are constrained by existing conceptual resources, the way the world actually works, and the structure of sub-disciplines; but they do not determine them. Although the

phenomenon of multiple discoveries might suggest some strong underlying process of social determination in science by which individuals (or
more plausibly research groups) do not matter, there is ample evidence
that the *timing* of discoveries is indeed contingent and, because of
entrenchment, the timing of discoveries may be economically crucial.[55]
Nor are economically crucial technical innovations clustered in periods
of economic depression where the 'need' for them is greatest within
capitalist societies.[56]

To the extent to which explanation (rather than analogy or
suggestion) is obtained in this literature it is usually functional in form.
Technics function (although not without contradictions) to maintain the
rule of the dominant class. As Elster has argued, there are major
problems with functional explanations of this sort. Functionalism is
often stretched to fit inconvenient facts by varying the relative weights
of different functions being served.[57]

The radical science movement provides no clear idea about why it is
that technics are functional. Often they rely on intentional explanations
which, as we have already seen, they cannot sustain. Is there anything in
the notion that commodities and scientific laws somehow come to
embody capitalist social relations because of their manner of
production, as contrasted with the idea that the *market selects out
products only some of which* embody such relations? I will take up this
argument in relation to science.

The radical science movement often seems to be unclear over which
conception of ideology they wish to deploy – ideology as distorted
knowledge or ideology as *any* class-based form of consciousness,
whether or not its world-view is relatively distorted. For example,
Young says that:

> If we say that science is not value neutral, that is value laden or
> ideological, then we say it expresses in complex ways – or mediates
> – how people treat each other. Ideology is not, on this argument, mere
> distortion or false consciousness. World views are ideological *and an
> ideology is a world view. Science is an ideology although* it is about
> the world we live in as well.[58]

Both the first and the second view of ideology can be read into the
quotation. Young and other members of the radical science movement
wish to argue for a better socialist science. They want to criticize
capitalist science for its conceptual distortion and warped understanding
of the natural world. However, the relativism of authors like Young

leaves no foothold from which such criticism can be mounted. The view that all knowledge is socially constructed and has no material referent denies that absolute inter-temporal or cross-cultural standards for judging science exist. There is a well-known problem of reflexivity with philosophical relativism of this sort: it leaves those who hold it no secure bridgehead from which to argue their own position and to criticize other philosophies of science.[59] What is there to say that socialist science would be better? As Hilary Rose has argued, the relativism of this strand of the radical science movement sits very poorly with its political aims. Thus the radical science movement must have some absolute standard for judging the distortion of science.[60]

Implicit in the radical science position is the idea that external influences on scientific production such as economic pressure or the borrowing of ideas from dominant ways of thinking about social and economic life leads to 'bad' science. It is true that the older 'internalist' tradition in the history of science now looks increasingly threadbare.[61] There is ample evidence that *among other* external influences the material interests and economic ideas of the dominant class have shaped theory construction and legitimation. (Of course the flow has been far from class structure to science.)

Consider the development of quantum physics in Weimar Germany in the 1920s. Forman has argued that the movement from classical mechanics based on determinate causal laws to quantum mechanics based on statistical regularity, and the impossibility of exact prediction of particular sub-atomic events, was strongly socially conditioned.[62] Physics and mathematics came under intense pressure in post-war Germany because they were said to paint a picture of the natural world which left no room for spontaneity. The world was governed by the 'rigid, dead hand of causality', and the rational/analytic method of mathematical physics was seen as opposed to nature as the source of feeling, inspiration, and action. Partly as a reaction to the trauma of what was seen by many Germans as a chance defeat in 1918, the dominant intellectual milieu was idealist and indeed existentialist. The most influential expression of this position was Spengler's *Decline of the West* which argues *inter alia* that the exact physical sciences are becoming a spent intellectual force, that they will be replaced by other forms of understanding, and that all knowledge is true relative only to its time and place. This book was very widely read among mathematical physicists, and it greatly influenced the intellectual reception of the new physics. Forman thus argues that

The programme of dispensing with causality achieved a very substantial following among German physicists *before* it was justified by the advent of the fundamentally acausal quantum mechanics. I contend, moreover, that the scientific context and content, the form and level of exposition, the social occasion and the chosen vehicles for publication of manifestoes against causality, all point inescapably to the conclusion that substantive problems in atomic physics played only a secondary role in the genesis of this acausal persuasion, that the most important factor was the social-intellectual pressure exerted upon the physicists as members of the German academic community.[63]

The point of this example is that quantum mechanics has been one of the most fruitful developments in twentieth-century physics despite its origins: if it was (in some sense) a class-based world view, it was, nevertheless, relatively undistorted compared to the perspective it replaced. For example, the theoretical model of semi-conduction phenomena developed by Wilson in the early 1930s derived from the work of Schrodinger, Heinsenberg, and Dirac. Although Wilson did not invent the transistor, his theoretical work was important to the more empirically and commercially orientated research of Shockley at Bell Telephone, which did.[64] Quantum physics is not an absolutely 'undistorted' picture of how the natural world *is*. We can never have such pictures even in principle. However, it represented a *progressive shift* in physics and was an improvement on earlier models, which became a fruitful research programme. Quantum mechanics also led to technologies, including micro-electronics, which may yield widespread benefits in certain possible futures. There are no good general grounds for believing that external influences necessarily lead to bad science, although they do so on occasion.[65]

I now turn to my second argument which is that scientific discourse may be appropriated into a number of different social ideologies and often can (though by no means invariably does) do ideological work for various classes or social groups. Barnes has argued that this open-endedness typifies the ideological use of science.

A belief may take on social functions in particular contexts if it naturally leads actors with their given pre-existing beliefs to adopt certain evaluations or courses of action. In other situations, or with different actors, the same belief may function quite differently.[66]

This is as true of the high-level metaphysical and ontological claims of science as it is of lower level claims: authors like Marcuse were wrong to see a simple connection between these high-level claims and 'one dimensional' thought.[67] If the ontology of quantum mechanics had a relationship with the ideas of authors like Spengler (and thus a complex relationship with Nazism) quantum mechanics has also been appropriated in completely different ways. Today greens like Capra use analogies between the 'world views' of quantum mechanics and certain mystical/religious traditions to emphasize: the unity of man and nature; the need for conservation; and the need for communitarian social forms. The practical successes of quantum mechanics lend legitimacy to the social ideologies of religious traditions with (what Capra sees as) ontologies related to quantum mechanics.[68]

The flexibility of technics

The most important technics often have a high degree of flexibility. This is crucial for, even if the distributional implications of a form of technics are biased at present, flexibility ensures that they may not be in the future. It is a fallacy to argue that society will continue to deploy a form of technics in the way it does at present.

There is a degree of indeterminateness about how society will develop. This comes not from any random element in the social world but from the fact that our social theories are not adequate, and probably cannot be adequate, to predict the future. Nevertheless those theories usually lead us to limit the possible future worlds to which we are willing to give credence. These possible worlds may also be seen as accessible from the present through deliberate action on the part of individuals and social groups. Along the various possible paths, a particular technic might be produced and used in quite distinct ways.

Perhaps the most convincing way to demonstrate such a case would be to try to show the degree of contingency which existed when major new forms of technics were introduced in the past.[69] However, I will take the more risky tack of looking at future rather than past possible worlds. Building upon the discussion of unemployment in an earlier section, I will argue that: (a) information technology places limits upon future possibilities but that (b) both corporatist and authoritarian forms of capitalism will be viable and that (c) the distributional implications of information technology would be quite different in the two forms.

It is often argued that parts of the hardware of information technology are relatively flexible tools as compared with other major twentieth-century innovations. Although information technology is being abused at present, the fault lies more with the applications, software, and systems design than with the underlying hardware itself. Thus Allan Burns writes in *The Microchip: Appropriate or Inappropriate Technology?* that

> The microprocessor itself, being by nature a raw material, may indeed be a neutral device but the design of the systems and equipment that incorporate it are not; they must reflect the influences, prejudices, and motivations of those who control their manufacture and use.[70]

Many authors would go further than this arguing that much of the hardware incorporating the microprocessor as a building block is also neutral even if much of the software, broadly understood, is not neutral.[71]

Both older studies of the introduction of mainframe computers and, more recently, studies of the introduction of newer forms of computerization and automation in the office often paint a picture of inflexibility and Taylorist methods of work design.[72] By introducing word processors much of the skilled aspect of typing in and laying out the work and correcting spelling and punctuation is lost. The number of typists may be greatly reduced in many offices where large amounts of routine paperwork are produced. The memory of the word processor is able to store paragraphs in standard form which may simply be called by the typist or her boss. The division of labour can be further extended by having a number of word processors share a common print-out facility with one person responsible for the printing out of all output. Similarly the maintenance of the computerized filing system can be separated from typing or input functions. Finally, in offices where decision making of a non-routine variety is important, the power to make decisions can be removed from those lower down the organizational hierarchy by presenting the relevant data in such an easily accessible form on visual display units that management is able to cope with many more decisions and has less need to delegate responsibility. In short, information technology allows the extension of Taylorism from the factory to the office.[73]

Nevertheless, there is much evidence for management interest in the 'human relations approach': systems designed to increase productivity by attempting to increase worker motivation, rather than to de-skill and tightly supervise them. Existing work practices are maintained when they are held to be conducive to worker motivation, and information flows are partially decentralized so that decisions of importance are carried out further down the hierarchy. The office or factory is organized along task lines rather along functional lines, so that workers see more than one part of the 'production process'. Much emphasis is placed upon work groups, and the set of social relations associated with different ways of using the technology.[74] Although some authors have argued that Taylorism is the ground over which the complex fugue of the human relations theorists is played, there is ample evidence that a human relations approach to job design may increase productivity.[75] Clearly, information technology does not lead in a determinate way to Taylorist work organization and the flexibility inherent in it can be used to make work more interesting. Moreover, information technology is being used in a variety of ways now and may provide some, though not an irresistible, impetus in this direction of more congenial work.[76]

However, some authors have argued that this sort of flexibility is beside the point. Within a capitalist system whose central dynamic is accumulation, there is no way in which the technology will be used to produce socially needed products or to humanize work. 'The new technology is not a moveable feast which may be used or abused at will. It is as much a product of capitalist society as war, famine, radicalism, sexism, and economic exploitation.'[77] I think that this argument is wrong. Along the corporatist path of development, information technology might be deployed in such a way that real gains are available to some working people. Whether those gains are large enough or will be spread widely enough to constitute a case of the neutrality of information technology will be discussed below.

I have already argued that investment in information technology may have the unintended second-order effect of reducing the rate of profit and calling into question the legitimacy of capitalist systems. If this is correct, there will be intense political pressure upon the state to increase employment, overall consumption power, and the rate of economic growth. Although the political strains of rates of unemployment of the 1970s were sustainable, it is unclear whether the high levels of unemployment associated with information technology are politically tolerable within a democratic system in the long term especially in view of the spread of technological unemployment to white collar and professional groups.

As part of one possible corporatist 'new deal' which would attempt to overcome these problems, the state might also attempt to implement some of the measures being advocated at present by unionists such as Jenkins and Sherman.[78] These include a shorter overall working lifetime, job sharing, improved health and safety measures, and better social security provision. A radical human relations approach to job design would be a necessary accompaniment to such measures for, if attractive leisure options are provided, work would have to be made more interesting if the correct number of skilled, alert, engaged workers were to be available.

The essence of corporatism as class compromise (and there are many other ways of viewing corporatism) is the idea that the state fosters agreement between the peak organizations of capital and labour. On the one hand, capital agrees to invest more and to support expansion of welfare provision; on the other hand, organized labour agrees to sacrifices of real wages in the short term. The state aids the enforcement of the agreement through restructuring industrial relations and giving the peak organizations power to discipline their memberships. Along the real income and employment dimensions corporatism, then, involves labour trading short term losses against possible longer term gains.

Corporatism has also been seen as an alliance between large corporations and their heavily unionized work forces against competitive capital together with the unorganized of society.[79] It is surely the case that those sections of the working class with the greatest power would gain most from such a compromise. Relatively speaking, the old, the sick, the currently unemployed, and those outside the trade unions would gain less. However, I would argue that the state would organize some trickle down of benefits because of electoral and bureaucratic interests, and in order to maintain social stability.

Some countries have a long history of corporatist industrial relations, and such a future is much easier to envisage where this is so. Similarly there is variation from industry to industry within particular countries. This matters because much detailed negotiation would take place below the state level. The Scandinavian experience with technology agreements gives some grounds for believing that corporatist structures of this sort can emerge. In Norway and Sweden in the 1970s various joint agreements were signed between employers (including the state) and unions regarding the introduction of computer-based systems. A typical agreement of this sort would give relevant union officials the right to be informed of the introduction of such systems, access to information on the system provided in a clear and comprehensible form, and the right to present a union viewpoint on the new system before final decisions are made.[80]

These developments are not peculiar to Scandinavia, although they have been taken further there. Technology agreements are, for example, a growing feature of British industrial relations. Evidence suggests that such agreements have largely failed to affect the way the work process is automated.[81] Nevertheless, British unions have had some limited success in 'humanizing' management plans.

Given that the world economic system begins to move out of depression, it is possible to envisage the power of organized labour being great enough for corporatist compromises more widely distributing the benefits of information technology to emerge. Along the corporatist path benefits from the new technologies might be quite widely spread. In contrast to the position taken by some neo-Marxist authors, we need not be pessimistic about this possibility: there are numerous cases of reform within the capitalist system which have had wide social benefits associated with them, and state managers have electoral and bureaucratic interests in such reforms even though they also face structural constraints preventing them pushing reform so far that the capitalist economic system is put into question.[82]

Corporatism is not the only path of development open, even in societies in which there is a history of class compromise. The corporatist strategy is premised upon two vital assumptions: control of real wages, and effective international collective action between states to simultaneously reflate the world economy. Even if attempts were made to ensure that those preconditions were satisfied, they might fail to be met completely enough for the incipient social problem of technological unemployment to be contained. For example the bankers of the developed world might fail to contain the debt crisis among the newly developed economies; or a major potential 'engine' of the international growth might attempt to free-ride on the reflationary efforts of other states; or overwhelming domestic pressures for trade barriers to protect older industries might undercut growth in the South.

If the corporatist strategy did fail the likely consequence would be a move towards authoritarian state forms and towards economic autarchy behind massive trade barriers, and this sort of capitalism could be sustainable for quite long periods.[83] In order to contain social conflict repression would be necessary, at least in the long run. No doubt the full range of electronic surveillance and data retrieval techniques which so worry the civil liberties lobby would be used.[84] Presumably some level of transfer payment and social welfare would be maintained, but these would be far lower than along the corporatist path, and much greater reliance would be placed upon overtly coercive methods of social control. Given the fact that domestic markets would be stagnant and foreign markets unavailable or costly to enter, the new technologies would be used defensively to cut production costs and the labour force. Given this and the fact that broader ideological developments would emphasize social discipline, nationalism, hierarchy and so on, management ideologies would probably be more Taylorist (although paternalism is another possibility).

Thus both current practices in introducing information technology and consideration of future paths of development illustrate a degree of flexibility and a degree of contingency in the possible distributional effects which may arise. The case presented here could be seen as substantiating the idea that *the technology itself* has no distributive consequences, that it is the socio-political choices about its employment which cause those consequences to come about. However, this would be a fundamental misconception. The reason for this is that the coming of information technology *constrains* the possible futures available to capitalist societies.[85] The potential problem of unemployment, in particular, makes some forms of capitalism unimaginable – for instance, the combination of monetarism and non-authoritarian state forms which would be unable to solve its legitimacy problem.

Liberals and orthodox Marxists are correct to say that many important technologies are flexible. They are wrong to see this as necessarily implying that the technology is neutral because *the technology itself* may constrain possible paths of social development, and certain groups may only benefit along impossible paths. I would argue that, although information technology is *not* like this, other important technologies are. The private car is a good example.[86]

A framework for the neutrality debate

Four high-level arguments about the neutrality of technics have been rejected. I doubt whether there are any convincing arguments of this sort which would enable us to establish whether or not technics as a whole are neutral. In this section I shall argue that what underlies disagreement about the neutrality of technics is not just differences of the sort discussed above but deep-seated moral and ethical commitments and fundamental theoretical differences about how societies work. Despite such differences, I think that all those concerned about this question might agree on a very open-textured definition of neutrality into which it is possible to 'slot' different moral commitments and theoretical positions.

A definition of neutrality

Following the discussion above, a particular technic might be considered to be neutral if its present distributional implications and (or) those along a future path or paths of social development, are not biased in favour of a certain group or groups.[87] This definition leads us to examine both the production *and* the use to which a particular technic is put. It differs from existing definitions, whether explicit or implicit, in emphasizing 'possible worlds' and the place of technics in them.

Clearly this definition lacks content until we have specified: what is meant by technics; a theory about how society works; and a set of values to be considered as pertinent. Disagreements over these lead to disagreements about the neutrality of technics.

Definition of science and technology

First, there are disagreements which arise from different conceptions of what science and technology are. As we have already seen, some authors wish to define science narrowly as a body of as-yet-unrefuted empirical laws, while others see science as a social institution within which we arrive at consensus about how the natural world works. Similarly, technology can be broadly or narrowly defined. For authors such as Lewis Mumford, Ellul, or Illich the hardware and software forms a continuum which cannot be usefully broken at any point.[88] Other authors resist these broad definitions of technology on the grounds that they make all social problems merely technological problems and that they overstate the ways in which hardware conditions organizational forms and scientific thinking affects culture more generally.

We have already seen how definitions of science and technology condition opinions on neutrality. First, narrow views of science define social, political and economic pressures upon individual scientists out of the neutrality debate. Second, if the software side of information technology were not part of the technology itself, this form of technics would be more likely to be seen as neutral, for as we saw above, it is largely the software which constrains social relations.

The role of social theory in the neutrality debate

The first, and perhaps most obvious, role of social theory is to tell us which social groups we are to consider in analysing the distributional implication of a form of technics. Are we to consider social classes, narrower social groups or individuals? How are social classes and social groups to be defined? Should international or inter-generational comparisons also be made? If we confined our analysis to rich Northern countries, we might conclude that information technology was neutral because of the corporatist path of social development along which gains for non-elite groups might occur. However, poorer countries in the South, and even the newly developed economies, might suffer in relative (or absolute, even) terms along this path. Similarly, there might be gains for the working class *as a whole* along the corporatist path, but certain groups within that class might not do well even along the corporatist path. An analyst who considered such groups as relevant might disagree with a class-based conclusion.

A second crucial role of social theory is in the construction of counterfactuals. To establish the distributional implications of a form of technics we need to ask what the distribution of well-being in society would be *in the absence of* that form of technics. This sort of counterfactual history is extraordinarily difficult to carry off convincingly, and has very seldom been attempted in relation to a major technological system.[89] The essence of the problem is to decide what else in society necessarily changes when you remove the technology in thought. This must be a decision guided by some social theory. Admittedly when major new developments like information technology are being considered one can sometimes justify using 'society before the advent of the technology' as a counterfactual (the assumption being that societal distributions would have remained unchanged in relevant respects). Clearly, in using evidence for past flexibility one needs to be sensitive to the sort of social entrenchment of technics discussed above: what was flexible *ex ante* may no longer be so.

Because it focuses on particular technics rather than technics as a whole, it might be argued that the methodology discussed here is reductionist, missing systematic interactions between technics. More correctly, we can only talk about the neutrality of parts of technics weakly linked to the whole. In order to construct the sorts of distributional counterfactuals implied here, it must be possible to remove the particular technic in thought. This is not possible for, say, the word processor. If this goes, so does much of the rest of information technology, relying as it does on similar components or scientific knowledge. However, we can remove information technology *as a whole*, and thus sensibly talk of its neutrality.

Clearly, the paths of social development which are considered plausible will depend upon prior theoretical positions. Given the crucial importance of the state to the development of science and technology, theories of the state are important to the neutrality debate. It is easy to see how different positions on the theory of the state could lead to different judgements about neutrality. For example, the idea that the actions of the state are functional for the long-run interests of the capitalist class as a whole would probably suggest that, no matter what path of social development was taken, capital could not lose from information technology. (In contrast, my argument was premised on the view that the state may act dysfunctionally although there are certain constraints limiting how far this process may go.)

The last important respect in which judgements about neutrality are theoretically guided is that they are based, in the last resort, on a theory of human nature and motivation. One way that this might generate disagreements is over the question of whether it is relative or absolute deprivation which matters to people. Along the corporatist path most groups in society could be made better off by information technology in absolute terms but the distribution of income might become more unequal. If so, some groups would suffer relative deprivation. Will that necessarily matter to them?

Values and the neutrality debate

Perhaps the most fundamental disagreements about distribution will stem from different ways of thinking about interests. Conflicts over whether real or subjective interests should be used and what real interests are will crucially affect the neutrality debate. Would a corporatist solution to the social problems posed by information technology serve the real interests of the non-elite groups? Even if subjective welfare improved, some would argue that anything that delays the advent of socialism harms the working class.

Besides differences over the way in which interests have been conceptualized, differences in primary social goods must also be considered. How are they to be understood, and what relative weights should be given to each of them? For example, it might be agreed that liberty is a primary social good. Advocates of pure negative freedom alone might accept that, with suitable forms of data protection, there is no reason why information technology should limit liberty. Even if information technology does not limit pure negative freedom it might constrain. Although some argue that the new technologies will lead to a plurality of different information sources, others argue that it is as likely that a centralization of the control of the media will occur, leaving us open to autonomy-limiting forms of manipulation.[90]

It is easy to see how rates of trade-off between various values might also be relevant. It might be agreed that both conceptual skills and skills of eye–brain and eye–hand co-ordination matter. But where those who emphasize conceptual skills might see the possibility of a 'computer aided craftman', others who weight the older craft-skills more heavily might see deskilling.[91]

How biased is biased?

The thread running through my discussion of this question is the idea that a biased technology is one which will, or is likely to, harm at least one group in all circumstances. There are numerous ways of unpacking this, however. It will be convenient to have some shorthand term for the way in which a particular technic is produced and used. Let us call this a 'realization'. It is quite possible for different realizations to coexist either currently or within a given path of development.

The first dimension along which judgements about bias may vary may be brought out by the following pair of definitions. The distributional implications of a technic might be said not to be biased if:

(a) There exists at least one realization under which some members of each social group benefits;

or alternatively if

(b) There exists at least one current realization and at least one realization along each possible path of social development under which some members of each group benefit.

Definition (b) is clearly stronger than definition (a) because (a) only requires one actual/possible realization under which each group benefits, whereas (b) requires that *every* actual or possible society contains such a realization.

Now it might be argued that different realizations may exist within a *particular* actual or potential world, but that some realizations may be important to the point of dominance. For example, it might be admitted that within a workers' co-operative the introduction of new technology might be beneficial to workers but that there is only a very limited space for this form of ownership within capitalist society.[92] Suppose that we can sensibly talk of some 'average' realization in any current or possible society. Then corresponding to (a) and (b), the distributional implications of a technic might be said not to be biased if:

(c) There exists at least one 'average' realization under which some members of each social group benefit.

(We should not demand that a neutral technic benefits each group under each 'average' realization, i.e. that in a statistical sense all groups may be guaranteed to benefit from it. We would not demand of an unbiased gambling game that both the punter *and* the bank should always win. Rather, the first requirement is that there are circumstances in which each might win. The second requirement is that these circumstances should be, in some sense, equally likely.)

This leads into the next dimension along which accounts of bias might vary. Our intuitive feelings about the future often lead us to say that some possible future worlds are more probable than others. If we are to introduce possible worlds into the analysis of neutrality, this would suggest that more unlikely worlds should, somehow, be discounted even though it is seldom possible to give a future world some precise probability value.[93] If it happens that a complete strong ordering of possible future worlds exists – and there is no reason why this should be so – stronger versions of definitions (a) to (c) could be given. In each case the set of realizations considered would be limited to those which are current and those along the most probable path of future development.

Finally, instead of considering each social group, some group or groups might be privileged and their interests serve as side constraints on what is to be seen as unbiased. The form of technics would be seen as biased *unless* the position of the group concerned was not made worse. It might be particularly pertinent to consider vulnerable sub-groups. For instance a Rawlsian might wish to privilege the positions of the poorest members of society – the members of a sub-group of a social class. Or future generations vulnerable to the actions of the current generation might be privileged because of the irreversibility of much of the (e.g. environmental) damage that we might do to them. The position of other social groups might then be analysed in any of the ways already discussed.

If this approach were taken, we would want to talk of neutrality *relative* to the target group. Presumably the justification for building such side-constraints into the definition of neutrality is that the concept of neutrality is, itself, morally loaded. To say a technology is biased is to say that a *prima facie* case exists for it being undesirable: at least one group will be harmed by the technology. (It should be clear that this is *only* a *prima facie* case.)[94]

Conclusion

It might be argued that this discussion of information technology futures best illustrates merely that questions about neutrality are undecidable. We just do not have adequate social theories to talk about the future impacts of major forms of technics. I would have some sympathy with this argument. But a better way of putting it is to say that we can only talk about neutrality *relative* to some social form or timescale over which we are confident that sensible discussion is possible. For example, my uncertainty about socialism means that I am only willing to talk of the neutrality of information technology relative to capitalist society. Similarly, my claim that information technology is not obviously biased is limited to the richer countries of the North: it is extremely difficult to think about distributional effects along the North/South axis, although a case can be made that the North will inevitably gain. Finally, my conclusion about information technology was based on a relatively 'middle range' rather than a strong concept of what an unbiased technology is: we need far more certainty than we currently possess to satisfy a strong definition of an unbiased technic.[95]

Although there is currently widespread disagreement about the neutrality of technics, I hope that the methodological and definitional points made in this conclusion might be broadly acceptable. The debate may be carried further by identifying differences in position along the dimensions discussed in this section. In addition to new technologies, it seems especially crucial to me that we use our foresight as well as current empirical studies when discussing neutrality. Although my specific focus here has been on technics, I do believe that most of the methodological points made in this chapter also apply to other important social institutions.

Notes

I would like to thank Bob Goodin and Lisa Hooper for comments on an earlier draft of this paper.

1 H. and S. Rose, 'The radicalisation of science', in H. and S. Rose (eds), *The Radicalisation of Science*, London: Macmillan, 1976, is a good historical survey.
2 A. Weinberg, 'Can technology replace social engineering', *The University of Chicago Magazine*, October 1966.
3 An ill-defined group. I have in mind authors like Aron, Bell, Kahn and Brezinski who were prominent in US social science in the 1950s and 1960s. For an excellent review see K. Kumar, *Prophesy and Progress*, Harmondsworth: Penguin, 1977, ch. 6.
4 D. Bell, *The Coming of Post-Industrial Society*, New York: Basic Books, 1973, p. 27.
5 See: M. Reinfelder, 'Breaking the spell of technicism', in D. P. Slater (ed.), *Outlines of a Critique of Technology*, London: Ink Links, 1980; H. and S. Rose, 'The problematic inheritance: Marx and Engels on the natural sciences', in H. and S. Rose (eds), *The Political Economy of Science*, London: Macmillan, 1976; S. Aronowitz, 'Marxism, technology, and labor', *New Political Science*, 1 (1978/9), pp. 105–19.
6 K. Marx, *Capital*, Vol. 1, New York: International Publishers, 1967, p. 422.
7 N. Rosenberg, *Perspectives on Technology*, Cambridge: Cambridge University Press, ch. 7.
8 See particularly S. and H. Rose, 'The myth of the neutrality of science', in W. Fuller (ed.), *The Social Impact of Modern Biology*, London: Routledge & Kegan Paul, 1971. Another important statement is D. Dickson, *Alternative Technology*, London: Fontana, 1974.
9 D. Albury and J. Schwartz, *Partial Progress*, London: Pluto, 1982, p. 179.
10 J. Lipscombe and B. Williams, *Are Science and Technology Neutral?*, London: Butterworth, 1979, p. 19.
11 A. Burns, *The Microchip: Appropriate or Inappropriate Technology?*, Chichester: Ellis Horwood, 1978, chs 1, 4 discuss these points.
12 R. Grossman, 'Womens' place in the integrated circuit', in 'The changing role of South-East Asian women: the global assembly line and the social manipulation of women on the job'. Special joint issue of *S.E. Asian Chronicle*, 66 and *Pacific Research*, 9 (1978).
13 J. Rada, 'The microelectronics revolution: implications for the Third World', *Development Dialogue*, 2 (1981), pp. 41–7 and the case studies in J. Rada, *The Impact of Microelectronics*, Paris: UNESCO, 1982, p. 11.
14 I. Illich, *Tools for Conviviality*, London: Fontana, 1973, pp. 65–71.
15 I do not propose to deal with the broader problems of the post-industrial perspective, implausible as it is. For these see: Kumar, *Prophesy and Progress*; J. Gershuny, *After Industrial Society*, London: Macmillan,

1978; C. Kerr, *The Future of Industrial Societies: Convergence or Continuing Diversity*, Cambridge, Mass.: Harvard University Press, 1983.

16 The most useful brief review is B. Wynne, 'Technology assessment: superfix or superfixation?', *Science for the People*, 24 (1973). See also L. H. Tribe, *Technology: Progress of Assessment and Choice*, Washington, DC: National Academy of Science, 1969.

17 D. Collingridge, *The Social Control of Technology*, London: Frances Pinter, 1980. S. Verba, 'Sequences and development', in L. Binder (ed.), *Crises and Sequences in Political Development*, Princeton: Princeton University Press, 1971.

18 Although not all such methodologies do so, biases are built into many existing, widely used methods. See N. J. Block and G. Dworkin, 'I.Q heredibility and inequality', in N. J. Block and G. Dworkin (eds), *The I.Q Controversy*, New York: Pantheon, 1976.

19 K. Griffin, *The Political Economy of Agrarian Change – An Essay on the Green Revolution*, Cambridge, Mass.: Harvard University Press, 1973, pp. 210–29.

20 For the effects of seat belts on pedestrian and cycling deaths see J. G. U. Adams, *Risk and Freedom: The Record of Road Safety Regulation*, Cardiff: Transport Publishing Project, 1985. Seat belts are a classic technical fix.

21 C. Taylor, 'Neutrality in political science', in P. Laslett and W. Runciman (eds), *Philosophy Politics and Society*, Oxford: Blackwell, 1967 3rd ser., pp. 25–57.

22 R. F. Bud, 'Strategy in American cancer research', *Social Studies of Science*, 8 (1978), pp. 425–59.

23 See B. Bohme, W. Van Den Daele and W. Krohn, 'Finalisation in science', *Social Science Information*, 15 (1976), pp. 307–30.

24 M. Black, 'Is scientific neutrality a myth', reprinted as Appendix One in Lipscombe and Collingridge, *Are Science and Technology Neutral?*

25 Rose and Rose, 'The myth of neutrality', p. 220. The authors go on to suggest that the fundamental science behind CS was neutral though part of a non-neutral paradigm.

26 See C. R. Littler, *The Development of the Labour Process in Capitalist Societies*, London: Heinemann, 1982, pp. 27–35; S. Hill, *Competition and Control at Work*, London: Heinemann, 1981, chs 3, 6, particularly the discussion of alternative managerial ideologies.

27 D. Noble, 'Social choice in machine tool design', in A. Zimblast (ed.), *Case Studies on the Labour Process*, New York: Monthly Review Press, pp. 37–44 especially.

28 Encouraged by supervisors who saw the possibilities for higher productivity. See B. Wilkinson, *The Shopfloor Politics of New Technology*, London: Heinemann, 1983, ch. 7.

29 Rose and Rose, 'The myth of neutrality', p. 218.

30 J. M. Levy Leblond, 'Ideology of/in contemporary physics', in Rose and Rose (eds), *The Radicalisation of Science*.

31 There is growing interest in state-centred or statist approaches both among Marxist and among liberal theorists. For useful surveys see P. B. Evans, D. Rueschewmeyer and T. Skocpol (eds), *Bringing the State Back In*, Cambridge: Cambridge University Press, 1985, chs 1, 11.

32 D. Gordon, 'Capitalist efficiency and socialist efficiency', *Monthly Review*, 28 (1976), pp. 19–40.

33 R. Nelson, S. Winter and H. Schuette, 'Technical change in an evolutionary model', *Quarterly Journal of Economics*, 90 (1976), pp. 90–118.

34 J. Elster, *Ulysses and the Sirens*, Cambridge: Cambridge University Press, 1979, ch. 1.

35 See T. Weisskopf, S. Bowles and D. Gordon, 'Hearts and minds: a social model of US productivity growth', *Brookings Papers on Economic Activity*, 2 (1983), pp. 381–441. Much stress is placed upon positive motivation.

36 That this is so may have been one of Marx's most central insights, and one of great potential value to modern social theory. See J. Elster, *Making Sense of Marx*, Cambridge: Cambridge University Press, 1985, especially ch. 1.

37 See, for example, CSE Microelectronics Work Group, *Microelectronics Capitalist Technology and the Working Class*, London: CSE Books, 1980, ch. 1.

38 E. Mandel, *Long Waves of Capitalist Development*, Cambridge: Cambridge University Press, 1980, ch. 4.

39 A. Gorz, *Farewell to the Working Class*, London: Pluto Press, 1982.

40 A good sectoral based survey in the British context is J. Sleigh *et al.*, *The Manpower Implications of Microelectronic Technology*, London: Department of Education and Science, 1980. The direct effects can be startling indeed. In a very detailed study of robotics, Ayres and Miller estimate in a near-term scenario for manufacturing involving the emerging generation of sensor based robots that 50 per cent of fabrication jobs and 25 per cent of assembly jobs could be robotized. See R. Ayres and S. Miller, 'Robotic realities near term prospects and problems', *Annals of the American Academy of Political and Social Science*, 470 (1983), pp. 28–55.

41 Mandel, *Long Waves of Capitalist Development*, ch. 4. For an alternative view see: C. Freeman, J. Clark, and L. Soete, *Unemployment and Technical Innovation*, Westport, Conn.: Greenwood, 1982.

42 See, for example, the numerous econometric studies surveyed in P. Stoneman, N. Blattner, and D. Pastre, *Micro-Electronics, Robotics, and Jobs*, Paris: OECD, 1982, most of which rely strongly on such neo-classical effects. For a good survey of the appropriate neo-classical theory, and criticisms of it, see C. M. J. Cooper and J. A. Clark, *Employment, Economics and Technical Change*, Brighton: Wheatsheaf Books, 1982, chs 3, 4.

43 S. Nora and A. Minc, *The Computerisation of Society*, Cambridge, Mass.: MIT Press, 1979, ch. 3.

44 Mandel, *Long Waves of Capitalist Development*.
45 See particularly: B. Young, 'Science *is* social relations', *Radical Science Journal*, 5 (1977), pp. 65–132; L. Hodgkin, 'Politics and the physical sciences', *Radical Science Journal*, 4 (1976), p. 39.
46 Young, 'Science *is* social relations', pp. 67, 79–81.
47 Young, 'Science *is* social relations', p. 67.
48 M. Sahlins, *The Use and Abuse of Biology*, Ann Arbor: University of Michigan Press, 1976.
49 A useful short summary of Sohn-Rethel's idea is A. Sohn-Rethel, 'Science as alienated consciousness', *Radical Science Journal*, 2/3 (1975), pp. 65–105.
50 G. Ciccotti, M. Cini, and M. De Maria, 'The production of science', in Rose and Rose (eds), *The Political Economy of Science*, p. 44.
51 T. P. Hughes, 'The electrification of America: the systems builders', *Technology and Culture*, 20 (1979), pp. 51–63.
52 Cf. D. Mackenzie and J. Wajceman (eds), *The Social Shaping of Technology*, Milton Keynes: The Open University Press, 1984, pp. 2–26, which uses this and other examples to argue that technics are socially shaped to fit capitalist relations.
53 Hodgkin, 'Politics and the physical sciences', p. 40.
54 E.g. S. Woolger, *Laboratory Life: The Social Construction of Scientific Facts*, Beverley Hills, Ca: Sage, 1979. I do not agree with the relativism of these authors, but their work does show how important agents are in negotiating scientific meanings.
55 A. Brannigan and R. A .Wanner, 'Historical distribution of multiple discoveries and theories of scientific change', *Social Studies of Science*, 13 (1983), pp. 417–35, surveys the literature and provides a test.
56 Freeman, *et al.*, *Unemployment and Technical Innovations*.
57 J. Elster, 'Marxism, functionalism and games theory', *Theory and Society*, 11 (1982), pp. 453–82.
58 Young, 'Science *is* social relations', p. 70.
59 S. Lukes, 'Relativism in its place', in M. Hollis and S. Lukes (eds), *Rationality and Relativism*, Oxford: Blackwell, 1982. See also the essays in that volume by Barnes and Bloor and by Hollis.
60 H. Rose, 'Hyper-reflexivity – a new danger for the counter movement', in H. Rose and H. Nowotny (eds), *Counter Movements in the Sciences*, Dordrecht: Reidel, 1979.
61 S. Shapin, 'Social uses of science', in G. S. Rousseau and R. Porter (eds), *The Ferment of Knowledge*, Cambridge: Cambridge University Press, 1980. This examines numerous case studies.
62 P. Forman, 'Weimar culture, causality, and quantum theory, 1918–1927: adaption by German physicists and mathematicians to a hostile intellectual environment', in R. McCormmack (ed.), *Historical Studies in Science*, Philadelphia: University of Pennsylvania Press, 1971, p. 3.
63 Forman, 'Weimar culture', p. 110.
64 E. Braun and S. Macdonald, *Revolution in Miniature*, 2nd edn, Cambridge: Cambridge University Press, 1982, pp. 19–22.

65 B. Barnes, *Scientific Knowledge and Sociological Theory*, London: Routledge & Kegan Paul, 1974, ch. 5; D. Bloor, *Knowledge and Social Imagery*, London: Routledge & Kegan Paul, 1976, ch. 1.

66 Barnes, *Scientific Knowledge and Sociological Theory*, p. 129. Those who dislike the philosophical relativism of Barnes and his co-workers may still agree with his sociological arguments about science and ideology. See D. Mackenzie, 'Notes on the science and social relations debate', *Capital and Class*, 14 (1981), pp. 47–61.

67 H. Marcuse, *One Dimensional Man*, London: Abacus, 1982; T. Roszak, *Where the Wasteland Ends*, London: Faber, 1972, part 2; W. Leiss, *The Domination of Nature*, Boston: Beacon, 1974, part 2.

68 F. Capra and C. Spretnak, *Green Politics: The Global Promise*, London: Hutchinson, 1984.

69 For a study of flexibility of technics at an earlier industrial divide see C. F. Sabel, *Work and Politics: The Division of Labour in Industry*, Cambridge: Cambridge University Press, 1982, especially pp. 37–45. For an excellent account of political possibility and the possible worlds approach to political theory see J. Elster, *Logic and Society*, New York: Wiley, 1978, especially ch. 3.

70 Burns, *The Microchip: Appropriate or Inappropriate Technology?*, p. 124.

71 E.g. E. Mumford, 'The design of work, new approaches and new needs', in J. E. Rijnsdorop (ed.), *Case Studies in Automation Related to the Humanisation of Work*, Oxford: Pergamon Press, 1979.

72 M. Weir, 'Are computer systems and humanised work compatible?', in R. H. Ottoway (ed.), *Humanising the Workplace*, London: Croom Helm, 1978; J. Barker and H. Downing, 'Word processing and the transformation of patriarchal relations of control in the office', *Capital and Class*, 9 (1980), pp. 64–99; R. Crompton and G. Jones, *White-Collar Proletariat Deskilling and Gender in Clerical Work*, London: Macmillan, 1984.

73 As Franco de Benedetti, joint director of Olivetti puts it: 'Information technology is basically a technology of coordination and control of [the] labour force, the while collar workers that Taylorian organisation does not cover'. Quoted in M. Duncan, 'Micro-electronics: five areas of subordination', in L. Levidow and B. Young (eds), *Science and Technology and the Labour Process*, London: CSE Books, 1981, p. 194.

74 E. Mumford, *Values Technology and Work*, The Hague: Martinus Nijhoff, 1981, ch. 10. For an introduction to the various branches of the human relations school and a thorough going critique see M. Rose, *Industrial Behaviour*, Harmondsworth: Penguin, 1981, parts 3 and 4.

75 For the classic statement of the idea that Taylorism underlies all more 'humane' developments see H. Braverman, *Labour and Monopoly Capital*, New York: Monthly Review Press, ch. 6. See also Hill, *Competition and Control at Work*, p. 50. For some additional case studies see Rijnsdorp (ed.), *Case Studies in Automation Related to the Humanisation of Work* and C. L. Cooper and E. Mumford (eds), The Quality of Working Life in Eastern and Western Europe, sections 1 and 2, especially the paper by A. Hopwood, 'Towards the Economic

Assessment of New Forms of Work Organisation' which surveys the evidence by the cost effectiveness of such methods. Hopwood argues that, despite some reporting bias from industrial psychologists, work reorganization is probably cost-effective (in a narrow sense) in many contexts. A good review of the Scandinavian job experiments in the seventies is F. M. Blackler and C. A. Brown, *Job Redesign and Management Control: Studies in British Leyland and Volvo*, Farnborough: Saxon House, 1978, chs 2, 3.

76 L. Hirschorn, 'The post-industrial labour process', *New Political Science*, 2 (1980), pp. 11–33.
77 Duncan, 'Micro-electronics: five areas of subordination', p. 202.
78 C. Jenkins and B. Sherman, *The Collapse of Work*, London: Methuen, 1979.
79 A view particularly associated with J. O'Connor, *The Fiscal Crisis of the State*, New York: St Martin's Press, 1973.
80 P. Docherty, 'User participation and influence in systems design in Norway and Sweden, in the light of union involvement, new legislation, and joint agreements', in N. Bjorn-Anderson (ed.), *The Human Side of Information Processing*, Amsterdam: North Holland, 1978, p. 116. For a broader cross-national survey of technology agreements see International Labour Organisation, *Technological Change: The Tripartite Response, 1982–85*, Geneva: ILO, 1985. There is some evidence for the breakdown of the tripartite approach to new technology in Sweden under pressure of economic events. See B. Gustavsen, 'Technology and collective agreements: some recent Scandinavian developments', *Industrial Relations Journal*, 16 (1985), pp. 34–43.
81 See R. Williams and F. Stewart, 'New technology agreements: an assessment', *Industrial Relations Journal* 16, (1985), pp. 58–74, which is based on a recent survey of 240 such agreements. Also see J. J. Richardson, 'Tripartism and the new technology', *Policy and Politics*, 10 (1982), pp. 342–61; I. Benson and J. Lloyd, *New Technology and Industrial Change*, London: Kogan Page, 1983, part 2.
82 Duncan, 'Microelectronics: five areas of subordination', p. 203.
83 Mandel, *Long Waves of Capitalist Development*, ch. 4.
84 For a good, brief survey see P. Hewitt, *The Abuse of Power: Civil Liberties in the United Kingdom*, Oxford: Martin Robertson, 1982, ch. 2.
85 By far the most theoretically interesting account of technological determinism is L. Winner, *Autonomous Technology*, Cambridge: MIT Press, 1977, especially pp. 88–100. To be more precise about what I am advocating, technology becomes part of a social structure which is continually *recreated* through the actions of agents but, at the same time, both facilitates and constrains these actions. That is, I am adding an overtly technological level to Giddens's theory of structuration. See, for example, A. Giddens, *Central Problems in Social Theory*, London: Macmillan, 1980, ch. 2.
86 There is no doubt that small, light cars with low top speeds and little acceleration can be made. Moreover, shared use of cars and co-operative ownership of 'green' cars could be arranged. But there are

characteristics of the very concept of the private car itself which will, I think, preclude those of anything more than a marginal development either in capitalist or socialist society. This is a technology inherently easy to turn into a status good, a product which panders to a desire to go faster than others, which is easy to make comfortable and which people would be loth to bear the costs of sharing once they have experienced it. In combination with characteristics of the product, strong continuities in human nature mean that technical flexibility *is* irrelevant.

87   As I have pointed out above, some technologies are non-neutral between generations. Thus when I am talking of social groups (in whatever sense they are precisely defined) I am talking about a group at a given time, *t*, to be distinguished from the group with the same label at some other time *t* + *s*. I skirt two difficulties: that the relevant social groups may change through time and that those changes may be propelled by the technology itself (as in the more technologically determinist versions of the white collar proletariat argument).

88   L. Mumford, *Technics and Civilisation*, New York: Harcourt Brace, 1963; Illich, *Tools For Conviviality*, p. 34; J. Ellul, *The Technological Society*, New York: Random House, 1964, ch. 1.

89   As Elster emphasizes, counterfactuals alone cannot establish causality. See *Logic and Society*, ch. 6. This chapter also reviews and criticizes the most important attempts at large scale counterfactual technological history.

90   T. Lowi, 'The political impact of information technology', reprinted in T. Forester (ed.), *The Microelectronics Revolution*, Oxford: Blackwell 1980.

91   The problem of defining what is meant by deskilling, and the 'social construction' of the notion of skilled work in conflicts between capital and labour is discussed in D. Lee, 'Beyond de-skilling: skills, craft and class', in S. Wood (ed.), *The Degradation of Work*, London: Hutchinson, 1982.

92   See J. Eaton, 'Cooperatives and the new technology', *Industrial Relations Journal*, 16 (1985), pp. 47–53.

93   Elster, *Logic and Society*, ch. 6 discusses two proposals. The first is a measure of 'distance' based upon how many changes between the actual and possible world have been made. Elster's preferred option is based upon the length of time since the nodal branching point at which the possible world and the actual world could be seen as diverging. This needs adaption for future possible worlds as Elster realizes.

94   For example, a non-neutral technology might be justifiable either on utilitarian grounds or because it did not violate rights abrogated by some alternative method.

95   Because some members of some social groups probably will suffer along the possible authoritarian path, the strongest definition of unbiased technics capable of sustaining my conclusion is (c) above.

9

Do neutral institutions add up to a neutral state?

Robert E. Goodin and Andrew Reeve

This concluding chapter is intended to pose, more directly, the larger questions of institutional design that have served as subtexts for previous chapters. There we have confronted the conceptual issues arising in various particular institutions or policy areas, and investigated what neutrality involves in various particular cases. But we still may be left wondering how best to arrange our social and political institutions, more broadly, to attain it. For example, should neutrality be pursued by everyone? Or should there be a division of labour, either amongst moral agents or social institutions, so that neutrality is the particular business of only some? Can neutrality emerge from a system of checks and balances? And if so, how?

In raising questions about the institutional design of the state, we are making two presuppositions, neither of which has been universally accepted. The first is that we can talk sensibly about designing institutions. Some say that the intentional design of institutions is impossible. Institutions, they say, evolve in ways beyond our grasp: both beyond our understanding and beyond our control. Our presupposition can equally well be challenged by those arguing that institutional design is so complex, and attended with so many unanticipated side effects, that any such discussion is worthless *ab initio*.

Clearly, the discussion throughout this book fundamentally presupposes that neither form of scepticism is wholly warranted. All that is, of course, a larger argument which cannot be pursued here. Nevertheless, if we are to talk of a neutral state at all, we will at a minimum require some specification of which institutions are part of the state, and hence subject to duties of neutrality. That much of that larger issue, at least, will be touched upon briefly later.

Our second presupposition is that institutional design is morally problematic. While the liberal position has been assailed by those whose theories of social life suggest the impossibility of institutional design, many other political moralists have too readily assumed that it is not for them to enter into the question: not because they accept that institutional design is in principle impossible, but because they assume it is unproblematic, or outside their competence, or because their moralizing underspecifies institutional outcomes.

The view that institutional design is not problematic is wholly understandable. It is taken to follow from the idea that The Good is good for everyone, that the right thing to do is the right thing for everyone to do. The very nature of morality as a system of universal prescriptions means that we all labour under the same moral law. Institutional design, on this account, is morally uninteresting: each and every institution is bound by the same moral imperative.[1]

The problem of institutional design is neglected, in addition, by moralizing which invokes an academic division of labour to justify leaving the problem to others. Questions of institutional design involve empirical issues of causes and consequences. The philosopher claims no competence in these areas, which involve a separate set of skills and a separate branch of enquiry.

Finally, the problem is neglected by the sort of institutional agnosticism which supposes that there are many possible organizational forms which will meet the requirements set down by our moral theory. Having specified the goal, the philosopher can be indifferent between these institutions, having assumed that they will all enable it to be met and that there is nothing in the theory to determine a choice between them.

If we try to give content to the goal of neutrality, however, this neglect cannot be sustained. If we simply assume that neutrality is a goal binding on all social and political institutions of the liberal state, and on all individuals in their capacity as agents of state authority, we make a ready passage from the individual's case, to the particular institution, to the state. But this is likely to ignore the most basic insights of institutional analysis: those that try to show the connections between individual action and the operation of institutions, and between the interaction of institutions and overall outcomes.

Granted the importance of the state's neutrality, we shall want to raise questions about the depth and breadth of the injunction that it be neutral. Questions of depth are concerned, essentially, with the different levels at which the injunction might operate. If the state is to be neutral, is there a requirement that all particular institutions within the state should be, and furthermore that all the individuals who give life to those institutions should be in their turn? Or is non-neutrality at a micro-level somehow consistent with neutrality at a macro-level?

Questions of breadth concern the range of actors on any given level to whom the injunction to be neutral applies. If the institutions of the state are to be neutral, does each have to exhibit that quality, or is it possible that the system as a whole could be neutral if countervailing biases cancel one another on any given level, and thus provide for neutrality?

The essays in this volume draw attention to the ubiquity of the idea of neutrality in liberal thought, a ubiquity which should alert us to the likelihood of significant differences between particular applications of the ideas. Three such differences are of concern here. First, neutrality has been invoked as a goal or virtue in many different contexts or domains. For example, neutrality has been recommended in education, the civil service, and broadcasting. For this reason, second, it has been predicated of, or commended to, a variety of agents and agencies: teachers as well as the education system, civil servants as well as the civil service, and journalists as well as the BBC and IBA, scientists as well as the Republic of Science. But third, and crucially, the objects of the neutrality appropriate to these contexts are various: for example, the neutral state displays its virtue in relation to lifestyles, the neutral teacher in relation to truth claims, the neutral civil servant in the DHSS in relation to claimants' rights.

It follows from this that when we enquire about the relation between micro-level and macro-level neutrality, we should consider two sets of possibilities. The first arises when the virtue of neutrality is the same one at the two levels. For example, even if the desired neutrality of the civil servant is the same neutrality as is sought in the civil service as an institution, we may still ask the questions noted above. The second set of possibilities arises when the version of neutrality appropriate to the two levels is not the same. For example, a neutral DHSS officer might exhibit the virtue with respect to the rights of claimants with whom he or she deals, without this saying anything about the neutrality of the social security system, whose appropriate virtue might be neutrality with respect to lifestyles.

The ubiquity of the recommendation of neutrality is connected to the view that the moral duties of all institutions and actors within them are the same. But that view makes neutrality something of an anomaly among the many values which the liberal state is meant to serve. Most of the state's moral goals are devolved upon particular branches of its organization. The task of protecting citizens' lives, liberties and estates is a general goal of the state, but it is also primarily the responsibility of agencies like the Ministry of Defence, the Home Office, and the judiciary. While the welfare of citizens may be a general goal of great moral importance, it is primarily the DHSS which attends to it. Neutrality seems to be a different case; it appears to engage all levels and all actors in the liberal state equally. It is this appearance which we shall discuss in this chapter. Have liberals fallen into a trap in supposing that the state's neutrality requires everyone to be neutral, or in supposing that if all actors are neutral the state's neutrality is guaranteed?

To address this question, we shall consider (pp. 198–202 below) the issue of breadth raised earlier. Having found no particular reason to suppose that the neutrality injunction need engage all actors on one level, we shall then turn to the issue of depth (pp. 202–7). Again, we shall find that there is no reason to suppose that the neutrality injunction has to be applied on all levels if it is to succeed at the level which matters most to liberal theory – the level of the state.

A more radical critique

Before proceeding to any of that, though, some preliminary clarification on the notion of the state employed here is required. We are supposing a distinction between state and society. Liberal theory has traditionally demanded neutrality of the first, but not of the second.

To be sure, society is by no means an object of indifference to liberal theory. Considerable attention has been given to the analysis of a just society, and to the circumstances in which free individuals should engage with each other outside the domain of the state. In this respect, society is both a more inclusive term than the state, and a term with which the latter is contrasted. For example, a liberal theory of a just society will clearly make prescriptions about the uses and organization of coercive power. Indeed, it may make precisely the prescription with which we are here concerned, that the state be neutral. But when society is contrasted with the state, the latter term standardly refers to political mechanisms for dealing with competing claims; again, the prescription of neutrality concerns just how those claims are treated.

There is inevitably a certain roughness, then, in our use of 'the state'. We have included institutions like science, education and the market because (as a matter of fact in the case of science and education, and analytically in the case of the market) the regulation of those institutions has a political character. The market provides an alternative to politics as a way of regulating claims, but it is also regulated in the name of claims which it cannot itself meet.[2]

The requirement that the state be neutral may be derived from a liberal theory of justice. But a radical critique has seen in that neutrality something closer to indifference. In Marx's essay 'On the Jewish Question', for example, the state's official indifference to the property or religion of its citizens is contrasted with the real effect that inequality of property or particular observance produces in civil society.[3] The state can recognize equal rights without producing a substantive equality. In general, the radical suspicion of the liberal concern with neutral procedures is that it is consistent with indifference to actual outcomes – and that largely because of liberalism's artificial and unreasonably sharp separation of 'state' from 'society'.

One approach to this is through an analogy between justice and neutrality. In both cases, the radical critique would invite pushing back the point of application of the idea. For example, equality of opportunity conceived in a meritocratic way can be pushed back to positive discrimination and perhaps even to genetic engineering.[4] Neutrality, similarly, sets out from the treatment of claims. There, the state is neutral between demands actually made of it. But the notion can then be pushed back, so as to require the state to take a more active role in assisting in the formulation of the claims themselves. In this way the requirements of neutrality are shifted from Marx's formal indifference towards something much more interventionist, and the borders between state and society softened.

We shall argue that it is a mistake to identify neutrality with either indifference or passivity. The analogy between equality of opportunity and neutrality may be developed, however, to put some restraint on too great an extension of the idea. Just as the distinction between equal opportunity and positive discrimination may be clouded if the former notion becomes too all-embracing, so the distinctiveness of neutrality becomes lost if it is to include everything appropriate to the design of a just society. But all this is perfectly consistent with treating neutrality as one of a number of virtues which the liberal state should pursue, rather than as a catch-all for those other values.

The breadth of the neutrality injunction

For the reasons which we sketched at the beginning of this chapter, state neutrality has been seen to require that all institutions and all agents of authority within it must be neutral in their turn. This section discusses and rejects these arguments.

We may best approach the view here being challenged by returning to the puzzle mentioned earlier. Why are we so comfortable in devolving so many of the state's tasks – and clearly these are moral tasks – to particular branches of the state, or to particular agents of it, while supposing that neutrality is a requirement directed at all of them? One answer might be given by referring to the nature of the moral tasks being contrasted. Perhaps the source or structure or some other feature of those tasks can account for the difference.

The argument might start from a distinction between those of the state's moral tasks which relate to 'consequentialist' values, and those which relate to 'deontological' ones. It would then assert that whereas responsibility for attaining consequentialist goals may be devolved upon others (for example, if they are better able to accomplish them), responsibility for discharging deontological duties is by its nature something which cannot be transferred; only the person with the duty can discharge it. This argument might be buttressed on the one side by the suggestion that transferable consequentialist duties are in the state's province precisely because it is thought that the state is better able to discharge them than individuals who are employing the state as an agent for these purposes, and on the other side by the claim that the virtue of neutrality is peculiar to the state's agents and the accompanying deontological duty attaches to all of them.

The point may be made clearer by marking the difference between harming and wronging a person. In the first case, the harm one person does to you may well be put right by help from another. In the second case, the wrong that one person does you cannot be 'put right' by the super-solicitious concern of a second person. The suggestion is that breaches of neutrality are wrongs of this kind: one person cannot be doubly neutral to make up for another's failure of neutrality.

Such an account meshes neatly with the analysis of neutrality which is motive-based. Neutrality in this conception is an attribute of a person's reasons for action, not of the results of his action. In Dworkin's terms, breaches of neutrality deny persons the 'equal concern and respect' to which they are all entitled.[5] Victims of bias and malice resent the reasons for their mistreatment, and this is a factor over and above their distress at any material injury that they may suffer in consequence.[6] Indeed, they can experience the resentment at the reasons for their treatment quite independently of any material outcome. Thus, it might be argued, everyone in the service of the state should display scrupulous neutrality towards all citizens.

This account suffers from two conspicuous problems. The first is that it works well only at one level of analysis. The argument looks at motives and intentions, the paradigmatic case of which applies to individual moral agents. They can be attributed to aggregates of persons, or socio-political institutions, or the state, only by an extension of this basic model. And those extensions are either imperfect or wholly unavailable. No doubt there are some well-organized collective entities, with formal internal decision procedures, which may be counted as genuine agents for purposes of attributing to them responsibility for their actions.[7] Indeed, recent legislation has so counted organizations like trades unions. Whether such attributions of responsibility can plausibly be based upon the intentions and motives manifested by collective actions is a rather different matter. Can we make any sense of the notion of collective intent when, for example, a large number of people back the same plan of action but for a number of different reasons?[8] The problem is not one of disaggregation, or lack of information; rather, it is the simple difficulty that it is wholly unclear that institutions and states can wrong people through malicious motives, in the way that individual moral agents clearly can, because it is unclear that we can attribute to them motives and intentions of the sort that individual moral agents certainly have.[9]

The second problem with the analysis concerns the relationship between resentment and non-neutrality. It supposes that people will rightly resent non-neutrality anywhere in the network of institutions, and that their rightful resentment will be in proportion to the non-neutrality. But resentment is appropriate when we experience a bias against us; non-neutrality sometimes just amounts to favouring others. If this favouritism towards others means that we obtain less of a scarce resource in consequence, then that fact will be a matter of regret. That is certainly a failure of neutrality, and would justify a charge of unfairness. Resentment, however, is directed at the motives of actors, not the consequences of what they do. If there was no ill-will towards us, then, we cannot feel resentful. No offence can be taken, because none was intended. The reasons the agent acted on had nothing to do with us.[10]

The relationships between bias, malice and resentment may be illustrated with practical cases. No one resents the fact that other people's parents are non-neutral, being biased towards their own children. Of course, someone might regret the fact that his own parents display less favouritism towards him than other parents do towards their children; but any resentment could only be directed at his own parent's malice (if it exists), not at other people's parents' favouritism.[11] Equally, no one resents the fact that other people's lawyers are non-neutral, being biased in favour of their clients, even though, of course, someone might regret the failure of his own lawyer to display an equal bias. Again, he would direct his resentment at the ill-will (if any) of his own lawyer toward him, not at the good will of other people's lawyers toward them.

For these two reasons, the analysis which treats neutrality as a duty binding on all agents of authority, and all institutions of the state, is incomplete. Inasmuch as it is grounded in a duty of equal concern and respect, it relies on an attribution of motives which may not be available despite a clear failure of neutrality. Inasmuch as the resentment individuals will feel when they experience a failure of neutrality is itself used to ground the duty to be neutral, it misses the wide range of cases in which resentment would not be an appropriate response to failures of neutrality.[12]

A second analysis which advocates maximum breadth in the application of neutrality runs broadly parallel to the analysis employing the consequentialist/deontological distinction, and it suffers from many of the same difficulties. On this view, neutrality is akin to the so-called 'executive virtues'. These are not necessarily good in themselves, but are preconditions of doing other things that are good. Perhaps examples are courage and intelligence. By analogy, neutrality is not in itself a morally worthy goal, but it is a quality which should infuse the pursuit of all our goals. Since it should infuse everyone's pursuit of those goals, it is an argument for maximal breadth in the application of the neutrality injunction.

This argument is beset by the same problems as the first. Insofar as neutrality, as an executive virtue, refers to an attitude or a mental habit, it is predicated of or recommended to individuals. And, once again, it is only by an extension of the model which cannot plausibly be made that such an executive virtue could be applied to institutions or states. The same examples, presented above, which suggest that people do not (and should not) resent the non-neutrality of others' parents and lawyers also suggest that neutrality cannot be an executive virtue in the sense of being a precondition for the pursuit of all other virtues. So we would need an argument that there is something about the role of an agent in the liberal state that makes neutrality an executive virtue for that particular role. Later, we shall suggest that whether that role does in fact make neutrality an executive virtue depends on the precise arrangements adopted by the liberal state. Further, we shall suggest that there are good reasons for those arrangements not to do so.

Although this view of neutrality as an executive virtue is not compelling, it rests on an important insight. It correctly maintains that our paramount concern is not with neutrality as such. Our goal is badly described by saying that the state should assist all its citizens neutrally; rather, our goal is that the state assist all its citizens, neutrally. The goal is assistance. 'Neutrally' simply specifies how that goal is to be pursued; neutrality is not a goal in itself. The model of neutrality as an executive virtue clouds that insight, however, when it goes on to characterize neutrality as a frame of mind to be adopted by all agents of the liberal state. The goal of attaining that mental attitude merges imperceptibly with the goal of treating people neutrally, for the sake of neutrality. The central insight – that neutrality is not valued as a goal in itself – can be detached from the erroneous development of that model.

This is a good place to recall the radical criticism that liberal procedural neutrality can be combined with indifference to outcomes, because this diagnosis of the problems with maximalist approaches to neutrality helps to draw out the connection between neutrality and indifference. At bottom, all arguments making neutrality the duty of all alike construe neutrality in terms of persons' reasons for action, rather than in terms of the consequences of their actions. That is not accidental. If it is the reasons that have to be right, then every agent must act on those reasons. If it is the results that have to be right, then some people could be excused from acting neutrally (and permitted to act non-neutrally) just so long as there is some systematic guarantee that the right results will be produced – when some other agency or device is taken into account.

The most fundamental problems with maximalist analyses of the neutrality injunction all derive from limitations in this reason-based notion of neutrality. In a nutshell, if neutrality of mind were all we wanted, indifference would be sufficient. One way, perhaps even the best way, to ensure neutrality in that sense would be through non-involvement. Instead of assisting everyone in equal measure, we could help no one. That, too, would manifest a neutral attitude. Dworkin's demand for 'equal concern and respect', construed with uncharitable literalness, is consistent with treating no one with any concern or respect. If neutrality is treated as a goal in itself, and if neutrality is construed as a frame of mind, then this conclusion is as inevitable as it is unacceptable.

That conclusion is avoidable if we define neutrality in terms of results, and appreciate that neutrality has no value beyond that which derives from the pattern of results. To show 'equal concern and respect' for all by showing it to none, on the grounds that at least that manifests neutrality, would in these terms be quite literally to make a fetish of neutrality. It would be to attribute to the notion powers that it does not possess, and to elevate it to a status it does not deserve.[13]

If results are the proper objective of neutrality, there is no necessary reason why everyone should be engaged in the same way by the injunction to be neutral; on the disposition-based analysis, there is. Hence the demand for neutrality can be waived with respect to some agents or agencies, provided that there are institutional guarantees to ensure that the right results are produced 'overall'.

We shall take it henceforth in this chapter that the results analysis of neutrality is the correct one in the context of the state. Even if there is a plausible reason to be concerned with motives or dispositions in the case, say, of education, when we move to problems of institutional design we do not want to produce the right motives or attitudes in people. Instead, we want to produce the right pattern of results. That is the relevant sense of state neutrality. It might still warrant close inspection of procedures. But this is to ensure that the network of procedures produces neutral results, rather than because procedural neutrality licenses indifference to results.

The depth of the neutrality injunction

There are three levels of analysis involved in discussions of neutrality. The injunction 'be neutral' is addressed, first and foremost, to the liberal state as a whole. But, at one level below that, it is often directed at the various institutions comprising the liberal state. One level lower again, it is readdressed to the various individual agents occupying official roles in those institutions. The question of the 'depth' of the neutrality injunction is simply the question of the level(s) at which the injunction is to apply.

On a conventional account, sketched earlier, the neutrality injunction is supposed to have maximal depth as well as maximal breadth. It is meant to apply to all levels of the liberal state equally, just as it is meant to apply to all actors or agencies on a given level. On this conventional view, the liberal state as a whole is neutral if and only if all its institutions are neutral, and they, in turn, are neutral if and only if all the individual agents within them are neutral. That, clearly, is the model suggested by the various rules and precepts discussed (often critically) in the previous chapters. That presumption is the one we wish to challenge.

To do so, we resolve the conventional account's broader claim into two components. First, we question whether neutrality at higher levels necessarily implies neutrality at lower levels. In short, does high-level neutrality reduce to lower-level neutrality? Second, we question whether, as the conventional wisdom maintains, neutrality at lower levels necessarily implies neutrality at higher levels. Again, in brief, does lower-level neutrality sum to a higher one?

Of course, both claims have a superficial plausibility, and in one respect it may be conceded that they contain a truth. It does seem unlikely that the state as a whole can be neutral unless its component parts are neutral; and it does seem unlikely that the state can fail to be neutral if all its component parts are. That this is indeed *one* way in which the state may achieve neutrality. We can concede that without conceding that it is the only – or, more importantly, the best – way to achieve that goal.

Does high-level neutrality reduce to lower?

In essence, this question asks whether macro-level neutrality is consistent with micro-level non-neutrality. No doubt we are likely to be sceptical of such a possibility but should we be? Composites standardly display attributes not displayed by their constituent parts – among them attributes like shape, colour, and size, which are products of the interrelationships and interactions between components. In a similar way, of course, 'equality' refers to a relation between constituents, and simply cannot be predicated of any of the constituents on its own. So too with neutrality: even if it can properly be predicated of constituent parts of the larger whole, it is perfectly possible, through deft arrangement of the biases of the parts, for neutrality to be an attribute of the system as a whole while not being an attribute of any of its components. Any scepticism about this possibility might be further dispelled by looking at analogies with other institutional matrices.

The market, at least in its idealized form, is supposed to be neutral between all consumers and producers, even though (and largely because) the particular producers and consumers operating within it are profoundly biased in favour of their own interests. Aggregate market outcomes, arising from the composition of a multitude of self-interested transactions, are alleged to be broadly neutral. The system is neutral while the components are not.

The system of adversarial justice provides a second example. The system as a whole might be perfectly neutral between all those engaged in proceedings, even despite (and largely because of) the countervailing biases of the lawyers who favour the interests of their own clients. The rules governing judicial proceedings, including the rules about the proper limits of those biases, should guarantee that the outcomes will be broadly neutral between the parties.

It may be that the same analysis can be applied to other components of the liberal state. For example, it is usually held that the neutrality of the civil service requires that each civil servant be neutral: this is a political neutrality, a willingness to serve with equal assiduity whatever government the electorate chooses. It may be true (subject to caveats discussed in the next section) that if all civil servants were neutral then the neutrality of the service as a whole will be secured. But that is not the only way to secure that result. The neutrality of the civil service is consistent with the non-neutrality of particular civil servants, so long as there is a plausible system of countervailing bias or a sufficient supply of partisans for any government that might be elected. There is no need for every civil servant to be equally assiduous in serving all governments, provided that all governments receive the same quality of service. Similar points could be made about education and the media. One aspect of the neutrality of education concerns the treatment of cultural groups in the community. One possibility is that every teacher and every school should be scrupulously neutral between all those cultures. Another is that there should be some teacher in every school, or some school, which caters in particular for those cultures. This plan might be objectionable on many grounds, but its non-neutrality could not be one of them. The equivalent possibilities exist with respect to the media. We might require that every commentator, every newspaper or every broadcasting station be neutral between all points of view. Another possibility would be that there should be some system of countervailing special consideration of particular points of view.

All this helps to demonstrate the possibility that macro-level neutrality is consistent with micro-level non-neutrality – and, indeed, that some macro-level claims to that quality depend upon micro-level bias. If we move to the level of the state, and the institutions within it, it is possible for the state to exhibit neutrality without all its institutions doing so. The older model of spending-department claims being filtered through the cabinet is a case in point. The Department of Trade and Industry presses the claims of business, the Department of Employment those of labour; the Treasury looks to the interests of taxpayers, the Department of Social Security to those of people who depend upon state spending; and so on. Despite the partisanship of each department fighting for its corner, the outcome might be neutral between the claims of all the conflicting interests. The problem of institutional design is to achieve a proper weight for all particular interests through counter-vailing biases.

Of course, we do not claim that the result of such partisanship will necessarily be neutral, only that it can be. The strong claim of necessary neutrality requires systematic engineering of the way in which partisans interact. The rules governing the interplay of contending forces must be such as to ensure that all interests are represented, fairly and effectively, in proportion to the strength of their legitimate claims. Further, there must be some guarantee that the outcome will be arrived at through processes which reflect only those factors. These are the sort of guarantees provided in the 'idealized' models of the market and adversarial judicial proceedings. Similar guarantees are needed whenever models of macro-neutrality are derived from micro-non-neutrality.

Nor is it claimed that such guarantees can ever be absolute. The ideal models of the market and of judicial proceedings are never fully realized. But the same may be said of the view of neutrality which provides an injunction to every particular agent and agency; there is no guarantee that such duties will be universally discharged, and many good reasons to suppose that they will not. In a second-best world, the issue is whether the imperfections in aggregating micro-non-neutrality into macro-neutrality do more or less damage than those which arise from failures in micro-level neutrality in a maximalist system.

Does lower-level neutrality sum to higher?

The answer to this question is, again, apparently straightforward. The conventional view of neutrality treats it as 'helping or hurting all in equal measure', or some such. Aggregating equalities inevitably yields another equality. So too neutralities on one level must inevitably yield neutralities on another, higher, level.

The first doubt about this idea follows from the distinction drawn earlier between the virtues of neutrality appropriate to different institutions and levels. The state is ideally neutral between interests or lifestyles; the legal system is ideally neutral with respect to the truth of a controversy; the media are ideally neutral with respect to the truth or interpretations of events. Hence even if a lower-level virtue of neutrality is fully realized, the higher-level virtue may not be, because it is a different virtue. When discussing the neutrality of individual agents, we are primarily focusing on a mental state or disposition. But when we look at institutions, we are focusing on neutrality of results.[14] To the extent that the appropriate virtue of neutrality is different at the different levels of analysis, it obviously would not follow that micro-level neutrality summed to higher-level neutrality.

A particular problem arises when we combine the idea of neutrality as a frame of mind with the idea of neutrality in terms of results. Persons can quite clearly produce non-neutral results without intending to do so. The discussion above (pp. 198–202) shows how misleading it is to move too readily between the two. 'Neutrality of mind' can be predicated only of natural individuals, whereas institutional design is concerned with producing neutrality of results. But neutrality of mind, even at the individual level, is not what really matters to liberals. If we use the idea of neutrality of results at both the individual and the institutional level, the grounds of the first doubt are removed.

Nevertheless, we may doubt the central claim for other reasons. One concerns the partitioning of the universe over which we are to be neutral. A standard point in the 'power debate' is that fairness of procedures for deciding among items on the agenda can be vitiated by unfairness in the procedure for deciding on the agenda itself. There is a straightforward analogy in the case of neutrality. All components of the state might be neutral in their operations, and summing those components would yield a neutral state, so far as it goes; but none of that speaks to the larger question of just how far neutrality does go. It may well be that what the state does, it does neutrally; but it could still fail to be neutral because of what it fails to do. Arguments about the non-neutrality of the laissez-faire state ultimately rest on this problem.

Another difficulty arises from the suspicion that there might be systemic effects which emerge in the process of aggregation despite the appearance of neutrality at the micro-level. For example, a simple plurality rule has the appearance of neutrality when applied to any particular constituency, although the 'cube rule' reveals the systemic effect for very small and very large parties to be under-rewarded in relation to the total number of votes cast for them.[15] We should therefore be alert to the possibility that similar systemic effects occur in the aggregation of other apparently neutral micro-level procedures or processes. Apparent micro-level neutrality might, when aggregated, produce the systematic disadvantage of certain sorts of people or certain sorts of preferences.

No one has ever supposed that neutral outcomes are equal outcomes. Both proponents and critics of the idea of neutrality have concentrated on the compatibility of neutrality with various sorts of inequality. If we construe neutrality, as we have done in this chapter, as an attribute of results, the requirement is presumably that gains and losses even out in the long run, that no one is systematically disadvantaged. A fair game of chance requires that over the long term a person gambling on particular outcomes would break even, yet in any particular round of betting will benefit some at the expense of others. Neutrality of results, too, requires a balanced assessment of gains and losses. But there are two dimensions to this aggregation. Just as the principle should apply to successive applications of the same rule over time, so too it should apply to the aggregate results of the workings of the various institutions that comprise the liberal state during any particular time period. This requires just the sort of overall assessment of results that is rendered unnecessary by too facile a claim that overall neutrality is guaranteed by the neutrality of component parts.

May the liberal state take sides? Does it have to?

It is simple enough to move from the injunction that 'the liberal state should be neutral' to the conclusion that 'the state should not take sides'. If the neutrality of the parts sums to the neutrality of the whole, and if the neutrality of the whole can be disaggregated into that of the components, then there is no scope for the liberal-cum-neutral state to take sides. At most, it is required to prevent any of its agents or agencies from doing so.

If we drop those assumptions, which we have cast doubt upon in this chapter, then the conclusion is quite different. Micro-non-neutrality, we have argued, is consistent with macro-neutrality, provided that there are proper 'laws of composition' to guarantee the neutrality of the aggregate outcomes. The debate about the possible neutrality of the state concerns both the content of those laws of composition, and the capacity of the state to guarantee or enforce them. In this sense, it is possible to regard arguments about constitutional provision, and more particularly arguments about a Bill of Rights, as attempts to fix a baseline of neutrality. Further, if we accept that it is only the state which can play the role of fixing the 'laws of composition', we can see how the problem of state neutrality is related to its activities as arbiter between particular interests or keeper of the ring in which those interests are fought out. It has been convincingly argued that the pluralist model of the state becomes incoherent when it represents the state as either arbiter or arena.[16] If the state is to be an arbiter between particular interests, it must take a view about which is more deserving, in the name of the public interest. But this public interest, according to pluralism, does not exist independently of the results of the interplay of particular interests. On the other side, if the state is to provide the arena in which that interplay is fought out, it merely legitimizes the success of the strongest particular interest.

A state striving to be neutral might, at a minimum, be expected to ensure that there is a level playing field for contending micro-level forces. Disputes about what constitutes a level playing field will undoubtedly turn out to be disputes about the locus of application of the idea of neutrality, which were discussed earlier. Just as equality of opportunity can be translated into positive discrimination, so too can the requirement of a level playing field be turned into a demand for the state to act as an intentional counterweight to the power of some interests or groups, aiding or organizing those who could otherwise be neglected.[17] Such intervention, apparently blatantly non-neutral, might nevertheless be justified in the name of neutrality.

In contrast to the pluralist theory of the state, this model does not suppose that the state is merely providing the arena in which political contests take place. The model here in view crucially claims that the state has a role in ensuring that all legitimate interests are proportionately represented in the interplay of micro-forces. That is a role the state is uniquely equipped, and peculiarly obliged, to perform. The public interest emerges not simply from the interplay of particular interests, but from the deliberately contrived neutrality of the political system.

Notes

1 Another problem this sort of account faces is its apparent failure to recognize the *special* character of the state. The two characteristics of (a) a claim to universal jurisdiction and (b) a claim to the use of legitimate force are precisely those distinguishing characteristics of state power which have led liberals to place special requirements on the neutrality of the state. Acknowledging the overarching power of the state with respect to (other) institutions like the market leads readily to a consideration of its peculiar responsibilities. We shall argue that neutrality is the particular virtue and responsibility of the liberal state.

2 This account takes for granted the sovereignty of the state, that is the claim that the state may legitimately regulate whatever it chooses to regulate. With respect to neutrality, this may pose a problem. The idea of neutrality may be used both to discriminate between those areas where the state may legitimately interfere, and those where it may not, and to characterize the proper stance of the state where it does in fact intervene. We return to this problem on pp. 207–8.

3 Karl Marx, 'On the Jewish question', in David McLellan (ed.), *Karl Marx Selected Writings*, Oxford: Oxford University Press, 1971, pp. 39–62.

4 Bernard Williams, 'The idea of equality', in Peter Laslett and W. G. Runciman (eds), *Philosophy, Politics and Society* (second series), Oxford: Basil Blackwell, 1962, pp. 110–31 especially p. 128.

5 Ronald Dworkin, 'Liberalism', in S. Hampshire (ed.), *Public and Private Morality*, Cambridge: Cambridge University Press, 1978, pp. 113–43 at p. 125.

6 Peter Strawson, *Freedom and Resentment*, London: Methuen, 1974, chapter 1.

7 Peter French, 'The corporation as a moral person', *American Philosophical Quarterly*, 16 (1979), pp. 207–15.

8 Gerald C. MacCallum, 'Legislative intent', *Yale Law Journal*, 75 (1966), pp. 754–87.

9 Certainly much of the activity of socio-political institutions is conducted by individual agents on behalf of the larger institution. These agents act in official capacities. We might in these cases talk of the motive(s) of the individual in applying the rules in that particular way. That may well give us leverage on the question of non-neutrality in the application of rules. Unfortunately, it does not help us with problems of non-neutrality in the formulation of rules, nor with the same difficulties with respect to the adoption of rules by collective entitities.

10 Our argument is, of course, concerned not with what people might say they resent, but with what they might appropriately resent. The appropriateness of resentment depends upon the theory of responsibilities, and may therefore be controversial. See Robert E. Goodin, *Reasons for Welfare*, Princeton, NJ: Princeton University Press, 1988, ch. 3.

11 People may also regret that their parents had less to spend on them than other people's parents did. But again, that could amount to actual resentment only if they thought that maldistribution reflected some malice (directed at them, or perhaps their forbears).

12 Of course, it may be appropriate to resent the fact that there is no systematic guarantee in a society that there will be someone biased in your favour to counteract the effect of others' bias. Again, the appropriateness would depend on a theory of responsibility. See note 10 above, and pp. 202–7.

13 Cf. the essays by Jeremy Waldron and Peter Jones in this volume.

14 Of course, what constitutes the 'results' will be a contextual matter. At the level of the state, we shall usually be concerned with interests or lifestyles.

15 For example, Iain McLean, *Elections*, 2nd edn, London: Longman, 1983, pp. 10–11.

16 Jack Lively, 'Pluralism and consensus', in Pierre Birnbaum, Jack Lively and Geraint Parry (eds), *Democracy, Consensus and Social Contract*, London and Beverley Hills, Ca: Sage, 1978, pp. 185–202.

17 David Miller, 'Market neutrality and the failure of cooperatives', in *British Journal of Political Science*, 11(1981), pp. 309–29, provides an example of how preferences for certain sorts of work organization might need intentional support if they are to have any chance of realization.

About the contributors

Adrian Ellis joined the Civil Service in 1981, and, by then a Principal, left HM Treasury in 1986 to be Administrative Director of the Conran Foundation, an educational charity. He is editor, with Krishnan Kumar, of *The Dilemmas of Liberal Democracies*, London: Tavistock, 1983.

Peter Gardner is Lecturer in the Department of Education, University of Warwick, where he specializes in the philosophy of education. He has contributed numerous journal articles in that field.

Robert E. Goodin was until recently Reader in Government at the University of Essex and is now Professorial Fellow in Philosophy at the Australian National University. An Associate Editor of the journal, *Ethics*, he is author of, most recently, *Protecting the Vulnerable*, Chicago: University of Chicago Press, 1985, and *Reasons for Welfare*, Princeton, NJ: Princeton University Press, 1988.

Peter Jones is Senior Lecturer in Politics at the University of Newcastle. The author of many articles, particularly in liberal political theory and the theory of democracy, he is at present preparing a book on rights for Macmillan.

Ken Newton, until recently Professor of Politics at the University of Dundee, is Reader in Government at the University of Essex. He is author of *Second City Politics*, Oxford: Oxford University Press, 1976, *Does Politics Matter?* (with L. J. Sharpe), Oxford: Clarendon Press, 1980, and *The Politics of Local Expenditure* (with T. J. Karran), Basingstoke: Macmillan, 1985. He is currently working on comparative urban politics and the politics of the media.

A. T. O'Donnell lectured in economics at the University of Glasgow before joining the Government Economic Service. He was formerly attached to the British Embassy in Washington and is now working in HM Treasury.

Andrew Reeve is Lecturer in Politics at the University of Warwick. He is author of *Property*, London: Macmillan, 1986, and editor of *Modern Theories of Exploitation*, London and Beverley Hills, Ca: Sage, 1987.

Jeremy Waldron was formerly a Fellow of Lincoln College, Oxford and a Lecturer in Politics at Edinburgh University. He is presently Associate Professor in the Jurisprudence and Social Policy Programme at the Boalt Hall School of Law, University of California at Berkeley. He is editor of *Theories of Rights*, Oxford: Oxford University Press, 1984 and *Nonsense on Stilts*, London: Methuen, 1987, and author of *The Right to Private Property*, Oxford: Clarendon Press, 1988.

Hugh Ward, Lecturer in Government at the University of Essex, has published articles on rational choice theory in various journals. He is currently working on problems in science and technology and in the theory of the state.

Index

ABC Network 143, 145
Abelard, Peter 111, 123
Ackerman, Bruce 10, 12, 17, 27, 33, 34–5, 68, 69, 82
Adam Smith Institute 96
adversarial justice system 204
affirmative action programmes 45, 54–5
agencies of neutrality 3, 7, 63, 70–1, 195–6, 198–200
aggregation, effects of 7–8, 206–7
aims of neutrality 3, 7, 68, 70–2
allocation system in markets 42
American Society of Newspaper Editors 148
anonymity: of civil service 99–101, 104; in markets 42, 45, 46, 48, 49, 50, 54
anti-discrimination legislation 54–5
anti-neutrality commitments 27–9
Armstrong, Sir Robert 85, 91, 92
Armstrong, William 100
Arnold, Matthew 112, 122
ascetics 30
Ascherson, Neal 150
association, freedom of 31
auction markets 50–3
audience ratings 131
authoritarianism 178–9
autonomy: and legislation 71, 77, 78; of pupils 112, 113, 116–17, 121–2; value of 6

Bancroft, Lord 97
banks 40
bargaining power 40
Barnes, B. 173–4
BBC 135, 147
Bell, D. 161
Bennett, James Gordon Snr 148
bias: in civil service 87–9; in media 132, 138, 139–40, 149–51, 153; in science 161, 183–5
Bill of Rights 32, 208
breadth of neutrality injunction 198–202
Bridges, Edward 94
British Society for Social Responsibility in Science 158
broadcasting, regulation of 135, 137, 145–8, 150–1
Burns, Allan 175

Cable News Network 145
cable television 145
cancer research 162
Capital Cities 143, 145
Capra, F. 174
care, private 191–2
causal relationships, breakdown of consensus on 95–6
CBS Network 143
changes of policy 91–2
Chapman, Richard 94
Chicago Mercantile Exchange (CME) 49

213

racial discrimination 31, 55
radical science movement 158–9,
163–4, 165, 168–9, 170, 171–2
radio 135
Rawls, John 10, 17, 18, 22, 27, 28,
30, 31, 32, 34, 36–7, 74, 76, 79
Rayner, Sir Derek 97
Raz, Joseph 26, 66, 68
RCA Network 145
Reagan, Ronald 145, 150, 153
Red Lion decision 137
referee, neutral, concept of 19
religious education 111–12, 119
religious faith 14, 75, 78
repression by state 178–9
research, distribution of 162, 165
resentment of non-neutrality 198–200
reservation price 50
resources, distribution of 17, 21, 22,
24, 29–30
responsibility, and neutrality 23–5
'Revenue-Equivalence Theorem' 51
Ridley, F.F. 86
rights 32–3, 136–7, 152
Rose, Hilary 158, 164, 165, 172
Rose, Stephen 158, 164, 165
Rousseau, Jean-Jacques 112
Rowland, Tiny 144
Royal Commissions on the Press
144–5
Royal Institute of Public
Administration 98

satisfaction, equal 15–16
sceptical cases for teacher neutrality
107–13, 120–1, 122–5
Schools Council Humanities Project
107–9, 111, 119, 127
science/technology, neutrality of 6,
157–92; and biased technologies
183–5; and elite intentions 164–5;
and flexibility of technics 174–9;
and market selection 166–8; myth
of 157–9; and planning/fixing of
technics 160–2; and science as
superstructure 168–74; and social
theory 181–2; and
'value-neutrality' of natural

science 162–3; and values 182–3
screen-based markets 50
sealed-bid auctions 51–3
Seaton, Jean 142
Second World War 65–6
secondary schools 107
secrecy, official 100
secularism 62
select committee system 100
self-management by civil service
97–9
self-regulation of media 148
Shah, Eddie 144
single markets 41
sociobiology 169
Socrates 110–11, 123
specialists in civil service 95–6
speech, freedom of *see* expression,
freedom of
Spencer, Herbert 138
Spengler, Oswald 172
state, neutrality of 9–38; as
administrator of ground-rules 9,
11, 208; and anti-neutral values
27–9, 73; and breadth of neutrality
injunction 198–202; and depth of
neutrality injunction 202–7;
illusion of 25–7; and institutional
design 193–4, 209; and intentions
of institutional actors 198–200,
209, 210; and international
conflict 9, 18–19, 25, 26, 35,
64–6; and liberty 30–3; and
life-style/aims of citizens 9, 32,
66–7, 75; and neutrality between
conceptions of the good 12–18,
22–4, 27, 28–9, 34, 62, 66–7, 70,
75–80; and neutrality between
individuals 11–12, 21–3, 27–8,
34–5; and principles of justice 10,
13; and responsibility 23–5; and
'taking sides' 207–8; and two
forms of neutrality 18–23, 35; and
wealth 29–30
state power 6
Stenhouse, Lawrence 107, 108, 111,
127
Stephen, James Fitzjames 113

For Product Safety Concerns and Information please contact our EU
representative GPSR@taylorandfrancis.com
Taylor & Francis Verlag GmbH, Kaufingerstraße 24, 80331 München, Germany

www.ingramcontent.com/pod-product-compliance
Ingram Content Group UK Ltd.
Pitfield, Milton Keynes, MK11 3LW, UK
UKHW021056080625
459435UK00003B/23